Voices of Our Ancestors

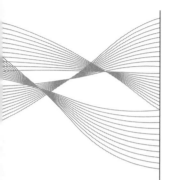

Voices of Our Ancestors

Language Contact in Early South Carolina

Patricia Causey Nichols

The University of South Carolina Press

© 2009 Patricia Causey Nichols

Published by the University of South Carolina Press
Columbia, South Carolina 29208

www.sc.edu/uscpress

Manufactured in the United States of America

18 17 16 15 14 13 12 11 10 09   10 9 8 7 6 5 4 3 2 1

LIBRARY OF CONGRESS CATALOGING-IN-PUBLICATION DATA

Nichols, Patricia Causey, 1938–
    Voices of our ancestors : language contact in early South Carolina /
    Patricia Causey Nichols.
        p. cm.
    Includes bibliographical references and index.
    ISBN 978-1-57003-775-7 (cloth : alk. paper)
        1. Languages in contact—South Carolina. 2. Ethnicity—South Carolina—History.
    3. South Carolina—Languages—Variation. I. Title.
    P40.5.L382U636 2008
    409.756—dc22   2008030350

This book was printed on Glatfelter Natures, a recycled paper with 30 percent
postconsumer waste content.

For Frank, my partner on life's journey

Contents

Illustrations

Acknowledgments

The people of South Carolina gave me an excellent education at a time when many of them were without indoor plumbing or electricity and too many of their children went to school only six months of the year. Their hard work and sacrifices I humbly acknowledge. This book is written for their descendants, to help them better understand the voices of the past and to encourage them to listen with care to all the voices of the present.

My senior high school English teacher, the late Evelyn Snider, deserves special acknowledgment for her efforts to teach so many of us to write well enough to compete with those outside the South, who thought we were less than intelligent because of the way we spoke. Her reading of and conversations about early versions of this manuscript provided boundless encouragement.

Family support during the research on Gullah came from my mother, the late Mildred Mitchell Causey, and her sister, the late Annie Laurie Mitchell Bonnette. Both teachers in South Carolina over many decades, these two women had extensive networks throughout the state that provided introductions to educators in Georgetown County. Children and staff at the former Parkersville School on Pawleys Island welcomed me into their classrooms, teaching me more about life and language than I could ever teach them. The people of Sandy Island welcomed me into their homes, church, and schoolhouse, where we held weekly writing classes. I am especially indebted to the hospitality of the late Prince and Rebecca Washington on those nights when the writing classes met, to Timothy Tucker for letting me be a passenger on the schoolboat that island children used, to George and Teresa Weathers for delicious meals and conversation after church on Sundays, and to Sarah Deas for sharing her daughter, Kelly. A dissertation grant from the Woodrow Wilson Foundation helped fund this research.

Family support for the research on European American English spoken in the community of Socastee came from my father's sister, the late Frances Causey, and her extended family network. The late Catherine Lewis, head librarian of Horry County Memorial Library, steered me to local publications and to local people knowledgeable about settlement history of the area. Small grants from San José State University helped fund this stage of my research.

A Rockefeller Postdoctoral Fellowship provided a year in residence at the University of North Carolina and an opportunity for research on Indian languages of the South. Ruel Tyson and James Peacock organized weekly seminars on comparative cultures of the South, which were open to the larger university community under the auspices of the UNC Institute for the Arts and Humanities. These seminars and sustained conversations with co-fellows Jim Crisp and Joyce Marie Jackson helped expand core concepts about the South from the disparate perspectives of history, anthropology, and linguistics. During this year the Lumbee Indian community of Prospect in Robeson County, North Carolina, welcomed me into an elementary school once a week. I am grateful for that opportunity to hear the voices of children of the same ages as those I had worked with on the Waccamaw Neck in South Carolina.

Many colleagues in the academic world have given support and advice over the years. Especially helpful were early discussions with fellow Carolinians Shirley Brice Heath and Charles W. Joyner. Students in a graduate seminar I taught at the University of South Carolina on English Language in America gave me insights about the uses of African American English that I had never considered, especially Evelyn Dandy and Katherine Mille. As a faculty member at the University of South Carolina, Michael Montgomery kept me abreast of his own work as well as that of his students and colleagues. Our exchanges at conferences have been a delight. Conversations with Carol Myers-Scotton about codeswitching have also informed this work, as well as other research on Spanish-English bilingual classrooms. In the final stages of preparing the manuscript, Anne Bonnette Harmon served as an invaluable first reader, and both Margaret Wade-Lewis and Michael Mongomery made observations and suggested corrections that have improved it considerably. None of these colleagues should be held accountable for any mistakes that remain or positions that are unsupported by the evidence. I alone am responsible for those. I am deeply grateful for the expert guidance of Alexander Moore, Karen Rood, and Jonathan Haupt at the University of South Carolina Press.

My husband, to whom the book is dedicated, prepared most of the maps and tables. He gave me room to be.

Prologue

If we can imagine ourselves transported back to an early spring morning in 1715 on the streets of Charles Town in what is now South Carolina, we might hear the voices of three continents mingled together in gossip, trade, labor, and nurture. Just before the outbreak of the Yemassee War, which would almost annihilate the young English colony, some American Indian headmen might be found in the governor's chambers speaking through an interpreter about the disreputable practices of Scots and English traders on their reservation lands between the Combahee and the Savannah rivers. Out on the streets a German family is talking with their Dutch neighbors, deciding jointly to ask a young son to negotiate with the Ladino-speaking Jewish shopkeeper, who speaks just enough English to serve his customers, for supplies for their farms. Above the street in an upstairs office, Huguenot merchants are talking together in French about the arrival of a new shipment of enslaved people from Angola, to be sold later that week by a Scots auctioneer they jointly employ. An older Barbadian planter and his young French neighbor are in town to attend to some legal business, hoping to get an early look at the Africans quarantined on Sullivan's Island before the auction and talking together in English about their spring planting and the prospects for selling rice to the European markets. Over on the island itself, men, women, and children from Central Africa who have survived the horrors of the Middle Passage are sharing whatever information they can piece together from conversations overheard between the African guards about the next part of their communal nightmare—those among them with some knowledge of the guards' language translating into whatever African languages are shared among the group. Back across the harbor on the Charles Town docks, Africans speaking together in Gullah or in a mutually known African language are loading a cargo of turpentine and barrel staves for shipment to Barbados. Resting for a noontime meal, they eat bread made of cornmeal that has been prepared by an Indian woman in their master's kitchen. Her *mustee* children have helped bring the meal down to the dock, hoping for a glimpse of their father, one of the African workers loading turpentine. These "country-born" children speak to each other and to their parents in Gullah, although the parents may sometimes speak to them in an indigenous Indian or African language.

Across town in a large dining room, an African butler is guiding the governor's family to their seats before a table set with fine china and silver cutlery, for a meal of venison caught and prepared by an Indian man who lives in a nearby village. Joining the governor's family today is a visitor from London, a clergyman sent out by the Society for the Propagation of the Gospel in Foreign Parts to convert Africans and indigenous peoples of South Carolina to Christianity. He has been talking with the governor about his difficulties and his hopes for a small core of converts. Over continued conversation about affairs of the colony and social events in town, the food is served by a young Glasgow woman, soon to marry a clerk working in the governor's office, after her indentured servitude is over. As a wedding present, the governor plans to give the couple a pair of enslaved Africans from the Guinea Coast to help them in their new household. He will choose two who already know English, so that they can serve as interpreters for additional Africans bought to work on the clerk's new rice fields, a promising crop for the future. In a cabin behind the mansion, a young woman nurses the governor's child, singing softly a Yoruba lullaby she heard in Barbados from her own mother. Two of her children play together in the yard with others who live in the slave quarters and are not yet old enough for field work. These children speak Gullah to each other, playing a pebble game from the Bight of Benin.

In this snapshot of an imagined day, the typical monolingual speaker in Charleston of the twenty-first century might wonder how so many different languages became one. How did speakers of 1715 come to understand each other as they came together from three different continents to live in the land called Carolina—separated into North and South only since 1712? This book tells the story of their many ways of speaking, both privately and publicly, from the earliest days of contact with each other. It discusses how all South Carolinians have come to use a common language in public settings, though with distinctive dialects echoing old ways of speaking. It describes how a new language, known as Gullah and sometimes locally as Geechee or simply country talk, was created in South Carolina and is still used among some families and friends in private settings, although virtually all of its speakers today also use some variety of the common language in public. This book is a celebration of the voices of our ancestors and of what they have created together in story and song.

Part 1 | *From Tribes to Races*
Inventing Ethnicity

Before meeting together in Carolina, the emigrants from America, Europe, and Africa had little notion of "race" as we have come to think of it. Most belonged to relatively small groups with whom they shared culture and usually language—either tribal or village. The replacement of a tribal kind of consciousness with a broader one happened as these three major continental groups came into frequent contact with each other and discovered the common values and behaviors that characterized their separate cultures. Like so many of us today, they understood themselves better when they encountered people who were different from them. In the South Carolina setting, differences *across* major cultural groups suddenly mattered more than those *within* one of the three groups. While small groups may have been engaged in tribal warfare on the continents of Europe, Africa, and North America, the new setting of South Carolina threw different tribes from old continents into situations that forced them to cooperate in order to survive. Native American groups found themselves uniting with ancient enemies against the inexorable penetration of their hunting lands by the Europeans. Africans, cut off from their native lands and languages, found strength in unity against the Europeans who enslaved them. Europeans, far fewer in number than Africans and less knowledgeable about the new country than Native Americans, united across national and religious differences to withstand uprisings from enslaved and indigenous peoples with grievances. Thus, survival needs fostered racial identification.

Race, as a way of classifying people by outward appearance (observable physical characteristics such as skin pigmentation, hair texture and color, head shape, and nose formation), provided a crude but effective method of dividing people into new groups according to features genetically transmitted and easily recognized. The categories of "white," "Negro," and "Indian" developed during this period, along with language varieties associated with each of them.

These new racial identifications were frequently problematic, of course, as some children were born in the new colony to mothers whose racial identification was different from that of their fathers. Such children became labeled as *mustee* or *mulatto*—adaptations of Spanish words for persons of mixed heritage—or half-breed.* As life among the newcomers and native peoples became better organized, labels of racial identity became crucial because the three different groups now thought of as "races" had very different rights and obligations in the new English colony of Carolina. Occasionally the choice of racial label was personal and made freely, but more often it was imposed from outside by the more powerful.

Almost imperceptibly the term *race* came to designate more than physical, inherited characteristics. Anyone who grew up in the South a century ago could point to friends of one race who had physical appearances closely resembling those exhibited by friends of another race. Within a large extended family, some members could exhibit physical characteristics more like one race than others within the same family. This is particularly true for groups who identify themselves as Indian and have done so since the contact period. Among some of these multiracial groups, those claiming the same ancestors might sometimes choose one racial label in one county,

---

*In the Carolina setting, common terms for the peoples of the three continents were *Indian* for native peoples of America (following Columbus's mistake), *Negro* for people of African ancestry (a Spanish word for the color black), and *white* for those of European ancestry. For people of mixed heritage, *mustee* referred to Indian and Negro, *mulatto* to Negro and white, and *half-breed* to white and Indian. In the early colony, *mustee* children were often the result of consensual unions between enslaved Indian females and enslaved African males. Mulattos throughout the colonial period were usually children of white male slave owners (or their relatives) and enslaved Negro females; often these unions were far from consensual. Half-breed children were often born to white male traders who lived with Indian wives in Indian villages in unions approved by the village; half-breed sons (and in at least one instance, a daughter) often became traders themselves.

another in an adjacent county. The choice usually depended on the rights and obligations accruing to each race in a specific location: where African Americans were in the majority with vibrant social institutions, it might be more advantageous to identity with them than with Europeans, and where Europeans were in the majority the opposite might be the case. For a special case such as Robeson County, just across the North Carolina line, where American Indians had a long presence and vibrant social institutions, the label *Indian* was long used with pride, even by those with physical appearances identifying them as being of African or European ancestry.

Perhaps because of ambiguities associated with racial labels that are based on physical appearance, another overlapping term for describing human categories has arisen in recent years: that of *ethnicity*.* This term goes beyond the easily observable and can more often be individually chosen rather than assigned from the outside, as is *race*. Ethnicity can embrace the easily identified physical features included in the notion of race, but it does not always do so. In practice some constellation of physical features, religious practice, food preference, language choice, nonverbal gestures, dress customs, and/or social and political organization serves to designate ethnic identity. However, no one of these factors is either necessary or sufficient. Like race, the designation of ethnicity is made from within or from outside the group. Both of these unsatisfactory terms continue to be used in ordinary language, with little examination, when designating "Us" and the "Other" for a given social setting. One's ethnic self-identity can change over time and place, as we will see for the early South Carolina setting. In contemporary times, more than one person born below the Mason-Dixon Line has "discovered" an identity with all things southern after experiencing life in the canyons of New York City. (To give a similar example from a contemporary context, Japanese or Chinese or Koreans who would never have even met in their countries of origin can become united as Asian "ethnics" in the cities of California.) What this book attempts to show for the South Carolina setting is that the very concepts of *Us* and *Other* have

*See Sollors's *Invention of Ethnicity* (1989) for discussion of how this concept has evolved in modern times.

changed over the centuries that peoples from three continents have interacted together on her shores. Perhaps a better understanding of how these
boundaries have functioned at an earlier place and time can help us address
current Us-and-Other challenges at different places around the globe.

Some of the central players in this story are individuals who have been
somewhere on the margins of the races or ethnicities of their time and have
served as essential "cultural brokers" between the groups—making possible
new ways of speaking and understanding. Because ethnicity is more likely
to include language use, it will serve as our organizing principle here rather
than race. As such, it will allow us to see more clearly those cultural brokers who moved *between* the ethnic groups, were often not trusted fully by
any ethnic group, and do not themselves fit neatly into any single ethnic or
racial category. For communication across the different cultures, however,
these people who were not always fully integrated into either culture were
essential.

We begin with a look at who was here first, who came, and what they
all became as they worked out ways of living together. Our focus will be on
the part that language has played in the creation and maintenance of ethnic identity for the three groups that have emerged from four centuries of
contact. In a final chapter, we will look briefly at several uses of language
as ways of maintaining and of bridging these identities. Language, though
not a constant feature of ethnic identity, is one that transcends biological
inheritance. After childhood a certain amount of personal choice attends
the variety of language that we speak. Most often we speak like those with
whom we identify, and they may or may not be those to whom we are related by blood. Throughout a person's lifetime, more than one language
variety may be chosen, depending on the social setting or circumstances.
As such, language is a barometer of our fluctuating self and group identity.
Changes in identity can be signaled by shifts in language choice—either for
a fleeting moment or for a lifetime. Through the voices of people who
spoke here, we can "listen" to some of these shifting identities.

1 | *Native Peoples*

Native peoples of Carolina identified with the land of their birth in ways the newcomers could not. Their ancestors had chosen names for the towns they lived in, the rivers they worshiped beside, game in the forests, and foods prepared from them. They named themselves and those outside their tribal groups. They listened to the songs of the mockingbird and bobwhite, not Shakespeare's lark or nightingale; they hunted for possum or bear, not the English badger or African lion. They breathed the fragrance of the yellow jessamine on spring mornings and fished in rivers stained dark by cypress knees. For many of them, the sun rose from the waters of the Atlantic in the east and set in the foothills or mountains of the west that looked toward the Mississippi.

Neither the Europeans nor the Africans had any notion of the vast time depth of these indigenous cultures. Indeed, as Mary Louise Pratt (1992) has argued, even later European travelers of the eighteenth century "saw" the American continents, with their vast forests and clear waters, through lenses distorted by images of their homelands. Land that looked empty or "virgin" to the newcomers had in fact been inhabited for many centuries before the coming of the Europeans. The people who had lived here first were—and still are—present. The conqueror writes the history, however, and many latter-day European Americans are still unable to see the "host tribes" or to hear the voices that were here before their coming. Unless we know something about those early voices, we will miss their overtones in American language and dialect of today.

Before Contact

For at least twelve thousand years before Europeans and Africans sailed onto the shores of North America, native peoples had inhabited the forests and shoreline of Carolina (Goodyear, Michie, and Charles 1990). They belonged to highly developed cultures and had organized themselves into towns loosely linked with others. Those living in South Carolina at the time of contact had previously participated in a complex Mississippian culture known as the Mound Builders—a reference to their distinctive burial and ceremonial earth mounds. These mounds, built by hauling baskets of earth from the rich river bottomlands of the Southeast, can be seen today at sites in eastern Texas and western Oklahoma, throughout Arkansas, Louisiana, Mississippi, Alabama, Tennessee, and Georgia, and at two places in far western and central South Carolina and one in south central North Carolina. Other related mound sites exist all along the Mississippi River and its tributaries, up into Illinois, Iowa, Minnesota, and Wisconsin (Texas 1984). The larger culture extended southward from the Potomac and Ohio rivers to the Atlantic and Gulf of Mexico and westward beyond the Mississippi for some two hundred miles (Crawford 1975; Weir 1983). One of the best examples of the ceremonial mounds typical of the culture can be seen today at Ocmulgee National Monument near Macon, Georgia, along with a reconstructed earth lodge where meetings were regularly held to observe purification rituals.

From the years 800 to 1200 A.D. this Mississippian culture flourished on a base of cultivated crops, supplemented by hunting and gathering. Maize, which had been domesticated earlier in Mexico, dominated crops of the Southeast and was accompanied by plantings of beans, peas, squash, and sunflowers. Tobacco was also grown and used for communal medicinal, political, and religious purposes but also for personal pleasure (Von Gernet 2000). Even though their tools were made of shells and stones rather than metal, the planting methods of the indigenous South Carolinians were more advanced than those of their contemporaries in Europe. Row planting was used, a technique not found in Europe for another century, and beans were interplanted with maize for a balanced diet. Cultivated crops were supplemented with wild fruits such as grapes and plums, and the primary drink was water that was easily obtained from springs or shallow wells.

The only lasting artifacts by which we know them are their complicated stamped ceramics. Living in a physical environment more benign than their contemporaries of the American Southwest, Carolinians of the precontact period did not build lasting stone dwellings like those found at Mesa Verde in Colorado or Chaco Canyon in New Mexico. Rather, their homes and villages were built of materials that have disappeared: wood, grass, and earth. The coiled pottery they used for cooking and storage has survived, however, along with the rare stones and minerals that they traded over long distances through an extensive network of villages along the rivers. It may be that the paucity of material artifacts from the native peoples of the

Southeast has made it easy to overlook their contributions in most accounts of South Carolina history. (For an exception to this general neglect, see Lewis P. Jones's 1985 history, written for schoolchildren but enjoyed as well by many adults. Walter Edgar's more recent 1998 history devotes part of one chapter to the first inhabitants of the state.) The size of the mounds and quality of the artifacts that have been found suggest that the Mississippian peoples were characterized by at least two distinct social classes, as well as by complex religious observances.

Around 1200 A.D., some three centuries before contact with the Europeans and Africans, something happened to cause the decline and abandonment of the ceremonial mounds. People began to live in smaller chiefdoms or kin-based groups. Some were simple configurations of a few towns and clans. Others were large chiefdoms, termed *complex paramount* by archaeologists, which integrated numerous different social and kin groups (Widmer 1994). To form the larger chiefdoms, small groups were absorbed by larger ones through military conquests but kept their identities through a loose political alliance. The smaller conquered groups had lower status than larger ones, while forming a loosely cohesive unit strengthened by marriage or placement of relatives in important official positions.

Early Contact

One of these paramount chiefdoms existed in central South Carolina at the time of contact with the Spanish in the 1500s. As we read the explorers' accounts of their travels from this period, archeologists caution us to remember that what these Europeans perceived as separate, isolated social groups were in fact part of larger and long-standing networks held together by traditional patterns of living and shared spiritual beliefs. Although the social groups of the native peoples had become smaller than those of the earlier mound culture, the chiefdoms of the Southeast continued to share beliefs and practices from the earlier period.

A widely known common language may have been one of the significant links between groups living in much of the area encompassed by contemporary South Carolina, but only a few people in each village seem to have spoken it. Several scholars have taken a fresh look at the early Spanish records of their expeditions across the length and breadth of the state and have concluded that this language was some variety of a Muskogean language (Booker, Hudson, and Rankin 1992).

Earlier scholars of Indian languages in the Southeast maintained that Siouan languages were dominant in precontact South Carolina (Mooney 1894; Siebert 1945; Swanton 1946). This belief was based largely on the limited information available from reports of English-speaking travelers such as John Lawson (1709), who made journeys into the interior in the 1700s. More recent analysis of the earlier documents from Portuguese- and Spanish-speaking travelers in the 1500s now presents convincing evidence that the dominant languages belonged to the Muskogean language family, prior to English contact and settlement. This difference in travelers' reports over the span of a century and a half (1550–1700) suggests that a massive language shift took place within the indigenous population itself, before many of their languages died for lack of speakers.

Early Spanish incursions into what is now South Carolina reveal their understanding of what settling this land would require. First and foremost on their list of needs was a cadre of interpreters who could serve as guides and cultural brokers between them and the native peoples. First they enslaved Indians to whom they subsequently taught Spanish, although later they occasionally used Spanish or French soldiers who had learned native languages by living among the Indians, sometimes as captives and sometimes as voluntary guests. An initial voyage by Pedro de Quejo and Francisco Gordillo in 1521 began as a venture specifically to capture and enslave Indians along the Santee River. Referring to the people there as "Chicora," the Spanish captured thirty Indians (who may have been, in turn, captives of Indian wars rather than native to the land called Chicora), and took them to Santo Domingo to learn Spanish. A surviving captive, whom they named Francisco Chicora, was subsequently taken to Spain and then back to North America (Hoffman 1990). He escaped from a later expedition along with his fellow interpreters, no doubt to tell fantastic tales about what he had witnessed in Spain.

In a second voyage made in 1525, Quejo had specific instructions to obtain Indians who could be trained as interpreters. However, on this voyage Quejo landed at the mouth of the Savannah River and found that his surviving captives from the 1521 expedition could not understand the form of Muskogean language spoken along the southern portion of the coast. Sailing north, perhaps to Winyah Bay near present-day Georgetown, he there picked up interpreters speaking an Algonquian language that was spoken north of Cape Fear. They then sailed to an island off the coast of northern Florida, where they enslaved some Indians speaking Timucuan. These accounts from the Spanish are significant because they suggest the linguistic diversity that existed prior to contact: at least three distinct language families along the coast of what is now South Carolina. A failed attempt at establishing a permanent settlement occurred in 1526, when Quejo's superior, Lucas Vázquez de Ayllón, sailed to the Santee River for the purpose of establishing a settlement. Bringing some six hundred persons (including some enslaved women and children from Africa) in six ships, Ayllón found the land not to be suitable for his projected settlement, so he set sail for Sapelo Sound further south. Before he could leave, however, Francisco Chicora and the other Indian interpreters escaped and remained somewhere in the Waccamaw Neck vicinity.

When the Spanish explorer Hernando de Soto marched north through the state from Florida in 1540 looking for treasure, he found the central town of the large Siouan confederation of Cofitachequi, located near the present town of Camden on the Wateree River (Hudson, De Pratter, and Smith 1984). The leader of the Cofitachequi was a woman, whose townspeople had recently been severely affected by disease, perhaps introduced by the earlier explorers along Cape Fear and Winyah Bay. She apologized to the Spanish visitors for the lack of corn in her granaries to share with them, telling them of the sickness that had afflicted her people at planting time the previous year. Soto and his men repaid her by depleting her corn supply and by abducting one of her kinswomen to serve as their guide on subsequent travels into neighboring North Carolina. This woman later escaped with one of the African men in living bondage to the Spanish, and they became mates (Baker 1974, 93). The man was of course probably African and bilingual in his native African language and Spanish; their union would represent one of the earliest recorded examples of sustained language contact between European, African, and indigenous people speaking together in the land to be known as South Carolina.

The need for bilingual guides and interpreters for the Spanish explorers was acute, as indicated by the earliest coastal expeditions and by written accounts from Soto's later journey into the interior in the 1540s. As the Spanish made their way from Georgia into South Carolina, they became thoroughly lost at one point because their Indian guide did not know the local terrain. He did, however, know a language understood by one of the Spanish soldiers, and for that knowledge alone the Spanish tolerated him: "Had not Perico been the only Indian who could translate from his language into the Indian language spoken by Juan Ortiz, who translated everything into Spanish, Soto would have thrown him to the dogs at this point" (Smith 1968, 59; cited in Hudson, De Pratter, and Smith 1984, 71). Juan Ortiz is an interesting example of a European interpreter who had learned to speak one or more of the indigenous languages of Florida when living as a captive for eleven years among the Indians in the Tampa Bay region.

Chosen as a translator by Soto on his expeditions to the interior South in 1539–42, Ortiz "sometimes served the expedition at the end of a chain of ten to twelve interpreters, each of whom spoke a different pair of languages" (Sturtevant 2005, 9). When Soto's initial expedition reached the major Carolina town of the Cofitachequi near present-day Camden, Perico was able to communicate with some of the Indian guides because they spoke a language that he understood.

Although the records kept by Soto and his men offer no details on specific languages spoken in the region, their difficulties with interpreters indicate that the indigenous people probably had no single common language among them, but instead relied on interpreters within each community. The Indian practice of adopting captives of war into their tribes and treating them as full community members made possible their widespread use of bilingual interpreters. Such interpreters would have been trusted by the tribe that adopted them and would have been fluent in both the use and the structure of the language of their tribe of origin and that of their adopted tribe. In his discussion of the languages of Southeastern Indians of the United States, James Crawford (1975) suggests that the extensive similarities in cultural traits among these tribes may have made possible their tolerance of language differences, citing reports from 1700 of towns only twelve miles apart using different languages. In ethnographic terms their rules for language use would have been similar, even though the languages themselves may have been mutually unintelligible.

Subsequent Spanish records kept by men who accompanied Juan Pardo on two expeditions into the interior of South Carolina between 1566 and 1568, as they retraced Soto's 1541 journey, offer convincing evidence to support this claim. Charles Hudson (1990) has examined documents from the Pardo expeditions, reprinting portions of them in both the original Spanish and in an English translation. In a collaborative effort that brings to bear insights from both ethnohistory and linguistics, Booker, Hudson, and Rankin (1992) have closely examined these same documents, as well other admittedly sketchy linguistic evidence. Focusing on the role played by Pardo's interpreter, a French boy named Guillermo Rufín, who had spent a year alone with Muskogean-speaking Indians near Port Royal Sound, Booker, Hudson, and Rankin conclude that Indians living from the southern coast up into the interior around present-day Rock Hill (and further into present-day North Carolina) spoke either a widely understood Muskogean language or closely related dialects of Muskogean languages. Rufín had no difficulty in understanding or being understood in most of the

Indian towns they visited. When he did have difficulty, the Spanish had to resort to multiple interpreters: Pardo would give his standard speech in Spanish; Rufín would interpret in the Indian language that he had learned; and some bilingual Indian present would reinterpret in the language known by the Native American leaders assembled to hear it. After the assembly had indicated by a response of "yaa" that they both understood and approved of the message that Pardo brought, the Spanish would distribute gifts: axes, wedges, chisels, beads, buttons, and cloth. Pardo seems to have given the same speech at each town, asking the leaders of the town and those of neighboring towns who had joined the group for this occasion if they would like to become Christians and give obedience to the pope and to the king of Spain. They were also asked if they would like him to send a Christian to instruct them.

The accounts of this journey and the repeated speeches are interesting on two counts for our purposes here. First, the Native Americans were accustomed to paying tribute to a "grand chief," as indicated by the ease with which Pardo got them to prepare storage places for corn to be used by the Spanish soldiers. Hudson describes three levels of political authority characteristic of the interior peoples of Mississippian societies of this time period. A village head, called *orata*, gave tribute to a regional chief, known as the *mico* (who was sometimes a female). The *mico*, in turn, owed allegiance to a grand chief, or *cacique grande*, whose influence and power was centered near the present town of Carters, Georgia, and extended into Tennessee and Alabama at the time of Pardo's expeditions. This *cacique grande* submitted to no one. The woman leader of the Cofitachequi whom Soto had encountered some two decades previously was just such a *cacique grande*. Apparently outlying groups paid tribute to each of these authority figures, with the stored corn serving as a food bank for the towns and their spheres of influence. Hudson points out that when the Indians became dependent on the demanding crop of corn, their social organization changed: tribes with allegiance based on kinship became chiefdoms with allegiance based on tribal groups. The coastal Indians whom the Spanish explorers first encountered were less centralized than those of the interior, using acorns and wild roots as a primary food rather than corn and living in small tribal groups only loosely affiliated with the stronger interior chiefdoms. Hudson (1990, 83) finds some evidence that the Cofitachequi chiefdom dominant at the time of Pardo's expeditions received tribute from small coastal groups from the Santee River north of Charleston to Port Royal Sound further south.

The foremost interpreter for Pardo's expeditions, Guillermo Rufín, had been a member of the French Huguenot colony located on Port Royal Bay in 1562. When Rufín's colleagues sailed for France, he had stayed behind with the Indians of Orista and later joined the Spanish expedition to the interior under Pardo. Booker, Hudson, and Rankin (1992, 404) believe Rufín learned a Muskogean language during the time he spent with these native inhabitants. Spanish records indicate that, as the Pardo expedition moved from the coast inward, Rufín was able to serve as interpreter some two hundred leagues into the interior. According to Booker, Hudson, and Rankin, "We are evidently seeing a situation in which a single language (or contact language) but not a single polity was present on the coast of Georgia and South Carolina" (416). Sometimes Rufín spoke with secondary interpreters—bilingual Indians who translated their local language into the Muskogean dialect that Rufín understood. Booker, Hudson, and Rankin note the political organization of the native peoples at the time of contact included peoples of diverse language backgrounds; they present some evidence that such multilingual confederations may have used a Muskogean-based lingua franca or simplified contact language internally long before contact with European peoples. In any event, languages of the Muskogean family (including those that later came to be called "Creek") were used by some speakers in most of the southeastern Indian towns. In the Piedmont, Catawba (a relative of other Siouan languages) was spoken; in western North Carolina and eastern Tennessee, Cherokee (belonging to the Iroquoian language family) was spoken; some Shawnee (of the Algonquian language family) was spoken; and Yuchi (a language isolate belonging to no known family) was spoken west of the Appalachians. Basically in South Carolina proper the major languages seem to have been Muskogean in the coastal plain and Catawba in the Piedmont. Hudson (1990, 83) observes that while the town of Arachuchi (present-day Rock Hill) was the northernmost town occupied by Muskogean speakers, the chiefdom had some power over towns further to the north, where Catawba was the language spoken, and perhaps over towns in the mountains, where Cherokee and perhaps Yuchi were spoken.

Although Rufín's success as a translator for the Spanish may have been due to the widespread knowledge of a Muskogean contact language, and although scholars now think that Indians of coastal South Carolina may have spoken Muskogean languages more extensively than previously believed, the early disappearance of the coastal peoples means that we will probably never know exactly which or how many languages they spoke. We have only the names by which the early colonial historians knew them, nothing about the structure of the languages themselves. Inland tribes were known by the name of Cheraw, Pedee, Santee, Saluda, and Wateree. Coastal tribes north of Charles Town went by names such as Waccamaw, Sewee, and Winyah. The densely populated coast south of Charles Town was home to nineteen different groups, with nine others living there from time to time (Waddell 1980). While both Waddell and Hudson (1990) believe that Indians to the south of Charles Town also spoke Muskogean languages, the evidence is lacking. These peoples along the lower coast—known by names such as Winbee, Combahee, Ashepoo, Edisto, Bohicket, Stono, Kiawah, Etiwan, Wando, and Coosa—interacted successively with Spanish, French, and English colonists, and a sizeable group lived within the early English colony as enslaved or as free Settlement Indians. Several small groups entered the state during the upheavals of the colonial period and settled along the Savannah River: the Natchez, who spoke a Yuchi-Gulf language and later merged with the Cherokees (Crawford 1975); the Muskogean-speaking Yamasees, or Yemassees, who migrated periodically to South Carolina from Florida; the Yuchi, who may have merged briefly with the Shawnees along the Savannah River in the 1600s (Eliades 1981; Kovacik and Winberry 1987). At the time of the English settlement in 1670, Creeks (speaking a Muskogean language) controlled lands in and around Charles Town (Eliades 1981). Thus, the emerging voices of the era just before European and African contact were primarily Muskogean, with some intermingling of Catawban in the northwest corner.

Consequences of Early Contact

Prior to contact, the native inhabitants of the North and South American continents had reached a population of perhaps one hundred million, with at least thirty-five thousand living within South Carolina's sphere of interest (Eliades 1981). Within a century that number in South Carolina had been reduced by two-thirds. Only ten thousand remained by the time of the English settlement at Charles Town in 1670. A little more than a century later, when South Carolina had become a state within a newly independent nation, indigenous peoples—or those readily identified as such—were rare: only five hundred could be counted in 1775 (see table 1.1).

To be sure, many descendants of the earliest Carolinians came to be identified as "Negro" or as "white." Those obviously of African-Indian heritage were commonly referred to as *mestizo*, while those of European-Indian heritage were sometimes called *half-breed*. The overwhelming loss of native inhabitants as cohesive social groups was nearly total except for a small band of Catawba in the north-central corner. The Creek Confederacy, made up of previously unaffiliated Muskogean groups, now lived mostly in Georgia and further west, while the Cherokee had moved further into the mountains beyond the state.

What happened within those two brief centuries? Disease, warfare, and trading practices caused widespread social upheavals and population decline. Microbes introduced from Europe and Africa had devastating effects on the peoples of the Americas. As Jared Diamond so convincingly argues in *Guns, Germs, and Steel* (1997), the lack of domesticated animals among the natives of South Carolina meant that they had not developed immunity to the germs that cross species, and they were highly vulnerable to diseases common to the high-density communities of Europe and Africa. Among the communicable diseases introduced by early Spanish expeditions were smallpox, measles, yellow fever, typhus, whooping cough, influenza, and plague. Smallpox was by far the most lethal of these (Kelton 2002); it has a long incubation period and is highly contagious for nearly a month; it can survive outside a human host (for example, on blankets) for several months, and it needs no other insect or animal for a host (as do, for example, malaria and plague).

Warfare and trading practices were lethal in a more direct way, but trade goods were also indirectly linked to the transmission of disease. As we have seen, Indians themselves used captives of war as slaves within their communities, although they did not consider them chattel for life. Spain had a long experience of slavery, but under the English enslaved human beings

Table 1.1. Estimated population by race in South Carolina, 1685–1790

	1685	1700	1715	1730	1745	1760	1775	1790
NatAm	10,000	7,500	5,100	2,000	1,500	1,000	500	300
EurAm	1,400	3,800	5,500	9,800	20,300	38,600	71,600	140,200
AfrAm	500	2,800	8,600	21,600	40,600	57,900	107,300	108,900
Total	11,900	14,100	19,200	33,400	62,400	97,500	179,400	249,400

(adapted from Wood 1989)

became commodities to be bought and sold like any other trade good. While all three of the contact groups (Native American, European, and African) practiced slavery within their societies, the kind of slavery developed during the colonial era "was an entirely new enterprise for all three cultural groups" (Gallay 2002, 8). After the English established a permanent settlement at Charles Town in 1670, Indians found that selling war captives to them was an efficient way to obtain the highly desirable European trade goods. One of the desirable goods was cloth, especially wool, which was warmer in cold, wet weather than their traditional deerskins. This cloth was one of the means by which smallpox microbes could be transmitted deep into Indian country, even without direct contact with the Europeans who had often developed immunity to it in childhood.

Consequence of Later Contact

The Spanish brought the first microbes; the English introduced another round of microbes and introduced trade practices that encouraged intertribal warfare on a scale that would decimate the native population. For the English, and the Scots who joined them, traffic in enslaved Indians constituted one of the most lucrative early enterprises of the new colony established on the banks of the Ashley and Cooper rivers in 1670 (Snell 1972; Gallay 2002). Gallay maintains that the drive to control Indian labor was "inextricably connected to the growth of the plantations and . . . the trade in Indian slaves was at the center of the English empire's development in the American South" (7). Eliades asserts that most were exported from the colony itself because they made unreliable slaves within a land that they knew well, and eventually the colonials were concerned over potential alliances between Africans and indigenous peoples. English colonies in the Caribbean were a favored destination, where "an Indian slave could be swapped for about seventy-five gallons of rum in the West Indies and the rum profitably sold or traded in Carolina" (Eliades 1981, 58), but they were also sold to mainland colonies to the north: Massachusetts, Rhode Island, Pennsylvania, New York, and Virginia. The best figures available indicate that more Indians were exported through Charles Town than Africans were imported into the colony during the years between 1670 and 1715, somewhere in the range of 25,000 to 40,000 southern American Indians in all (Gallay 2002, 298–99). Some remained in the colony as slaves, primarily women and children used for domestic labor. Colonial records show 350 enslaved Indians in 1703 and 1,400 in 1708 (Snell 1972, 61n).

The distant Lords Proprietors, from their vantage point in England, had wanted the colonists to integrate the Indians into their new community, tried repeatedly to regulate relations with the Indians from afar, and were strongly against the slave trade (Snell 1972). The colonists who had immigrated and hoped to make their fortunes in the new land had other ideas. Prior to settlement at Charles Town, the English, like the Spanish before them, had made several preliminary explorations and attempts at settlement. One of these reconnaissance trips along the coast near Port Royal had included a London surgeon named Henry Woodward. In 1666 Woodward volunteered to remain with the Indians there for several months to learn their languages and customs (Hahn 2002). He was captured by the Spanish and taken to St. Augustine, escaped in 1668, and returned to South Carolina in 1670. Immediately the officials of the new colony employed him for exploration, primarily because of his knowledge of five different Indian languages. Woodward and others in the new colony believed that wealth could be gained quickly through expansion and trade with the native population, and their classification of enslaved Indians as trade goods prevailed (Eliades 1981, 57).

In 1674 Woodward went to establish an alliance with the Westo Indians along the Savannah River and from there further into the interior to learn more about the land and its inhabitants (Hahn 2002, 87). The Indians he encountered, later known under the collective name *Creek*, became the new colony's most important trading partner for deerskins and enslaved Indians. Building on the Indians' own practice of enslaving war captives, the Carolinians led by Woodward provoked or encouraged hostilities between the various Indian tribes (Wright 1981) and then exchanged their captives for European trade goods. This trade ultimately included deerskins and Indians exchanged for guns, metal tools, textiles, and rum from the Caribbean colonies. The Westos were a useful early trading partner because of their position controlling west and south pathways and because of their desire for weapons to fight the Cherokees to the west. Initially their Indian enemies would not trade with the Carolina colonists (Gallay 2002). For a short period the Westos supplied the colonists with Spanish-allied Indians whom they captured further south, as well as coastal Indians nearer to Charles Town. In the 1680s a trading post at Savannah Town was established on the north bank of the Savannah River across from contemporary Augusta, which attracted many Indians, among them Yemassees, who were relative newcomers to the South. In 1684 a number of Scots traders came into South Carolina, establishing Stuart's Town in the Port Royal area.

Important in the developing Indian trade, this town ultimately failed, but Scots remained in this area and grew in their understanding of the Yemassee in particular and Indian affairs in general (Gallay 2002, 90). Trade with distant Indians began, and local Indians were employed as slave catchers with rewards of arms and ammunition. A colonial act of 1701 made anyone north of the Santee River or south of the Savannah River subject to seizure if they did not have an official "pass" sanctioned by the officials in Charles Town. By employing friendly Indians as a police force, "the ruling elite had found a way to use coastal Indians to secure the internal order of the colony by allowing no one, African, Indian, or European, to leave without permission" (Gallay 2002, 97).

Three Scots from the Stuart's Town area played major roles in future relations with the Yemassee, Creek, and Chicasaw: George Smith, John Stewart, and Thomas Nairne. As trade increased, local hunting grounds became depleted, and Indians had to travel further into the interior to obtain the deerskins and other animal pelts for trading. James Moore Sr., one of the early governors (not yet elected by the colonists but rather appointed by the Lords Proprietors and thus free to use his position for personal gain), was a vigorous trader in human captives and led expeditions into Florida to obtain more enslaved Indians for sale. As a result of his invasions between 1700 and 1703, many previously separate Indian groups began to form alliances and to use the term *Creek* to cover a confederation of mostly Muscogulge peoples who spoke related languages. Other groups within the newly forming confederacy spoke quite different languages, and thus their closer association under stress from the English slavers set up conditions for language change. As Governor Moore and his troops attacked the Spanish missions where many Indians lived, some Indians who managed to escape enslavement relocated north to South Carolina.

The uniting of the kingdoms of England and Scotland in 1707 under the Act of Union meant that the Scots still living near Stuart's Town gained new rights in the colony as full citizens. One of them, Thomas Nairne, made an official visit for the colony to the Chicasaw and Choctaw, delivering presents and keeping a journal that supplied important detail about the cultural practices of these two groups. He became a resident Indian agent, required to be in Indian territory for ten months of the year and living only two months in the English settlement. His job was to settle disputes between Indians and traders, which had become numerous. When Governor Nathaniel Johnson was accused of promoting illegal wars for booty, he had Nairne imprisoned on a charge of treason (Gallay 2002). After being in jail for six months, Nairne was elected to the House of Commons and worked to reform Indian relations. One of his moves was to urge the Society for the Propagation of the Gospel (SPG) to send ministers to the Yemassee, having observed the benefits of the presence of French and Spanish clergy in their communities. The church officials in England were reluctant to do so, but the SPG missionary Francis Le Jau was receptive to this idea and did what he could, attempting to identify the most widely used language among the Indians. Traders told him that the language known as Saona or Savannah could be widely understood, in addition to Creek, both probably Muskogean languages. Le Jau himself had difficulty attracting the free Indians in his neighborhood to religious instruction, although some masters were bringing their enslaved people of color to Sunday services. The free Indians, Le Jau reported, came among colonists only when they wanted something. He also reported that Indian children in his neighborhood spoke English (Gallay 2002). The missionaries experimented with another method for converting the Indians by sending a young Yemassee man to England for education, planning for him to return and missionize among his people. This young man, "Prince George," went to London in 1713, learned to read and write, and was baptized by the bishop of London. Unfortunately, when he returned to South Carolina in 1715 during the Yemassee War, he found that his family had fled south. They were later captured and sold into slavery, and Prince George himself disappeared from the records.

Before this crucial war of 1715, the South Carolinians had come to the aid of North Carolina when war broke out with the Tuscarora Indians there in 1711. Significantly for what followed, almost the entire army commanded by the South Carolina leader, John Barnell, was composed of diverse Indians from the Carolina lowcountry, Piedmont, and Savannah River (Gallay 2002, 267). This joint venture prepared the diverse Indians for future cooperation against the colonists in South Carolina in the Yemassee War to come.

By 1714 the Carolina traders were out of control. Most went into the backcountry without a required license from the colonial government; they sold rum illegally; and they employed a credit system whereby Indians incurred debts they could not possibly pay. The deer population was declining, and Indian captives were harder and harder to obtain. The Creeks traveled to Charles Town to present their complaints against the traders, and the governor met with them and tried to appease them.

On Good Friday, April 15, 1715, a coalition of Indians attacked the traders and representatives of Carolina, killing most of the resident traders, including Nairne. Plantations were burned and residents either killed or taken as captives to the Spanish in St. Augustine. Surviving colonists in outlying areas fled to Charles Town, and raids continued for a year. Finally a small army was organized to defend Charles Town, which now constituted the boundary of the colony. The Indians did not try to eradicate the constricted colony itself, but focused on the individual traders (Gallay 2002).

By 1717 the Carolina government had made peace with most of the Indian groups but had lost its most important allies and could not defend itself further than one hundred miles to the west. Many Indians moved away, into the foothills or mountains. The Indian slave trade declined, though it did not stop completely. The wars to obtain and enslave Indian captives did stop, and the government took full control of the Indian trade. No more private traders were allowed. Trade as a purely commercial enterprise gave way to trade as an instrument of policy and diplomacy. The colonial government annually presented gifts to Indians, even as Indians themselves developed political strategies that would keep the Europeans at a greater distance while still maintaining a flow of trade goods. Many remaining coastal Indians joined either the Creek, who moved back into the foothills and mountains of Georgia and Tennessee, or the Catawba in the north-central corner of the state.

The group of Indians known as Catawba emerged as a group of natives who "learned to live in their own new world" (Merrell 1989, ix). The term *Catawba Nation* was rarely used before 1700, and the Indians referred to by this name actually included a number of smaller groups in the Piedmont that had existed separately but shared a similar cultural tradition. Located on a strategic trading path between Virginia and South Carolina, they traded with both colonies. Although now dependent on English trade goods, they still retained a choice of trading partners. After 1715 the Carolina traders were more circumspect in their behavior. One trader, Thomas Brown from Ireland, began trading in the 1720s and followed advice from older traders to take Indian wives and participate in village life. Such traders became important for peace, carrying governor's letters along with merchandise to Piedmont villages and sending back messages with animal pelts to Charles Town. According to Merrell (1989), both sides called on traders during times of crisis.

After the Yemassee War, memorialized in William Gilmore Simms's novel *The Yemassee*, many coastal Indian tribes simply disappeared from the colonial records of South Carolina. Those who remained were known as Settlement Indians, with no tribal affiliation. As coastal peoples were destroyed by disease and war, were enslaved in European settlements, or were forced into the interior to join with other native groups, they would have shifted their language use within two generations to that of the dominant group they joined. In the European settlements, that language would have been some variety of English, while in the interior it would have been the indigenous language of those peoples best able to survive the European encroachments.

How did Catawba (related to Siouan languages) become the dominant language of native peoples of South Carolina in the two centuries between Pardo's visit in the late 1500s and the establishment of statehood in the late 1700s? In the most recent accounts of the early native peoples of Carolina, Charles Hudson (1990; Hudson and Tesser 1994) and James H. Merrell (1989) have reviewed the available evidence on internal migration within the Native American groups. Internal shifts in power and prestige came about for a variety of reasons, including a changed physical environment, disease, and war. Prior to the English settlements of the late 1600s along the coast, native peoples had been moving to Carolina in response to two separate sources of pressure: an English colony to the north in Virginia and a Spanish stronghold to the south in Florida. In Carolina they found a temporary haven from European encroachment on their traditional hunting grounds. As we have seen, they could not escape the invisible disease organisms introduced by the Europeans, even though they might not have been in direct contact yet. The resulting population decrease forced smaller groups to band with larger ones for protection against historical enemies among the native peoples, as well as against the encroaching Europeans. Thus, a classic context for language change was established. Smaller, less prestigious groups generally learned the language of the larger group as a second language and then became bilingual within a generation or two. The consequences of widespread bilingualism will be discussed in a later chapter.

Writing two centuries after Soto's initial contact with the Cofitachequi, James Adair (1775) claimed that the court language of the confederation would have been Catawba. He could not have been right, although that may have been the language Adair himself heard in the 1700s. In the first adequate description of Catawba, made when the language was almost extinct, Frank Siebert (1945) concluded that it was a Siouan language. There is little evidence to indicate even how close to the twentieth-century Catawba the language heard by Adair in the 1700s would have been. The people who were called Catawba or Cherokee were quite different entities between the initial contact in the sixteenth century and subsequent English settlements in the eighteenth, much less the Catawba people of the twentieth. In the intervening centuries the Catawba language of the north central part of South Carolina apparently absorbed several related Siouan languages and perhaps even some Cherokee, whose speakers were historically enemies of the Catawba (Merrell 1989). Citing Adair's 1775 claim that the Catawba people of 1743 spoke twenty different dialects and languages, some of which were not Siouan, Hudson points out that the Santee River drainage area, which was the traditional territory of the Catawba, was "a prehistoric meeting ground for the hill tribes and the southern chiefdoms" (Hudson 1970, 14). With such a geographic location, it is not surprising that they might embrace a variety of dialects and languages. After European contact, trade grew in this strategic location: by the mid-1700s the influence of language and culture contact became apparent as the Catawba began to adopt English surnames (Hudson 1970, 43). The European traders in this area had Indian wives and children who lived with their mothers' people. Hudson reports that Thomas Brown, the emigrant from Ireland, was one such trader in the Congaree township and that *Brown* today is a very frequent name among the Catawba.

In his sensitive study of the Catawba's new world after European contact, James Merrell observes that the English-speaking traders living in Indian territory were lead players in language and culture contact: "Adoption or marriage brought one into a kinship network that carried duties and rights understood by all in a village" (1989, 31). Because the traders had to follow traditional customs to get along in the Indian towns, they became knowledgeable about indigenous medicine, cooking, weather prediction, enemy signals—and language. In their turn the indigenous inhabitants learned to read the brands that the European traders placed on deerskins and to decipher the marks used for weights. The bilingual children of the traders became an even more important link between the Indian and European cultures because of disparate customs: by Indian matrilineal rules they were full members of native society, and by colonial custom they were their fathers' children (Merrell 1989, 122–23). The results of this intimate contact within Indian villages were bilingual interpreters who understood both the language and many customs of the Europeans. By 1729 the Catawba were speaking to the colonists through their own interpreters, and after 1750 a European traveler to the backcountry could count on finding an English-speaking interpreter in any village he entered.

Three separate accounts having to do with written English indicate how well the Indians came to understand the respect that the colonists gave to the written word. After the pivotal Indian uprising of 1715, the Catawba requested that the colonial governor's letters be carried into the Piedmont to their villages, where they could be translated and discussed with the bilingual traders. By the middle of the eighteenth century the colonial governors had begun the practice of awarding written military commissions to selected Indian leaders, under the governor's signature and the colony's seal. These written documents were so valued by the Indian leaders that colonial records show frequent requests to replace the original pieces of paper when they wore out (Merrell 1989). Finally, and most important, the Catawba themselves requested that the colonial government survey their lands in the upcountry after a devastating smallpox epidemic that greatly reduced their numbers in 1759. They were aware that the only way to ward off encroaching European settlers from their lands was to produce "a paper to restrain them" (Merrell 1989, 200). This survey and resulting land deed of 1764 provide a clear example of how the indigenous peoples of South Carolina had, after a century of language contact with English, adopted both a new language and a new use of language to aid their own survival as a people. They had come to recognize that written legal contracts in English were honored by the colonial government as binding in a way that oral agreements had been in their native societies. They secured a written document on terms as favorable to themselves as possible at that time—a document whose terms are still respected and debated by those now governing twenty-first-century South Carolina.

The few remaining Catawba still living on the prerevolutionary Catawba Reservation in the north-central part of South Carolina reflect what happened to the indigenous languages after European and African contact. Today the Catawba children go to integrated schools in the nearby town of Rock Hill, and most of the community attends a Mormon chapel. The last speaker of Catawba died in the 1960s, and all Catawba today are monolingual speakers of English.

Table 1.2 is a timetable that summarizes the major contact incidents for the native inhabitants of South Carolina with European and African immigrants to their lands between the 1500s and 1700s.

Table 1.2. Indian contact with Europeans and Africans

1500s	1600s	1700s
1500s—Simple & complex chiefdom societies throughout Southeast. Complex collect tribute from simple chiefdoms.	1600s—Spanish missions exist from northern Florida to northern Georgia along coast & survive until 1686.	1700s—S.C. governor Moore leads raids on Spanish missions. 10,000–12,000 Christian Indians enslaved. Scots on Savannah River trade with Indians.
1510s—Agriculture based on maize; kin networks for social structure; mounds for religious rituals	1610s—Spanish missions	1710s—Yemassee War, 1715. Creek confederacy develops between Muscogulge peoples.
1520s—Spanish explore upper S.C. coast, enslave Chicora Indians from Santee. Attempt at colony	1620s—Spanish missions	1720s—In 1729 S.C. becomes Crown colony based on rice & labor of Africans. Catawba use own interpreters with English.
1530s	1630s—Spanish missions	1730s—Settlement Indians used as African slave catchers, help to suppress Stono Rebellion of 1739.
1540s—Hernando de Soto marches from south through S.C. to Cofitachequi chiefdom on Wateree River.	1640s—Spanish missions	1740s
1550s	1650s—Spanish missions	1750s—Every Indian village has an English speaker to interpret in exchanges with English; Catawba object to rum trade.
1560s—Brief French & Spanish settlements on Parris Island, S.C. Juan Pardo marches through S.C. twice.	1660s—Hilton explores S.C. coast. Henry Woodward lives with Indians to learn languages. English settlement on Cape Fear River, N.C.	1760s—Indian traders have Indian wives & children. Rum & deer hide trade increases with Muskogee & Choctaw.

Table 1.2. Indian contact with Europeans and Africans (continued)

1500s	1600s	1700s
1570s—Spanish have mission on Parris Island. Indians force them to leave, but Spanish rebuild.	1670s—English settle Charles Town, raid Spanish missions & enslave Indians. Spanish destroy Port Royal.	1770s—Naturalist William Bartram travels from N.C. to Florida & describes S.E. Indian life, along with plants.
1580s—Spanish Armada defeated by English in Europe. Spanish on Parris Island; French at Port Royal, S.C.	1680s—English & Indians raid Spanish Sea Island missions & Indians disperse; Yemassee go to S.C. Scots in Stuart's Town	1780s—Silver Bluff on Savannah River is center of deerskin trade & borderland between Indians, Europeans & Africans.
1590s—Spanish missions along Atlantic coast destroyed in 1597; rebuilt on Sea Islands	1690s—S.C. colonists begin trade with coastal Indians: rum & manufacturing goods for animal hides & Indian slaves.	

2 | *European Peoples*

Like the Native Americans, Europeans came from many different tribes before they landed on the shores of South Carolina. Some came from groups that had come to consider themselves as "nations" on the world stage—or at least the European one of that era. Others came from regions or metropolitan areas that were not yet considered to be part of any larger national group. As with those native to the shores and forests of South Carolina, the newcomers gradually replaced their tribal consciousness with a pancultural one as they came into contact with those from the continents of North America and Africa. As the Carolina colony developed, differences across major cultural groups would have seemed far greater than those within one of the three groups. While the tribes of Europe, Africa, and America may have been at war with each other on their home continents, in the South Carolina setting they joined together to face tribes from other continents in a united front. Europeans, fewer in number than the incoming Africans and less knowledgeable about the country than the Native American residents, eventually banded together against the threat of uprisings by both the enslaved Africans and the displaced Indians.

As larger cultural units were formed, the more global notion of race came to replace the smaller tribal or national group as the way the newly formed ethnic groups thought of themselves and of each other. The categories of "white," "Negro" or "black," and "Indian" developed during this period, along with language varieties associated with them. How cultural differences became translated into distinctions of skin pigmentation, and how skin pigmentation in turn came to be associated with language variety, is the South Carolina chapter of a larger American story.

Spanish

The peoples of Europe are not usually thought of as "tribal" at this stage of their history in the sixteenth century, but they did not belong to nations in the modern sense of that word. The Spanish, as the first Europeans on the Carolina shores, are a case in point. The Iberian Peninsula, now divided into the nations of Spain and Portugal, was at the beginning of the sixteenth century divided into several kingdoms ruled by Catholic monarchs. As late as 1492 the territory of Granada along the Mediterranean coast had been under Muslim rule (Lovett 1986). The large Jewish population in Spain, which had played such an important intellectual and economic role under Muslim rule, had been persecuted under the Christian Inquisition and then expelled from the country in 1492. Some 28,500 Spanish Jews were burned at the stake, and another 50,000 fled the country, first to Portugal and then to other countries of Europe and to the Americas (Raphael 1985, 115, 150). The Christian kingdoms of Spain and Portugal, reconquering the peninsula from the Muslims and then exterminating or expelling the Jewish population, were positioning themselves as monarchies holding allegiance to the Roman Catholic pope, kingdoms that commanded both religious and political allegiance from their subjects. More individual kingdoms than a single empire, these monarchies financed economic and religious expeditions to the Americas beginning with the voyage of Columbus in 1492.

The commercial expedition of Columbus focused on the quest for spices, gold, and slaves (Lovett 1986). In the 1500s Spanish expeditions explored the interior of South Carolina and established forts and missions among the Native Americans on its southern coast. By 1600 the Spanish had established towns in the West Indies, in Central and South America, and along the east and west coasts of the Florida peninsula on the North American mainland. Unlike the indigenous peoples of America, the Spanish had steel swords, guns, and explosives, along with leaders accustomed to taking quick, concerted action without having to secure group consensus ahead of time (Weber 1992). They also traveled with huge mastiff dogs that were trained to herd, harass, or kill whatever their masters sent them after (Hudson 1997). These dogs gave the Spanish a great advantage in controlling captive Indian laborers, guides, and translators—despite the Spaniards' lack of familiarity with the terrain.

The explorations of South Carolina by the Spanish between 1521 and 1561 were launched from the Spanish settlements to the south, primarily to claim more Spanish territory and slaves. In 1526 Lucas Váquez de Ayllón established a settlement at San Miguel de Guadalupe, thought by some scholars to have been near the present town of Georgetown on the Waccamaw River (Quattlebaum 1956; Rogers 1973). This short-lived settlement of about six hundred people included enslaved Africans from Santo Domingo. In the fall of 1526 the enslaved mutinied, probably joining recently enslaved Native Americans. These Africans would have spoken Spanish as a second language, as well as one or more African languages. According to a former Horry County librarian, local residents of Horry and Georgetown counties today speak of the "Spanish Geechees" of Georgetown (Catherine Lewis, personal communication, 1981), but any continuity as a social unit has long since disappeared, along with the use of the Spanish language.

Although no Spanish Europeans settled permanently in South Carolina, they left behind a legacy of European diseases that were devastating to the indigenous peoples: smallpox, measles, influenza, whooping cough. As we have seen from the account of Hernando de Soto's journey through Georgia, South Carolina, and North Carolina in 1540, the microorganisms introduced earlier in the failed coastal settlement by Ayllón's people had already made their way to the interior town of the Cofitachequi near present-day Camden, causing the Cofitachequi leader to apologize to Soto for the lack of food in her granaries. During the previous planting season, her people had been ill with the new European diseases, to which they had no resistance. Although Soto's journey through South Carolina left valuable accounts of the Spanish impressions of the countryside and its people, it had relatively little impact on either the land or its people, except to increase the Native Americans' wariness about Europeans. In 1567 the Spaniard Juan Pardo made another exploration of the interior, similar to that of Soto, as discussed in chapter 1.

Much more important to the lifestyles of the indigenous peoples than these expeditions to the interior were the forts and missions established along the coast, from below the southern branch of the Edisto River and extending to the Spanish central settlement of St. Augustine in northern Florida. Becoming a Spanish stronghold in Florida with its establishment in 1565, St. Augustine was joined the following year by a smaller settlement at Fort San Felipe on what is now Parris Island in South Carolina. Using enslaved Indians as labor for the building of this fort and for the planting of crops to sustain it, the Spanish saw these indigenous peoples rise in revolt a decade later and demolish Fort San Felipe. Forced to retreat temporarily to St. Augustine (Rogers 1973), the Spanish built another fort the following year near the demolished one and established Christian missions between the Edisto River and St. Augustine that survived for another century, overlapping the coming of the English. We can only surmise that in the meantime the Spanish learned how to interact more effectively with the indigenous peoples they encountered.

The linguistic legacy of the Spanish is alluded to by historian David Duncan Wallace in his description of the landing of three English ships a century later: "[the] first words that the English heard from the Indians in 1670 were a welcome in broken Spanish" (1934, 55). During their century of contact with the missions along the coast of South Carolina, the Indians along the coast would have come to associate the Spanish language with Europeans. Many would have learned at least some Spanish, and some may have become fluent in its use. The place name of St. Elena (later anglicized to St. Helena) remains today as an important linguistic legacy from the Spanish presence in South Carolina during this period (Dabbs 1983).

French

The initial French attempts at settlement on the Carolina coast overlapped the Spanish period. In France the Protestant reformer John Calvin had attracted a growing number of followers with the publication of his *Institutes of Religion* in 1536. Known as Huguenots, the French Protestants experienced increasing conflict with the Catholic monarchs of France, culminating in three decades of religious wars between 1562 and 1598 and by the widespread massacre of Protestants on St. Bartholomew's Day in 1572.

At the beginning of this conflict, a French Huguenot named Jean Ribaut was sent to Florida and South Carolina to establish a colony as a refuge for the Huguenots. His initial attempt in 1562 was probably on what is now Parris Island in Beaufort County (Rogers 1973). This first venture failed, as did two further attempts in Florida, which were met with stiff resistance from the Spanish.

The situation in France for Protestants improved with the Edict of Nantes in 1594, guaranteeing freedom of worship throughout France. A century later, however, the edict was revoked by the Catholic monarch, Louis XIV. In the decade following 1685, more than fifteen hundred French Huguenots left to join the new English colony in South Carolina, which was sympathetic to dissenters from the Roman Catholic faith and allowed freedom of worship (Rogers 1973).

A historian of the French Huguenots in South Carolina reports that several Huguenots were on board the first three ships that sailed from England in 1669 to found an English settlement in Carolina, and about forty-five Huguenots sailed together for Charles Town in 1680 (Hirsch 1928). Their early participation in the English settlement indicates that, from its beginning, a pancultural group was in the process of formation among the

Europeans. One of its key ingredients would be a Protestant predisposi-
tion, leading to an eventual acceptance of a separation of church and state
that distinguished it from the countries of Europe. Each of the European
"tribes" that came brought with it a particular version of the Protestant
interpretation of Christianity, leading to a multitude of churches competing to become the established church, supported by taxes from the colony's
citizens. The most practical solution proved to be having no "established,"
and thereby tax-supported, religion.

The French founded five French Huguenot churches in Charles Town
and its outlying areas. Initially French was used in their services. Colonial
records indicate, however, that the congregations switched to English fairly
quickly and gradually identified with the Anglican Church, which was also
Protestant. For most of the colonial period, beginning with an act of the
General Assembly in 1706, the Church of England was the established
church of the English colony, with a church built in each parish at public
expense (Rogers 1973). As the Huguenots changed to the Church of England, it provided ministers of French nativity to those congregations who
were French speaking. After the theological schools in France were closed
in 1719, it had become increasingly difficult to find Huguenot pastors to
invite to serve South Carolina churches (Hirsch 1928). By joining the
colony's established Anglican church, the Huguenots achieved the double
advantage of hearing services conducted in their own language and of
having these pastors paid with public monies. It is notable that by providing a minister who spoke French, the Church of England hastened the
assimilation of the French Huguenots into the English society. Colonial
records indicate that by 1706 the Goose Creek Huguenot church near
Charles Town had a French minister who had been ordained in the Church
of England, and by the following year it had been absorbed into the Church
of England. By 1732 the Huguenot church in Charles Town had assimilated
with the Church of England under similar circumstances.

Largely through this accommodation by the Church of England to their
early language needs, the French Huguenots became fully integrated into
the English society. By the year 1733 some French congregations were
requesting ministers who spoke both English and French, revealing the
growing bilingualism of their congregations, and the Church of England
apparently met that request also. The Huguenot parish in the Orange
Quarter on the east branch of the Cooper River was the final one to give
up the French language for its services. In 1758, a little more than half a
century after initial Huguenot immigration, this church also united with an

English-speaking Anglican church, signaling members' assimilation with the English. By this date the original French refugees were all dead, and their descendants all understood English (Hirsch 1928, 78).

Two factors closely associated with this assimilation, in addition to religious affiliation, were marriage patterns and educational practices. Intermarriage between the English and French was common in the new colony. Like the English, many Huguenots were planters on a large scale, and they followed the practice of the English in sending their male children to England for an education. (As members in good standing of the established Church of England, their children could attend English schools, unlike the children of "dissenters" in the New England colonies—a fact that gave rise to early institutions of higher education in New England but not in South Carolina.) A clear indication of how quickly the Huguenots switched from French to English as their primary language can be seen in their wills, which were seldom written in French after 1720, and by the family names, which were often Anglicized (Hirsch 1928, 101). Indeed, the printer of the *South Carolina Gazette* when it began publication in 1732 was named Lewis Timotheé in 1732, but by 1734 (issue 10) the masthead indicates that he had changed the spelling of his name to the more English-sounding *Timothy*. After Timothy's death in 1738, his son became editor, using the name Peter Timothy.

French-speaking settlers continued to come into South Carolina through the colonial period, but the later entrants did not merge with the planter class along the coast, as had the Huguenots. In 1732 a group of Swiss settlers founded the small town of Purrysburg in what is now Jasper County. They had both French and German speakers in their group, but only a French-speaking minister for their Protestant services. Their identity as a Swiss group was soon lost, perhaps largely because the two language groups coexisted and the settlers were not able to provide educational or religious instruction in either language. The final French speakers to enter the colony were Protestants who established the town of New Bordeaux in the Abbeville District, a long distance from the earlier coastal settlements. These newcomers were severely impoverished, having to petition the lord of trade in London (where they had been living on charity) for both passage money and for a subsidy for their beginning settlement (South Carolina Historical Society 1858). In 1764 they established a French Protestant church at New Bordeaux, Hillsboro, just a little more than a decade before the end of the colonial period. By this time they were greatly outnumbered in both the upcountry and along the coast by speakers of English.

Germans

Like the French before them, some German speakers came to the American colonies fleeing religious persecution in Europe; many others came seeking economic opportunities not available at home. Germany was even less unified than France and Spain during this period, being essentially a patchwork of ecclesiastical principalities and free cities under the umbrella of the Holy Roman Empire, which extended from the North Sea into northern Italy. The Roman Catholic pope excommunicated Martin Luther in 1520 for his denial of the church's authority in religious matters, and over the remainder of that century tensions increased between his Lutheran followers and representatives of the Roman Catholic Church. The Thirty Years' War from 1618 to 1648 was conducted mainly on German soil and represented a struggle among the various European monarchies for religious and economic power. Its effect on the peasants of Germany was devastating, decreasing their population and laying waste their agricultural base. By the time of the next conflict between the Europeans, during the years 1701–1714 (known as the War of Spanish Succession in Spain or as Queen Anne's War in England), conditions for many Germans had become unbearable. Some twelve thousand German Protestants accepted Queen Anne's offer of protection, and about half of these continued on to the English colonies of New York and South Carolina (Bernheim 1872). Individual Germans began appearing in Charles Town after 1708. No cohesive group of Germans came, however, before the Swiss Germans and French who settled Purrysburg in 1732 along the Savannah River. As we have seen, this settlement of Protestants had difficulty in providing religious instruction and education in their own languages. The pastor at Purrysburg is reported to have preached in French, reading sermons in German or conducting prayer meetings with a German translation of the English Book of Common Prayer (Voight 1922). Some of their children were sent to the Georgia settlement at Ebenezer for schooling in German, but the distinctive German and French identification of this settlement had disappeared by the end of the colonial period. On the basis of what we know about other bilingual communities, the need for a common language would have become acute as the original settlers intermarried with speakers of a different language and as their children acquired the language spoken by most other Europeans in the growing colony. That language would eventually be English, just as it had been for the earlier Huguenots.

The largest group of Germans to settle in South Carolina in the early days of the colony were those who founded the interior town of Orangeburg in 1735. These newcomers had better luck maintaining their distinctive

German identity than had those at Purrysburg, helped in no small part by
their success in obtaining a German-speaking pastor in 1737 and organizing the first Lutheran church in South Carolina. The pastor apparently
spoke only German and conducted his services in that language (Bernheim
1872). Few English speakers lived in this district, and German speakers continued to join it at late as 1769—both factors that would have helped maintain the language and their tribal identity as Germans. German men served
as justices of the peace, traders with the Cherokee, and translators of German for the colonial government (Roeber 1993).

The settlements most successful at retaining their German heritage
were those established even further inland than the one at Orangeburg. The
Saxe Gotha settlement of 1737 (in present-day Lexington County between
the forks of the Broad and Saluda rivers) attracted large numbers of German speakers between 1744 and 1750. To minister to their spiritual and
educational needs, a German-speaking pastor served both a German Reformed and a Lutheran congregation for almost half a century. In Newberry
County migrants chiefly from Pennsylvania settled in the Dutch Fork area
in the 1750s, an area isolated from Charles Town, Orangeburg, and Saxe
Gotha (Roeber 1993). In the twentieth century the county of Newberry
was the only one in South Carolina to have maintained a larger number of
Lutherans than any other denomination (Glenmary Research Center 1982).
Another German settlement was attempted just before the end of the colonial period at Hard Labor Creek in Abbeville County, but it was not as
successful as the Orangeburg and Saxe Gotha settlements in retaining its
cultural identity. The settlers were unable to obtain a pastor who spoke
German, except for the first few years, and by 1811 their community had
lost its identification with the Lutheran Church.

Like the French, the tribal identify for the Germans was associated
primarily with a language and with distinctive Protestant church services.
Unlike the French, the Germans did not merge on a large scale with the
Church of England, but retained their allegiance to the Lutheran Church.
Their most successful settlements were in the interior of the state (in Lexington, Newberry, Richland, Fairfield, and Orangeburg counties), away
from the English-dominated coast.

Dutch

A small group of immigrants closely associated with the Germans were
the Dutch. Unlike the Germans, they established no cohesive settlements
that can be identified as Dutch. Perhaps because of the greater religious
tolerance in the Netherlands than in other European countries of the

seventeenth century, fewer Dutch immigrated to America in general. After the loss of New Amsterdam (now New York) to England in 1664 and the turbulent decade that followed, some of the Dutch in the New York colony returned to the Netherlands. Others went to the Dutch colony of Surinam, and two boatloads went to South Carolina in 1674. Thus, Dutch in small numbers were present in the South Carolina colony from the almost the beginning of English settlement. Their numbers did not increase dramatically, however. The 1790 census indicates that South Carolina had only five hundred citizens who could be identified as Dutch, less than half of 1 percent of its white population (De Jong 1975, 261). Advertisements in the *South Carolina Gazette* describe runaway Dutch servants only about once or twice a year during the 1740s and 1750s. Some of the Dutch may have joined German-speaking communities, since there was little difference between spoken dialects of the Netherlands of that period and those of adjacent parts of Germany (Gleason 1961). An added problem in distinguishing the two groups at this period is that Germans were often referred to as "Dutch" by English speakers (Smit and Smit 1972). To top it all, the Germans, French-Swiss, and Dutch were all frequently referred to as the Palantines. Determining who was who at this late date is often next to impossible—a further illustration of how European tribes assimilated with each other (or were perceived to be one) in the new colony.

Welsh

One of the economic factors attracting a variety of European groups to South Carolina after 1730 was the direct encouragement of the colonial government of South Carolina. In 1731 this government imposed a seven-year duty on all enslaved Africans brought into the colony, and it set aside the money collected from these duties to aid European settlement. This policy probably attracted many of the German settlers described above. It was certainly a factor in the establishment of a large Welsh settlement in 1736. In that year the colonial General Assembly granted Welsh settlers from the northern colonies of Delaware and Pennsylvania a large tract of land on the Pee Dee River: 173,000 acres in Queensboro Township (present-day Florence and Darlington counties on both sides of the Pee Dee River). The Welsh called this settlement "Welsh Neck," a name it retains to this day. In 1738 they established the Welsh Neck Baptist Church, a church that mothered no fewer than thirty-eight additional Baptist churches in the colony (Hartmann 1967).

For the original settlers, the Welsh language was an important part of their cultural identity. The language was commonly heard in Philadelphia, where many of them had settled first after their emigration from Wales. At least one of the Philadelphia Welsh Baptist churches used a Bible written in Welsh until well into the 1700s (Hartmann 1967, 46). The Bible had been translated into Welsh as early as 1588 in Wales, and church schools had been established to foster literacy among the children. Under the Stuarts, beginning in 1660, the dissenter groups in Wales had been persecuted, and many Welsh had immigrated to America, taking both their language and a tradition of literacy associated with religious observance.

Although dissenters from the established Anglican Church of Great Britain included more denominations than Baptist, those British dissenters migrating from Delaware and Pennsylvania to South Carolina were Baptist. This denomination was a "separatist" one, believing strongly in separating church from civic politics. A relatively new denomination in Wales, it dates back only to 1649 in that country. No doubt the newness of the sect and the threat of persecution provided strong motivation for their establishment of an all-Welsh settlement in South Carolina when conditions became attractive to do so. Initially they limited their group to those of Welsh birth, fostering this cultural identity not only with a Bible written in Welsh but with a concordance as well (Townsend 1935). Their strong missionary spirit mitigated retention of their Welsh identity, however. The new churches they mothered and the welcome they extended to any who would worship with them ensured that the services could not long remain in Welsh. It also meant that Welsh young people came into close and frequent social contact with non-Welsh churchgoers; inevitably they married outside their linguistic and cultural group. By the time the St. David's Society was established in 1777 to found a public school "for educating youth of all Christian denominations being protestants in the Latin and Greek Languages, writing, mathematics, arithmetic, and other useful branches of Literature" (Coker 1976, 28), the medium of instruction had to be English. When the school was finally built a decade later in 1786, teachers were imported from the leading Baptist institution, Brown University in Rhode Island (Coker 1976). English was the language spoken by these instructors.

The use of Welsh as a community language seems to have ended within a generation for this Welsh Neck settlement. The influence of the cultural group lingers in surprising ways. One prominent high school in the region (Conway High School in Horry County) used the Welsh tune "All through the Night" for many decades as its alma mater hymn. The hymn singing still treasured in Wales is also a tradition among many Baptist congregations in the Pee Dee region of South Carolina. The Welsh connection with the Baptist denomination has been largely forgotten by the wider population, as the number of Baptists in the backcountry was augmented with the Great Awakening revivals throughout the colonies in the eighteenth century. The Scots-Irish settling the backcountry of South Carolina during this period were attracted to both the evangelistic services and to the separatist politics of the Baptist preachers; they abandoned their Presbyterian faith in large numbers and joined the Baptists. The Pee Dee Welsh, the upcountry Scots-Irish, and the lowcountry English Baptists in Charles Town found a common bond across tribal boundaries in this new Protestant denomination, blurring original tribal affiliations for later generations. Today this denomination is the dominant one in the state, with thirty-five of the forty-six counties having more Baptists than any other denomination. Methodists, representing another evangelical sect of the Great Awakening but one that maintained ties with the Anglican Church until after the Revolutionary War, are in the majority in eight counties; Lutherans maintain their German-affiliated majority only in Newberry County (Glenmary Research Center 1982). Since colonial days this propensity of Protestants to move from one denomination to another has been one of the most significant factors in blurring, then erasing, old tribal identities among the Europeans.

Scots

The Scots and Scots-Irish made up the largest European group to settle in South Carolina and the one for whom the old tribal affiliations had already begun to blur by the time of their settlement in the region. A few of them came directly from Scotland itself, but most came from families who had already spent several generations on the plantations of northern Ireland. Known originally as Ulster Scots, then as Scots-Irish within the British Isles or as Scotch-Irish in America, these Scots had been "planted" in northern Ireland by King James VI of Scotland (who became James I of England) during the early 1600s in an attempt to bring the "wild Irish" under control (Leyburn 1962). King James made grants of Irish land to landlords in Lowland Scotland and to English merchants, who in turn leased these lands to tenants in Scotland and England willing to emigrate for a chance at a better life. Ulster, with its nine counties about twenty miles across the channel from the Galloway region of Scotland, was attractive to the impoverished farmers of the Lowlands.

By 1640 some one hundred thousand Scots and twenty thousand English had settled in Ulster (Dickson 1966, 3). Of the nine Ulster counties, only Monaghan remained truly Irish: Donegal and Tyrone were almost wholly Scottish, Armagh and Derry were mostly English, Fermanagh and Cavan were both English and Scottish, and Down and Antrim were first settled by Scots with some English coming in later into Antrim (Leyburn 1962, 92). The Scottish counties that sent most settlers to Ulster were those of the Galloway district; others had lived in counties around the city of Edinburgh and in the district between Aberdeen and Inverness. The Irish counties of Ulster, then, experienced contact between the tribes of Scottish Lowlanders, the English farmers and a few city dwellers from London, and the natives of Ireland itself. They practiced several varieties of Christianity (Presbyterianism for the Scots, Anglicanism for most of the English, and Roman Catholicism for the Irish) and spoke distinctive varieties of English that often correlated with their religious practices.

Though the Scots had lived for more than a century in Ireland before many of them immigrated to America, there is little evidence that they assimilated with the native Irish. Overwhelmingly Presbyterian in faith and outlook, most seem to have maintained a social distance from the Catholic Irish whose lands they had usurped, and there is little indication of inter-marriage on any significant scale (Leyburn 1962, 139). With those English who were non-Anglican, there was greater chance of intermarriage, espe-cially after King Charles II was restored to the throne of England in 1660. At that time dissenters from the Anglican faith from the southwestern coun-ties of Scotland, English counties between London and Wales, and English counties in the north came pouring into Ulster. In addition, after the 1685 revocation of the French Edict of Nantes, which had allowed Protestants to practice their faith, some French Huguenots went into Ulster and united with the Presbyterian Church of the Scots. By the end of the 1600s Ulster had become a meeting place for Protestants from several European tribal groups—foreshadowing the tribal contact and cultural leveling that was to occur during the next century on North American ground.

Economic hard times hit Ireland in the early 1700s, and the Scots-Irish and other Protestants in Ulster, whose families had already experienced one uprooting, were receptive to a second immigration to America. Protective laws for English textiles had hurt the Irish wool trade; rents had increased; and wages had fallen drastically. Under the reign of the Roman Catholic King James II in the 1680s, Protestants in Ireland had suffered hard times, as the native Irish attempted to drive them out with the aid of a Roman Catholic army (Leyburn 1962). The fresh economic troubles were all too painful a reminder of their precarious existence and dubious rights to the lands they occupied in Ireland. Between 1717 and 1766 some 250,000 Scots-Irish immigrated to the American colonies. The attractive offer of help with land and rent, and even sometimes tools, to "poor Protestants of Europe" that had been extended by the colonial government of South Carolina was a significant factor in the decision of so many of these immigrants to settle in that colony. Census records from 1790 indicate that the greatest numbers of Scots-Irish had settled in the colonies of Georgia, South Carolina, North Carolina, and Pennsylvania (Leyburn 1962, 186).

The initial Scots-Irish settlements in South Carolina originated from northern Ireland itself, while later ones originated in American colonies to the north. One of the earliest was in the present county of Williamsburg, about thirty miles inland from the coast. In 1732 a township there was granted to some Presbyterians from County Down in Ireland, who had originally immigrated to Ireland from Glasgow in Scotland (Wallace 1856). The Provincial Council of South Carolina paid for their passage and supplied their tools and provisions for a year (Dickson 1966, 50). Several years later they were able to secure a minister for their Presbyterian congregation from Ireland, an important factor in maintenance of tribal identity, as we have seen for the Germans at Orangeburg and Saxe Gotha. In 1734 another Scots-Irish settlement was attempted at Kingston in present-day Horry County, but it was not initially successful (Quattlebaum 1956). The original settlement name is retained by the Kingston Presbyterian Church in the present town of Conway. In all, some 650 Scots-Irish sailed from the port of Belfast directly to South Carolina in the years 1736–1737, before the initial bounty money put up by the colonial government was exhausted (Dickson 1966).

A second wave of Scots-Irish came to South Carolina from earlier settlements in Pennsylvania and in Virginia that were becoming crowded. On the small upcountry farms they established, these Scots-Irish grew tobacco and other provisions for the lowcountry (Rogers 1973). Between 1760 and 1769 many Scots-Irish came into South Carolina because of the renewal of the colonial government's promise of financial help. This new offer was financed by a duty on enslaved Africans imported to the colony and had been prompted by the increasing numbers of Africans in the population relative to Europeans (see table 1.1). Protestant immigrants to South Carolina from Europe were now offered passage money, exemption from taxes for two years, money for tools and provisions, and land amounting to a hundred acres for the family head and fifty acres for each family member (Dickson 1966). Sometimes even indentured servants were offered an annual wage plus land and free passage in return for service of only four years. Remembering the harsh economic conditions in German cities and counties of northern Ireland and the religious persecution in France, we can understand why so many were willing to pull up stakes and undertake the grueling passage across the Atlantic and take up a more promising future in the new colony of South Carolina. Dickson (1966) estimates that between three and four thousand Scots-Irish settlers came into South Carolina and Georgia during this second wave, from both Ireland directly and from earlier settlements in the middle colonies. The European population of South Carolina doubled between 1763 and 1775. Most of the Scots-Irish came of their own free will, with the expectation of eventually owning land in the colony even if some had to undergo the hardships of indentured servitude first.

In the earliest years of the South Carolina colony, smaller groups of Scots had come directly from Scotland itself. To distinguish them from the larger number of Scots-Irish, we will here call them the Scots. A few of them were among the first passengers to establish the colony in 1670. Protestant Scots were motivated to immigrate by the poor economic conditions that characterized their country and by the religious persecution that followed the Restoration of Charles II to the throne in 1660 and the subsequent reign of his Roman Catholic brother, James II, in 1685. An early Scots town called Stuart's Town was founded as a refuge for Scots Covenanters in the southern portion of South Carolina in 1684, but this settlement was destroyed by the Spanish two years after its founding. Although the original settlers of this town seemed to join with other Europeans for protection, they retained their sense of Scottish nationality for some time, as well as the Scots dialect of English, which was considered "uncouth" by some English aristocrats (Graham 1956, 111). A Scots merchant of Charles Town was elected to the colonial assembly in 1702, indicating a fair degree of assimilation with other Europeans, but he was far outnumbered in this body by men from England, France, and the Caribbean islands (Waterhouse 1975).

The 1707 Act of Union between England and Scotland made the move to Carolina attractive for many Scots merchants, because it meant that Scots could now live and trade on equal terms with the English (Rogers 1973). By 1729 enough Scots lived in Charles Town to organize the important social club known as the St. Andrews Society. The coastal Scots were more nearly assimilated with the elite of the colony than were the Scots-Irish of the inland and of the upcountry. They were merchants, physicians, planters, and sometimes tutors for plantation schools, while the upcountry Scots-Irish were primarily farmers of small landholdings. However, even though they mixed with the English and the French colonial aristocracy on a political level, the coastal Scots seemed to have retained their sense of Scottish tribal identity more firmly than the migratory Scots-Irish. The St. Andrews philanthropic society that they established in Charles Town testifies to that, as does the distinctiveness of their speech. According to social historians of the period following the Revolutionary War, one of the great fears of the planter class was that now their children would not have proper speech models as teachers. No longer could the planters send their sons to schools in England, but would have to rely instead on Scots tutors who spoke the Scottish dialect (Wright 1969). This concern with the varieties of English spoken in the colony surfaces in the advertisements for runaway European indentured servants, just as it does in those for runaway Africans and Indians who had been enslaved to European masters. Chapter 4 will discuss these attitudes in more detail.

The smallest groups of Scots to enter the colony were those of the Scottish Highlands, speaking the old Celtic language of Gaelic. A group of the Highland Scots settled in the Cape Fear region, which was then part of South Carolina but is now in North Carolina, just north of the Pee Dee section settled by the Welsh. Like the Lowlanders of Scotland, these Scots were Presbyterians. For their temporary minister in 1732, they had a Scots-Irish pastor who could not speak Gaelic. Soon, however, they obtained a permanent minister who could preach sermons in both English and in Gaelic—an indication that both languages were spoken in the congregation from almost the beginning of settlement (Meyer 1957, 116). Like the Lowlands Scots, this congregation conducted its church school instruction in English. There was little printed in Gaelic at that time; even the New Testament was not available in Gaelic until 1767. The spoken language seems to have been vigorous, however, lasting more than a century from the initial time of settlement. The recorded date of the final sermon preached in Gaelic for the community is 1860 (Meyer 1957, 119). There must have been a long period of bilingualism in this community, as indicated by their strong support of formal education conducted in English. By the 1770s the community was recruiting teachers and ministers from Scotland and was supporting numerous schools, in which English was the only medium of instruction (Meyer 1957, 148).

The fragmented Scots (Scots-Irish, Lowland Scots, and Highland Scots) had distinct histories in the old country, and they came to play different roles in the new colony. Most of the Scots-Irish had no memory of Scotland itself, having lived outside the mother country for more than two generations. Often they thought of themselves as "Irish" with a difference, distinguishing themselves from the "mere Irish" (E. Wright 1969). In some sense they foreshadowed a common American experience, having become during their stay in Ireland "people of a new nationality with its own traditions and culture and points of reference" (Leyburn 1962, 142). They were Protestant, with a fierce hatred for all Catholics, and this new identity overshadowed an older national identity as Scots. True, they shared with other Scots a great respect for education, a term that they identified with a narrow biblical rather than a broader classical tradition. Unlike the Lowland Scots of coastal South Carolina and the Gaelic-speaking Highlanders of the North and South Carolina border region, the Scots-Irish of the backcountry in South Carolina were strongly anti-British and became some of the staunchest patriots of the Revolutionary War. The South Carolina battle at Kings Mountain during the war was fought primarily between Scottish Loyalists and Scots-Irish patriots, bringing old tribal animosities to a head on new terrain. These old animosities, plus their different settlement patterns in the new colony, prevented the three types of Scots in South Carolina from claiming a strong tribal identity with each other. Those who settled in the upcountry focused on the concerns of the small landholder, while those of the lowcountry identified more closely with the large landholders of the plantations. The Gaelic speakers along the Cape Fear River became oriented toward North Carolina after the modern boundary lines were drawn between the two states in 1737.

Irish

Often confused with Scots-Irish in early South Carolina's social history, immigrants with long family histories in Ireland were usually quite distinct from the Scots-Irish who had settled in the northern counties of the island of Ireland on lands formerly held by Irish Catholics. Much animosity existed between the two ethnic groups as a result of this occupation. Although available population figures on the origins of European immigrants to South Carolina indicate larger numbers of Irish than Welsh, German, or French (Edgar 1998, 58), we have little documentation of their language use or its change over time. Early Irish settlers came as individuals rather than as groups. While some of them played significant roles in the colony's early government and commerce, we have no records of colonial-era schools, churches, or social societies founded by the Irish—except for those of a small group of Irish Quakers who settled near present-day Camden (Edgar 1998, 60). The Irish who did come as groups during the 1760s often did so under conditions not conducive to the development of new communities. Lured by the Bounty Act of 1761, which promised passage money to "free poor Protestants" who would settle in the colony, many Roman Catholic Irish were recruited under false pretenses by enterprising merchants who saw a chance to profit by this offer. Some Catholics may even have been kidnapped, and the government often would not pay the promised bounty as a result (Edgar 1998, 59). Although at least one township, Boonesborough, was established for Irish immigrants in Abbeville County near the Georgia border, it is not clear that it grew as a cohesive community with an Irish identity. The lack of cohesive communities and self-directed schooling suggest that within a generation these Irish immigrants probably adopted the speech patterns of more cohesive European groups living near them. In the upcountry, where most of them settled, the nearest groups would have been Scots-Irish or German, but in the lowcountry they might have been English or Scots. Some Irish individuals lived as Indian traders in the upcountry or further to the west, and they would have learned the languages of the Indian groups with whom they lived for ten months of the year. It was only after statehood and an act granting free exercise of religion that the Roman Catholic Church of Charleston was established in 1791; an Irish benevolent society (the Hibernian Society) was founded in 1801; and the first Roman Catholic bishop of South Carolina was sent from Ireland in 1820 (Rogers and Taylor 1994). These late dates serve to indicate both the early challenge and ultimate success the Irish had in maintaining their ethnic group identity in the context of South Carolina.

Sephardic Jews

A European group that is not often thought of as an integral part of colonial South Carolina was the large Jewish population centered in Charles Town. Originating in the Iberian Peninsula and known as Sephardim, this Jewish group was distinct from those originating in the German lands and known as Ashkenazim. Most of those immigrating to South Carolina came from London, having settled there after religious persecution in Portugal and Spain. Some few may have come from the Caribbean colony of Barbados, where a congregation of Sephardim had settled after emigrating from an earlier Portuguese colony in Brazil.

The presence of the Sephardic Jews in South Carolina was an early one, and they rapidly established common political affiliations with other Europeans, although they maintained separate religious practices. As early as 1695 a Spanish-speaking Sephardic Jew was serving as interpreter between the English-speaking governor of Carolina and the Indians from near St. Augustine (Elzas 1905, 19). In 1697 four Jewish men were included in a group made citizens under a special act of the General Assembly granting "liberty of conscience to all Protestants" (119). *Protestant* here seems to have meant non–Roman Catholic. The aversion of the Sephardim to Roman Catholicism had been firmly established during the massacres of the Spanish Inquisition in the fourteenth century and in the expulsion of Jewish survivors from Portugal in the fifteenth. As we have seen, a history of religious persecution had prompted many of the Protestant Christians to come to South Carolina, and their acceptance of Jews who immigrated under similar circumstances may have been prompted by the common hostility to Roman Catholics felt by Protestant Christians and Sephardic Jews. Elzas (1905) indicates that there is some evidence that Jews in South Carolina were voting in popular elections by 1703, although officially only Christians could vote between 1716 and 1790. Despite this official requirement that citizenship rights go only to Christians, a Jewish man was elected to represent South Carolina at the first and second provincial congresses in 1774, becoming the first Jew in American history to serve in an elective office (Goodman 1973, 41).

The social and economic integration of the Jewish population with that of other Europeans was equally early and far-reaching. Jewish men belonged to the Scottish St. Andrews Society in Charles Town, a social and philanthropic organization established in 1729. By 1735 many of the merchants in Broad Street of Charles Town were Jews, trading goods such as wine, sugar, and citrus products for rice and bread products produced in the colony (Elzas 1905). Some Jewish men served as officers in provincial forces, as inspector of indigo and appraiser of dyes and drugs or as "a Linguister or Interpreter for the Spanish Language" in the House of Commons for the colony during the 1740s (Hagy 1993). By 1761 some had established branch businesses up the coast in Georgetown, then the center of the prosperous rice plantations that provided the colony's economic base. By the end of the eighteenth century Jewish men had come to dominate the civic life of Georgetown (Joyner 1999).

Most of the Sephardic Jews in South Carolina seem to have spoken Spanish. In 1750 a large number came to South Carolina from the London congregation, which had used Spanish in their religious services. In the Charles Town synagogue, largest in the nation at the end of the colonial era (Joyner 1999), the Spanish language (or Spanish-related Ladino) was used along with Hebrew. In 1824 members of this Charleston Jewish congregation organized the Reformed Society of Israelites, the beginning of modern Reform Judaism (Rogers 1973). Although this movement was short-lived in Charleston, the petition of the congregation at this time to use English for the prayers and the sermon indicates that Spanish was no longer the language of the home. Like other European groups in South Carolina, the Sephardic Jews had shifted to the common language as the original immigrants died out.

English

The English constituted just slightly more than one-third of the European immigrants to South Carolina (Edgar 1998, 50), but they were the true elite of South Carolina. The free English immigrants who came during the initial two decades were fewer in number than the indentured servants who came later from Scotland and England, but these early English settlers set the tone for the colony's social, political, and economic life for the next century. A number of them were younger sons of English gentry, from the mother country as well as the English colony of Barbados, who had no rights to their family estates because of the English practice of primogeniture, under which the eldest son had exclusive rights of inheritance. Barbados, a Caribbean island colonized earlier by the English, was experiencing a severe land shortage by the late seventeenth century. Settled largely by younger sons of the English gentry and by Irish servants and enslaved Africans (Dunn 1972), Barbados lands had become increasingly concentrated in the hands of a few wealthy planters through consolidation of its vast sugar plantations, which were exhausting the soil. One governor of the island claimed that land in Barbados in 1676 was more expensive than that in England (Waterhouse 1975, 267). A few Barbadians were among the colonists who first sailed to South Carolina in 1670, and their numbers and influence grew during the first decade of the settlement. Among the settlers in that first decade whose place of origin can be identified, fully one-half came from the West Indies (Baldwin 1969). Since Barbados was the most developed and land-poor of all the Caribbean colonies, it would have contributed most of the settlers who could immigrate again to the new colony of South Carolina. These West Indies immigrants would have included both rich and poor settlers in their number: planters, merchants, and artisans as well as small farmers, sailors, servants, and slaves. A small number of them were both rich and influential. One historian reports that nearly half of the South Carolina governors between 1669 and 1737 had either lived in the islands themselves or were sons of islanders (Dunn 1972, 81). Their influence continued to be felt through their descendants, as a large

proportion of the wealthier inhabitants of the colony through the mid–
eighteenth century could trace their ancestry back to families who had entered the colony in those first two decades (Waterhouse 1975, 280).

The free English immigrants, as opposed to most indentured English
servants, were speakers of the standard dialect of England, then centered
around London and the East Midlands. More than half of them were literate (Shatzman 1989). The wealth and prestige that they had within the
early colony, coupled with their use of written English for communication
with each other through the colony's weekly newspaper that began in 1732,
through weekly religious services in their Anglican churches, through legal
documents exchanged with the mother country, and through the many
letters they exchanged with family members and acquaintances in England
helped establish the variety of English they used in speech and in writing
as the standard for the new colony.

Colonial Peoples in Motion

Indentured servants from England and other European countries, who
entered into labor contracts with landowners in return for their passage
money to the new colony, could join the land-owning class with relative
ease if they survived to collect the benefits awaiting them after servitude.
Most who came to the North American colonies were between the ages of
ten and forty, with women immigrating somewhat younger than men
(Galenson 1981). The younger ones immigrated under indenture at ages
similar to those who entered service in England—thus extending an already
existing pattern of "service." In England the prospective servant signed a
contract or "indenture" with a merchant, who in turn sold the contract to
a colonial planter or farmer in the second market. In return for labor a servant received passage to a colony of his or her choice, maintenance during the contract, plus certain "freedom dues" (money due them) at the end
of the contract.

In the first decade of the South Carolina colony, about 65 percent of the
241 indentured servants came directly from England, with more than one-
third of them being literate in English (Shatzman 1989). Those who came
to South Carolina entered into their contracts as free persons, not as pris-
oners or rejects from the streets of London as was so often the case for
those who had gone to earlier English colonies of the Caribbean or to the
Chesapeake colonies further north. Best estimates are that fewer than 200
felons in total were ever transported from England to both of the Carolinas (Ekirch 1987). Those binding themselves to a period of servitude came

in search of the opportunities implicit in the grant of 70 to 150 acres of land due them at the end of their period of service; the number of acres seems to have varied by time period and/or their contract (Galenson 1981; Shatzman 1989). Since both male and female servants were eligible for this offer, a servant couple could pool their resources and have a realistic chance at upward mobility. One such husband and wife eventually owned some 2,230 acres between them (Shatzman 1989). Probably more than half of the indentured servants, however, did not survive the rigors of settlement in the new land. Many fell ill in the unhealthy climate of South Carolina, with its seasonal bouts of malaria and dengue fever, and those who were knowledgeable beforehand about South Carolina often rejected indentured contracts there because of the hard labor associated with working in the rice swamps during the summer heat. Galenson (1981) maintains that the colony's gradual reliance on enslaved African laborers rather than indentured European ones was engendered by its bad reputation for health, climate, and grueling labor required. By 1708 some 4,100 enslaved Africans and 1,400 enslaved Indians far outnumbered the remaining 120 European servants (Shatzman 1989). About 85 percent of the early indentured servants who did survive, after periods of service averaging less than four years, are on record as acquiring property of their own (Shatzman 1989, 135), some of them with holdings of more than a thousand acres. A few of these new landowners were elected or appointed to public office, a clear indication of their integration into the elite ruling class of the colony.

The relative ease with which indentured English servants, and later servants from other European groups, could join the land-owning class would have provided strong motivation for adopting the dialect or language used by the elite as an outward symbol of their own membership in this landed group. In addition to the lands they acquired for planting, these former servants could own lots in town, socialize with others of the planter class, perhaps marry "upward," and see their sons educated in English schools. Women, in particular, were able to move up socially by entering into advantageous marriage contracts because of the shortage of them in the new colony. In 1680 men servants outnumbered women servants by five to one, although the numbers became more nearly equal two decades later as the colony moved toward being a permanent community (Shatzman 1989). Single women could inherit and sell land in their own right, and many women in Charles Town engaged in occupations that would have brought them in contact with the ruling elite. A number of advertisements in the *South Carolina Gazette* are from women selling property and livestock or offering their own professional services as teachers of drawing, needlepoint, reading, music, dancing, or French and English. Such activities would give women who had been educated an opportunity to interact with members of the ruling elite in situations that would require use of the language variety used by the elite.

Those who had land and a reasonable amount of leisure had ample opportunity to socialize with each other in the growing city of Charles Town. The landowners and merchants attended numerous concerts, theatrical performances, and balls. They participated in philanthropic clubs associated with their national origins: the St. Andrews Society for the Scots, St. George's Society for the English, the German Friendly Society, St. David's Society for the Welsh, South Carolina Society for the French, and an Irish society. They also had a garden club, a library society, military and hunting clubs, a fire insurance company, and purely social clubs such as the Batchelor's Society, the Smoaking Club, and the Loyal Society, "vulgarly called the *Laughing Club*" (Cohen 1953, 20). The weekly newspaper the *South Carolina Gazette*, published in Charles Town for forty-three years (1732–1775) with only a few interruptions, kept colonists abreast of international events, of news from other American colonies, and of their own colony's political and social happenings. These opportunities for face-to-face interaction among the elite in Charles Town, as well as for continued communication through print when isolated on their plantations, helped the planters and merchants maintain and strengthen social bonds among themselves. As we have seen, the social bonds established at church fostered assimilation between the French Huguenots and the English elite. In a similar fashion bonds established between Jews and Scots at the meetings of the St. Andrews Society, between English, French, and Scots in the men's hunting clubs, and between the women and men of the library and music societies would have influenced their behavior patterns in language, in dress, and in manners. Former servants who managed to join the planter class would have begun to speak like their associates, abandoning the dialects of northern England and Scotland for that of London, and the languages of Dutch and German for English.

Most former servants settled away from the coastal influence of Charles Town after their period of servitude because the most desirable lands around the city had been parceled out to prominent colonists in the early days of settlement and inherited by their eldest sons. Younger sons moved north to settle the lands around Georgetown or south around Beaufort. The lands of the upcountry were less fertile and more open to hostility from the native inhabitants; thus the colonial government in the 1760s enticed prospective settlers to that frontier with offers of rent-free land and money toward their costs of passage. During the same time period, upcountry Indians now known as Catawba requested a survey of their lands, along with a written deed, because of the encroachment of the settlers coming into their historical territory. The settlers from more crowded northern colonies moving down through the Appalachians to claim the lands offered by the colonial government joined former servants moving from the crowded coastal settlements to claim land in the upcountry as their promised "dues" at the end of servitude. As we have seen, most of those following the Great Wagon Road to South Carolina were Scots-Irish, along with some Germans (Roeber 1993). The coastal indentured servants moving to the upcountry at the end of their servitude were also Scots-Irish or English, as well as German. Those Germans who founded or joined established German-speaking communities in the interior continued to use German for at least another generation until they gradually intermarried and assimilated with their English-speaking neighbors. English had long been the primary language of both the Scots and the Scots-Irish, but it was not the variety of English heard among the elite of the coastal city of Charles Town. Living widely apart in the sparsely settled upcountry, these small frontier landowners had little leisure, as indicated by their ownership of only one or two slaves, if any. They did not meet regularly in social clubs or for music concerts, nor did they send their sons to England to school. Their primary social institutions were the Protestant churches they founded in large numbers and the church schools associated with them. The written language used in the holy texts they read was the same as that used along the coast, but the spoken dialects were more like those of northern England and Scotland than like that of London. The differences between the lowcountry and the upcountry became so great that a college (now the University of South Carolina) was opened for classes in the center of the state in 1805 primarily to promote greater unity between the two sections through the interaction of their young men.

Racial Unity

Although their languages and places of origin may have differed greatly, Europeans who successfully settled South Carolina had several cultural traits that served to bind them together and make possible a unity beyond their original tribes. In the frontier edges of the colony, where Indians had lived for centuries before their coming, European settlers would have

sought common allegiances across their old tribal differences and would
have recognized fellow Europeans almost always by outward appearances
of skin pigmentation and clothing. In this relatively hostile environment,
other Europeans of whatever national origin would be perceived as friends
rather than foes. Along the coast Africans and "country-born" Afro-
Carolinians began to outnumber Europeans as early as 1715 (see table 1.1).
In this area where a coalition of Indians had risen against the European settlers and almost exterminated them in that same year, Europeans of any
background would also be perceived as part of "us"—neighbors with common interests who could be counted on in times of trouble.

Equally important as physical appearance, although not as often recognized as a cultural bond, was literacy for all Europeans—whatever the language they spoke. Not all settlers were literate, true, but many were, and
all groups sought educated preachers and teachers for their churches and
young people. This was a fairly new phenomenon for Europeans in general and related to the breakup of the medieval Roman Catholic Church
with its Latin-based holy texts accessible only to a limited few. With the
Protestant Reformation that got underway in the 1500s, the holy texts of
Christendom were gradually translated into the vernacular languages used
in the developing nation-states, were disseminated in multiple copies by
the newly invented printing press, and were read by many ordinary people
without the mediation of an educated clergy. In the eighteenth century the
novel and the newspaper emerged, linking people who did not know and
would never meet each other into what Benedict Anderson (1983) has called
"imagined communities." Vernacular languages replaced Latin as the language of government, and those who had never had access to written documents (such as merchants and women) were united with other readers in
their "language field." As Anderson puts it, "These fellow-readers, to whom
they were connected through print, formed, in their secular, particular, visible invisibility, the embryo of the nationally-imagined community" (47).
Certainly the weekly *South Carolina Gazette*, published initially in 1732,
served to unite literate readers throughout the colony who might never
meet each other face to face. Their perceived common interests and concerns about activities of the other two "races" were given voice by this
newspaper in Charles Town. The choice of English as the language for this
newspaper that had been started by a French Huguenot solidified English
as the language in which the colony did its business and conducted its
affairs. Although English was the spoken language of only one portion of
the European settler population, every European group had its own literate

practice. Literacy and the uses of printed language for religious purposes and governmental affairs were common to all the European tribes that settled in South Carolina, and the wide use of written English by those who ran the colony's affairs served to unify them all across time and space.

Native Americans in North America had not developed literacy among themselves at the time of contact, although a half-Cherokee named Sequoyah developed a syllabic alphabet for Cherokee in the nineteenth century, which enabled his people to achieve a high level of literacy among themselves (Crystal 1987). Few Africans were literate, except for some Muslim males who had learned to read the Koran. The conditions of slavery in South Carolina ensured that they could neither teach each other the Arabic used in this holy text nor use it to communicate with the wider Arabic-speaking world. As the colony developed, many Africans sought actively to read and write English, recognizing the practice of literacy as an avenue of personal and social empowerment in their position as chattel property.

Religion was another unifying factor among Europeans. Virtually all the settlers were Protestant Christians except for the important group of Jewish settlers along the coast. As merchants with extensive contacts around the Atlantic world, these Jews held a vital position in the economy of the colony from the earliest days. Though not of the same religious faith as other settlers, they shared with them a belief in the God of the Old Testament and an abhorrence of the Roman Catholicism that had persecuted their ancestors in the Iberian Peninsula. Both Jews and Protestant Christians were "people of the Book," with written texts that contained religions truths serving as guides to religious rituals. In contrast, except for the few Muslims, the people of America and Africa held religious beliefs tied to a locality rather than to a book. Indians throughout the Southeast typically located their village along a river in a position where they could see the sun rise and perform rituals associated with the natural world that surrounded them. Separated from their own natural surroundings and local gods, the Africans more quickly than the Indians adopted Christian beliefs and rituals—though often in forms that encompassed rhetorical forms and practices of their ancestral homelands.

In sum, while physical appearances may have been the most obvious source of racial unity among the Europeans, literacy and religion were other broad unifying factors. Their position as a minority outnumbered by both Africans and Indians in the early decades of the colony was of course the most obvious factor leading to both racial consciousness and racial unity.

3 | *African Peoples*

Unlike indigenous Carolinians and immigrant Europeans, Africans did not choose South Carolina as their home. Enslaved Africans accompanied the Spanish explorers on their interior marches in the 1500s; then the English imported Africans by force to be used as laborers in their new colony, beginning with the first ships to arrive in Charles Town in 1670. Peter H. Wood's analysis (1974) of the origins of Africans in the early settlement of South Carolina indicates that those arriving in the first generation came from other English colonies in the Caribbean. Since it was not until after 1700 that Africans outnumbered Europeans in South Carolina (see table 1.1), many Africans in the first three decades of the colony usually became bilingual in English, as did the white servants from non–English-speaking parts of Europe. The majority of Africans in this early period came from the overpopulated English island of Barbados, where they had already been exposed to English. In the less densely populated South Carolina, where they often worked side by side with their owners in the early days of the colony, the opportunities to become fluent in English would have been much greater than on the sugar plantations of Barbados. Slave and servant alike would typically learn to speak a variety of English used in the landowner's household as they worked together at the myriad of tasks associated with life in frontier settlements. A smaller number would become bilingual in the French or German spoken in some households, but even they would soon add English as second and third generations of the household came to use it as their primary language.

As the economy of South Carolina began to shift to one based primarily on rice, and as prospective European servants showed more and more reluctance to serve their terms of indenture in subtropical Carolina, the larger landowners began to import shiploads of workers directly from Africa. In the emerging global economy around the Atlantic, African slave traders and European merchants alike treated human laborers from sub-Saharan Africa as a commodity. In the process the meaning of slavery as an institution changed radically: what had been in Africa a term of servitude similar to European serfdom with negotiated terms of labor (Carney 2001) became the absolute control of human beings in the European trade system and for any children born to an enslaved woman. In early South Carolina enslaved Africans were able to negotiate a "task system" of assigned jobs, with free time to cultivate their own gardens or hunt game and fish when these tasks were complete, but their mobility and freedom to profit from their own labor were severely curtailed. Slavery as reinterpreted by Europeans in their colonies became a chattel system, with enslaved persons listed in wills as property to be divided among heirs, right along with horses, hogs, and houses. From its inception the colony of Carolina had been a commercial enterprise funded by absentee English landlords. Initially the sale of deer hides, enslaved Indians, and wood products were profitable for Carolina traders and European merchants, but as these natural resources became depleted, various crops were tried with an eye to their sales potential. Rice proved to be the winner in Carolina's subtropical climate, and it was a crop that required intensive labor to satisfy the demand for this first cereal to be traded globally. The slave trade itself—with a peak of one hundred thousand people annually taken from Africa during the eighteenth century—increased the global demand for this rice that was easily stored and consumed by enslaved Africans on the voyages across the Atlantic (Carney 2001).

Many Africans were skilled in the growing and processing of rice for local consumption if they had grown to adulthood along the rice-growing West Coast of Africa, and the Carolina planters preferred laborers from this area for their knowledge of a crop not grown in Europe. After a period of quarantine on Sullivan's Island, which Peter H. Wood has called the "Ellis Island" of black Americans (1974, xiv), Africans were sold in the slave markets of Charles Town to be domestic laborers, field hands, and skilled artisans within South Carolina or were transported to other English colonies in North America. Representing perhaps hundreds of different tribal groups from the western coastal and inland regions of Africa and speaking even more languages than the Europeans, these Africans also came to self-identify and be identified by outsiders as one race in the South Carolina context. Like their European and Indian fellows, they had perceived many distinctions among themselves in sub-Saharan Africa and continued to do so in Carolina. Under conditions of bondage in Carolina, they forged new elements of language and culture.

To discover exactly where these Africans originated, historians have relied primarily on records kept by the European slave agents in Africa, Atlantic ship captains, and South Carolina slave traders and owners for documentation. (See especially Curtin 1969, Wood 1974, and Littlefield 1981.) A more complete understanding of the processes by which the tribal groups of Africa became the "Negro race" in colonial America awaits more indirect evidence supplied by anthropologists, folklorists, ethnohistorians, and linguists. Because of the overwhelming numbers of Africans in bondage in South Carolina, how an African American consciousness manifested itself through language is of central significance to how this racial identification developed. In South Carolina, where Africans arrived speaking as many as forty or fifty different African languages, together they created and learned a common language that can still be heard in many homes, churches, and school yards of the lowcountry: *Gullah*.

Under conditions of slavery that were quite different from those in other European colonies of South America, the Caribbean, and elsewhere on the North American continent, Africans in the Carolina colony forged a common identity that drew on the Bantu heritage of the Congo-Angola region, the related heritage of the Niger Delta region, and the traditions of the Guinea Coast between modern Nigeria and Senegal. The geographic area encompassed by the enslaved Africans imported to South Carolina was far larger than that from which the Europeans came. Despite the vast area encompassed by their homelands, Africans, like Europeans and Indians, shared many religious beliefs and social customs that enabled them to shape and maintain their own distinctive traditions. Most important, the Carolina colony, unlike other mainland colonies, contained more Africans than Europeans and Indians for most of the colonial period. On the larger plantations Africans were able to construct a distinctive culture of their own in slave quarters that were apart from the main plantation house. Because many plantation communities were broken up upon a slave owner's death and because skilled enslaved adults often had fairly extensive freedom of movement, the spread of many elements of this common culture took place throughout the plantation belt of the American South. African Americans made economic, cultural, and linguistic contributions that social historians have only recently begun to recognize, ones that have given the old American South many of its distinctive social and artistic forms: music and dance, food preferences and preparation, spiritual beliefs and respect for the wisdom of elders, storytelling and language.

Windward and Leeward Coasts of Africa

The national boundaries in postcolonial Africa have changed so much and so often from the original tribal territories of the 1700s that the origins of

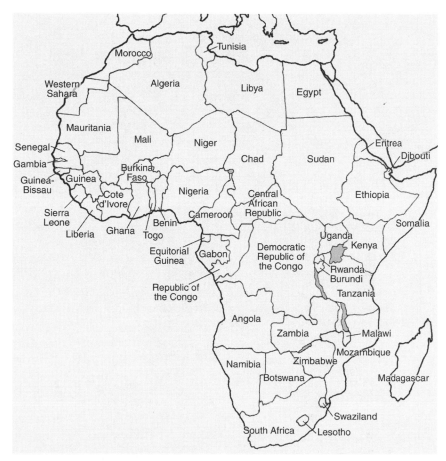

FIGURE 3.1 National boundaries in modern Africa

Africans who came to South Carolina are best described in terms of regional rather than national boundaries, though these modern national boundaries must serve as a point of reference (see fig. 3.1).

The early Africans brought to South Carolina from Barbados and other Caribbean islands probably had been born along the Guinea Coast. (While sources vary as to what *Guinea Coast* refers to, it is used here to mean that portion of West Africa that lies between the Senegal and Niger rivers (see fig. 3.2.)

Dunn (1972) indicates that the sugar planters of Barbados, Jamaica, and the Leeward Islands of the Caribbean were the first Englishmen to practice slavery on a large scale, bringing some 250,000 Africans to these islands before the end of the seventeenth century. About 30 percent of the enslaved

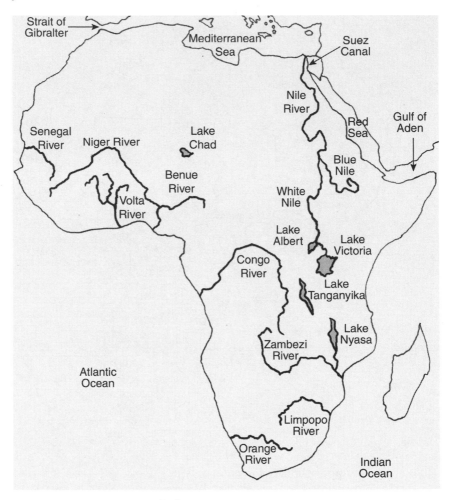

FIGURE 3.2. Major rivers of Africa

Africans in the Caribbean originated in Senegambia and in Angola, while
the remaining 70 percent were from the lower Guinea Coast, specifically
the Windward Coast (Liberia), the Gold Coast (Ghana), and the Slave
Coast (Togoland, Dahomey, and Western Nigeria). Dunn indicates that
the Caribbean planters considered Angolans to be the least desirable of all
West Africans, characterizing them as rebellious and lazy. Bridenbaugh and
Bridenbaugh (1972, 240) seem to confirm Dunn's assessment of the low
numbers of Angolans in the Caribbean, indicating that both the Dutch and
the English secured the bulk of their captive Africans at the mouth of the

Gambia River or on the Gold Coast. Those from the upper Guinea Coast were more expensive than those from the Gold Coast, a factor that may have weighed heavier with some slavers than with others. In any event both Dunn's and the Bridenbaughs' analyses suggest that the earliest Africans brought to South Carolina from Barbados originated along the Guinea Coast rather than in the Congo-Angola region.

Perhaps influenced initially by Caribbean planters, a number of whom became leaders in early South Carolina life, planters on the Carolina mainland showed a decided preference for laborers from the upper Guinea Coast region, Gambia in particular. This preference is clear in the planters' letters and in the advertisements in the *South Carolina Gazette*. Peter H. Wood (1974) has proposed that African knowledge about rice growing was essential to the successful cultivation of this crop that formed the economic base of the South Carolina colony. Europeans knew virtually nothing about its growth when they entered the colony, but the climate and rivers of coastal South Carolina were ideal for the crop, which became its major export to Europe and to other English colonies. Daniel Littlefield (1981) has further developed Wood's thesis to show that more than 40 percent of the Africans brought to South Carolina during the 1700s came from rice-growing areas along the upper coast of Guinea, extending from present-day Senegal to Sierra Leone. The clear preference of South Carolina planters for labor from this area meant that they would have kept these Africans in South Carolina rather than selling them to other colonies, especially since other North American colonies did not show such a preference.

Who were these peoples eagerly sought by the Europeans as participants, even though involuntary ones, in the newly established colony? Some had been slaves in the rice fields of West Africa, according to Littlefield (1981, 78–80). He cites one slave trader's report of slaves on the coastal rice plantations of Sierra Leone being brought from the interior to cultivate the local crop before being sold to Europeans for transportation across the Atlantic. The linguist P. E. H. Hair (1965) has observed that a large proportion of the vocabulary of blacks on the Sea Islands of South Carolina and Georgia listed in the work of linguist Lorenzo Dow Turner (1949) as "African" come from the Sierra Leone region, although Littlefield's demographic analysis does not indicate the existence of a disproportionate number of Africans from this region. South Carolina groups identified by Littlefield as familiar with many varieties of rice, as well as with a wide range of cultivation methods associated with the different growing environments of Africa, include the Malinke, Soninke, Serer, Joola, Balante, Kisi, Papel,

Baga, Mende, and Temne. The slavers and planters used more generalized names, often associated with geographical region, as indicated by the newspaper advertisements for runaway slaves. The *South Carolina Gazette* described 188 of the 1,327 runaways between 1732 and 1775 as simply *Guinea* (Littlefield 1981), a term that was often generic for all of West Africa between Senegal and Angola (Equiano 1789; Harris and Levey 1975) but sometimes referred only to the region between Senegal and modern Nigeria. More specific identifications list 277 runaways with origins on the Windward Coast and its hinterland (Gambia, Mandingo, Jolonka, Bambara, Fullah, Araba, Limbo, Temna, Windward Coast, Boler, Kishee, Rice Coast, Grain Coast), an area extending from the upper Guinea Coast to a portion of the lower Guinea Coast (Littlefield 1981, 118–19). Only 64 were identified as coming from the Leeward Coast and its hinterland (Gold Coast, Coromantee, Cromttey, Fantee, Yaney, PawPaw, Whydah, Nego, Carbady, and Simbey), an area encompassing the remainder of the lower Guinea Coast between present-day Liberia and the Niger River delta.

Littlefield compares the runaway slave figures for different tribal groups with the import figures from Curtin (1969) and finds that the Gambians were overrepresented among runaways. He suggests that the case for the planters' preference for Gambia workers is made even stronger by their propensity to escape, indicating that the value of their agricultural skills outweighed the risk of their running away. He notes, however, that it is not always clear exactly what the Europeans meant by the Gambia; it may sometimes have been used as a general term for any African from the upper Guinea Coast. He notes also the slavers' and planters' practice of assigning a country label to an African who was shipped from a port associated with that country, even if brought to the port from further inland. Littlefield believes that the available evidence suggests that most Africans brought to coastal South Carolina originated in coastal areas of western Africa rather than the interior. As we shall see, this may not have been the case for the Congo-Angola area.

What is clear is the planters' preference for slaves from the upper Guinea Coast and their significant numbers as both imports and as runaways. There is some indication that South Carolina planters did value slaves from the Gold Coast (roughly present-day Ghana), but it is also clear that the majority of Africans from the Gold Coast who were transported by the British ended up in Jamaica. Littlefield suggests that one of the reasons for this may have been the lack of women available in the Gold Coast traffic, given the South Carolina planters' well-established practice of importing both men and women to the colony. Unlike the planters in the Caribbean, the Carolina planters encouraged family life among their slaves in order to increase their slave holdings. They could afford to do so, Littlefield suggests, because the plantations of South Carolina were self-supporting and produced most of their own foodstuffs, unlike the Caribbean sugar plantations. An established plantation owner of coastal South Carolina might see the long-term benefit of supporting women of childbearing age, knowing that within a few years their children would be contributing to some of the less strenuous domestic labor needed for the plantation. Many planters also valued the skills of older slaves who were no longer able to contribute their physical labor but who were well able to supervise others, to attend to less physically demanding craft work found on the Carolina plantations, and—perhaps most important of all—to provide the cultural glue that held the large and constantly changing group of enslaved peoples together as a community.

Recent work by Judith Carney (2001) on the cultivation of rice in colonial South Carolina and Georgia helps us to understand why Africans from the Senegambia coast were preferred over all others: the knowledge base they brought with them. *Oryza glaberrima* had been cultivated in Africa for centuries in an area from Senegal south to Liberia and inland for about one thousand miles to Lake Chad; it probably was originally domesticated in the wetlands of the inland delta of the middle Niger River in Mali. Different systems of cultivation had been developed to adapt to specific climate and soil conditions: a wetland crop in the river floodplains of Senegal, Gambia, Niger, and Bani, which was alternated with cattle raising; and a mangrove crop along coastal estuaries further south, which was alternated with other crops and for which elaborate canals and embankments were used to control water flow. Less than one hundred years after the first successful settlement near modern Charleston, South Carolina had become the richest southern colony, and Charles Town had one of the greatest concentrations of wealth in the world—all based on the production of rice by the knowledge and labor of enslaved African women and men.

Carney discovers three distinct stages of production over the first century of the colony's life: (1) initial rain-fed swamp cultivation and complementary cattle raising, with cow pens developed in remote areas by slaves doing open-range cattle raising; (2) inland swamp cultivation with lands cleared and banks built to hold and release water, as in the mangrove system of Africa; (3) tidal cultivation between the 1750s and 1770s, when some fifty-eight thousand Africans entered the colony, many of them coming from Senegal, Gambia, and Sierra Leone—many of them female. As Dale Rosengarten (1987) has documented, even the fanner baskets used by plantation women to winnow the rice were patterned after those found in Senegal, though woven with Carolina grasses. Women were a crucial part of rice cultivation early in the colony history because, as Carney documents, rice cultivation is largely a woman's occupation (planting, weeding, and processing) in most of the African rice-growing region. The knowledge base of West African women for rice (and also indigo) might account for why women were brought in greater numbers to Carolina than to the Caribbean sugar colonies. Their presence led to an earlier population growth of "country born" slaves in Carolina than in the Caribbean. Because of their numbers, the Afro-Carolinians became significant agents of language spread on the coastal plantations and in the urban centers.

Niger Delta Region

Those Africans deemed least desirable as slaves in South Carolina were Calabars of both genders and Igbo men from east of the Niger River. Curiously enough Igbo women were found in disproportionately high numbers and seem to have been thought desirable for the South Carolina colony. Littlefield (1981, 10) cites a wide range of evidence indicating that the planters thought Calabar and Igbo people to be not only small and weak but also melancholy and apt to commit suicide. He also gives convincing evidence that, despite their general disdain of people from this region, South Carolina planters imported more Igbo women than women of any other region. Although in general enslaved women of all groups ran away less frequently than men, those women labeled *Igbo* or identified as from the Bight of Biafra were unlike any other group of enslaved women in the colony. The runaway advertisements in the *South Carolina Gazette* show that, in proportion to their numbers in the colony, more of these women ran away than women from any other group, even those born in the colony itself (Littlefield 1981, 143). The total number of runaway slaves (both Igbo and Calabar) from the Niger Delta was only eighty-nine, just a few more than those from the lower Guinea Coast, but Littlefield's careful analysis indicates that the relative proportion of Niger Delta women who escaped was high (20).

Clues as to why the planters might have wanted Igbo women in South Carolina, despite this undesirable tendency, can be found in the 1789 autobiography of a former enslaved Igbo man, Olaudah Equiano. Kidnapped as a boy of eleven from what is now the province of Benin in Nigeria, Equiano attained a wide view of the world, serving as a slave in Barbados, Virginia, and England, in the British navy, and on colonial trading ships. In 1767 he bought his own freedom in England, and two decades later he wrote his memoirs, probably with the aid of an editor, in connection with his work for the antislavery movement in Britain (Jones 1968). Equiano describes the Igbo people with details one would expect from a man who had encountered a wide range of customs in his travels around the Atlantic, noting their distinguishing characteristics in almost ethnographic terms. These people, he says, are a nation of dancers, musicians, and poets, celebrating every great event with dancing, accompanied with appropriate songs and music. He describes their musical instruments as drums of different kinds, a stringed instrument something like a guitar, and a percussion instrument similar to a xylophone. They use a local indigo to dye their clothes a shade of blue that Equiano thinks brighter and richer than any used in Europe. Both men and women, as well as children, work the crops, with the women spinning, weaving, and dyeing cotton with indigo. Equiano reports that the Igbo grow yams, beans, and Indian corn for vegetables and keep cattle, goats, and poultry for meat. Tobacco is grown and smoked in clay pipes that they make. They have a variety of peppers, which they favor for spices, and make a fermented drink from the sap of palm trees. Some of these food crops, of course, had come originally from the Americas as part of the global trade around the Atlantic: Indian corn, tobacco, and peppers.

Indigo became an important export crop in the Carolina colony by the mid-1700s, second only to rice. Details of the struggle to find the right seeds and suitable growing conditions for it can be found in the letters of a remarkable young woman born in the West Indies, educated in England, and sent to South Carolina along with her mother to look after her father's plantations there (Pinckney 1972). From the young age of sixteen to twenty-one, while her father remained in Antigua, Eliza Lucas Pinckney managed two Carolina plantations, one located along the Waccamaw River, where she experimented with indigo and other crops. By 1745 she had shown that indigo could be grown in South Carolina of a quality that would be desirable for the textile industry in England. Her letters make only fleeting references to the slaves on her plantations, and we have no direct evidence of their help with her experiments. She mentions her efforts to teach two enslaved girls to read so that they could become "school mistres's for the rest of the Negroe children" (Pinckney 1972, 34) and her "superintendentcy over a little small pox Hospital" some years later when she managed another plantation after her husband's death. She gives no details of trials in the fields by which she selected suitable land for the indigo, though she does mention the seeds that her father sent her from Antigua and those distributed to other planters from crops she raised. We can only infer that, as with the growing of rice, knowledge of the growing and the processing of the indigo crop came in large measure from Africans who were familiar with it. We can speculate, though we may never know, that this young woman found it quite natural to accept advice from the African women of her father's plantation about growing and processing a crop new to her and to the colony. Igbo women, according to Equiano's account, would have had those skills. Like the Gambians, whose tendencies to run away were tolerated because of their rice-growing skills, these Igbo women's tendency to run away and their melancholic dispositions were probably tolerated by many of the South Carolina planters because they understood the growth habits of indigo, as well as the fermentation process that resulted in the valuable cakes of blue dye.

Congo-Angola Region

Even though the planters preferred workers from Gambia, at times they imported more from the Angola region further south of the Niger Delta, particularly in the years of the colony just prior to the Stono Rebellion of 1739. During the initial growth of the rice plantation economy, more enslaved people were imported from Angola than from any other region, a situation that probably had more to do with availability than with preference. Wood's figures for 1735 to 1740 indicate that nearly 70 percent of the Africans arriving in Charles Town during those five years were Angolans, with about 6 percent from Gambia, less than 1 percent from the West Indies, and the remainder from elsewhere in Africa (1974, 340–41). The Stono uprising, which took place about twenty miles from Charles Town on a Sunday while the planters were at church, included many Angolans among the conspirators. From an initial number of twenty, the rebellious group grew to sixty or one hundred, as they marched some ten miles toward St. Augustine, where they anticipated a warm reception from the Spanish. The Spanish were both hostile to the English and also spoke a language closely related to Portuguese, which many of the Angolans may have learned when Portugal occupied their native region. The uprising was suppressed before it reached the South Carolina border, late on the same day that it began, when the group stopped to rest on the banks of the Edisto River. Most of their number were either killed or recaptured, but they shocked the planters into recognizing the great potential for further uprising in a situation where Africans now outnumbered Europeans by more than two to one. In 1740 the colonial assembly adopted a strict slave code that was to regulate activities of enslaved Africans until their emancipation after the Civil War.

After the Stono Rebellion, the number of Africans brought to the colony from the Congo-Angola region declined. While in the 1730s and 1740s they had made up 39 and 31 percent of the runaway slaves, respectively, they constituted roughly 21 percent for the overall period between 1732 and 1775, or 276 out of a total of 1,327 runaways advertised (Littlefield 1981, 20–21). This is about equal to those from the upper Guinea Coast, a figure that includes the Gambians and the Igbo women from the Bight of Biafra, who are overrepresented in the numbers. The early stage at which the Congo-Angola peoples were in South Carolina and their proportionately large numbers meant that their languages may have provided a significant component of the common language base among the Africans. As "seasoned" workers who had learned to survive in the new environment and who had learned something of the language of the planters, enslaved men and women from Congo-Angola would often be the ones who introduced the new arrivals to strategies of survival in the new colony. Hazel Carter's 1978 examination of Turner's texts of the speech of African Americans in coastal South Carolina from the first half of the twentieth century indicates late survival of some Congolese and Angolan lexicon and syntax.

Who were these people, and what customs and traditions did they bring with them to the new colony? Unlike Africans along the upper and lower Guinea Coast, those of the Congo-Angola region had developed elaborately organized trading states prior to European contact (Curtin 1990). The practice of slavery had been long established in the Congo-Angola region by Africans themselves, before the period of European contact that began in the late 1400s (Birmingham 1966). This well-developed trade in slaves among the Africans was capitalized upon by the Portuguese, the first Europeans to enter into trading relationships with central West Africa. They traded slaves within Africa itself, and they also supplied mainland Portugal and its new colonies with this eagerly sought source of labor.

Three trading states participated in this commerce with the Europeans over the three centuries before the slave trade ceased. The Kongo kingdom was the dominant power in western central Africa in that first century of contact, an agricultural people who used slaves bought or captured in war to till their crops. Palm trees were a major agricultural crop, with the oils used for lighting and cooking, the sap for an alcoholic beverage, and the bark for fibers from which to weave cloth. Other crops were yams, bananas, peppers, a bitter kola nut used as a stimulant similar to coffee, and millet. They raised some small livestock as well. With the exception of rice and indigo, the crops of the Kongo kingdom were similar to those of the Windward and Leeward coasts and of the Niger Delta. By the sixteenth century the Mbundu kingdom of Ndongo (Angola) had risen to dominance over the Kongo. People in this kingdom raised cattle, in addition to crops of millet, beans, yams, and radishes. They had eggs and honey, but used no milk (Birmingham 1966). Women cultivated the land and reared the livestock, while men hunted birds, hares, rats, snakes, hippopotamuses, and crocodiles. Fishing appears to have been unimportant for them. They held daily markets throughout the country to trade their foodstuffs. The Ngola people were skilled hunters and warriors who had learned to forge iron. In the eighteenth century the Ndongo kingdom was replaced by the interior kingdom of Kasanje, as the slave trade along the coast disrupted traditional patterns of life among the Kongo and Ndongo. The town of Lunda dominated the flourishing slave trade with the Portuguese, sending slaves from the interior to the coastal ports. It is probably these interior peoples who were resold to English slavers for transportation to the American colonies during the years of greatest slave importation to South Carolina.

"This Country Born"

Littlefield's figures on runaway slaves indicate that a large proportion were born in the South Carolina colony (1981, 122), as high as 40 percent in the decade of the 1740s immediately following the Stono Rebellion and nearly 27 percent for the entire period between the 1730s and the 1770s. These African Americans who succeeded in escaping captivity, if only for a brief time, represent the beginnings of identification by race rather than by tribe. The advertisements in the *South Carolina Gazette* characterize them as "Negroes" (the Spanish word for black) who were "this country born," giving such details as the clothes they were wearing when they escaped, who their previous masters were, or on which plantations they had relatives. Their ancestry or parents' country of origin is never mentioned. Almost without exception they are said to speak "good English," whenever language is mentioned. (Littlefield finds only two who do not in his survey of 1732–75, and I find none in my smaller sampling of four decades of advertisements between 1732 and 1765.) Robert Olwell (1998), in his exploration of the power dynamics in South Carolina in the period after the Stono

Rebellion, concludes that by the decade of the 1750s, the majority of enslaved Africans then living in South Carolina had been born in the colony. Thus, from the reports on language use found in the *South Carolina Gazette*, the majority of those classified as "Negro" would have been speaking a variety of language classified (at least within the colony) as English. This was a distinctive variety of English according to an early advertisement in the *South Carolina Gazette*, placed by the printer himself in 1734: "To be Sold for ready Money Four choice young Negroe Men Slaves and a Girl, who have each been bred in some useful way, and speak very good (Black) English. Enquire of the Printer himself" (no. 9, March 23–30, 1734; repeated with additions, nos. 10 and 11, 1734).

No doubt those who had spent all their lives in the colony developed better facility in understanding each other's speech patterns than did outsiders. In 1751 the South Carolina governor, in a report to the Lords Commissioners for Trade and Plantations, said that many of the forty thousand "Negroes" in the province were natives of Carolina and "that the rest can all speak our language," since no new Africans had been imported for the decade after the Stono uprising (Merrens 1977, 182–83). By contrast, in 1780 near the end of their occupation of South Carolina during the Revolutionary War, British troops found communication with African Americans exceedingly difficult, reporting that "none of us could manage to talk with these people because of their bad dialect" (cited in Olwell 1998, 246). Taken together, these three evaluations on the kind of English spoken by Africans and African Americans during the 1700s suggests a wide disparity in language use as well as in listener comprehension.

For a brief time British troops occupied the lowcountry and Charles Town itself between 1778 and 1780. Olwell reports that the British offered slaves a kind of emancipation, but only that of joining the British army. Like the South Carolina planters, the British troops saw slaves as confiscated property. They did, however, hire African Americans to work for wages and allowed them to go home in the evenings, and in the last years of British occupation all-African regiments were created. According to Olwell's interpretation of the evidence, enslaved Africans were torn between their desire for freedom and a wish to preserve the plantation community and family ties they had established in that community. Neither side's promise of freedom could be relied upon. Many slaves were missing by the time of the British defeat in 1782, when they left Charles Town. Olwell estimates some twenty-five thousand slaves were gone—smuggled out of the colony, evacuated, taken as spoils of war, or lost to the diseases and privations that accompanied war. Probably one-fourth of the lowcountry Africans had disappeared from the region between 1775 and 1782.

Our concern here with early language contact in South Carolina ends with the Revolutionary War, but it is worth noting that a large number of new Africans entered after the transition from colony to statehood was completed in 1788. Even though the slave trade was banned from 1784 until 1803 and again after 1807, probably as many as ninety-four thousand slaves entered South Carolina illegally and legally between 1783 and 1810, most directly from Africa (McMillin 1999). At the same time the number of free blacks in Charleston (incorporated and renamed as a city in 1783) increased from six hundred in 1790 to eleven hundred in 1810 (Deaton 1999). Anxiety about slave revolts gave rise to new laws affecting the behavior of those African Americans who were not slaves. A turbulent period was ahead in terms of the new racial identities formed in this new land and of the rights of citizens that went beyond race, but the formative period for language contact had passed. Henceforth newcomers to the state would learn the dialects and languages that had evolved during the early contact period. The center of government would shift to the new capital at Columbia in the middle of the state, but the locus of wealth and power would continue until the Civil War to be situated in the lowcountry, where African Americans made up most of the property by which that wealth was measured.

At the close of the Revolutionary War, our time boundary for early South Carolina, the native-born Afro-Carolinians far outnumbered the portion of the population born in Africa. They would be the ones responsible for teaching any newly arrived Africans the ways of existing in the new country, and those ways included a new language.

Part 2 | *Languages to Dialects*
Speaking Together

What is the difference between a dialect and a language? Mostly it is a political distinction: in traditional usage, a "language" has a recognized government or social organization associated with its use. In the centuries before the English settled Carolina, many who lived in the northern part of the European island of Britian called their speech Scottis, a language with a separate literary and legal tradition from that of Inglis to the south and the Gaelic of the Highlands and the Hebrides. After the union of the Scottish and English crowns in the early 1600s, the influence of English spread—especially in written texts such as the Authorized Version of the Bible promoted by the Scots King James, who had become ruler over the unified country. Scots was thought of as a dialect of English by the time that the Carolina colony was settled.

Just the opposite had happened to Spanish and French. Once considered dialects of Latin, they gained the status of distinct languages as their speakers became organized into political units no longer identified with the old Roman Empire. For Spanish the standard was associated with the most powerful political region: Castile. For French an official language academy had been established in the early 1600s to rule on standard usage. For German, an ancient sister dialect to English, a standard dialect had emerged through Martin Luther's choice for his translation of the Latin Bible—this despite the fact that Germany itself was still an assortment of city-states. Like German, Welsh had been used for a translation of the Latin Bible, but in Wales itself the official language of government became English with the union of Wales and England in the 1500s. Unlike Scots, Welsh had

remained a distinctive language used in written texts and religious observances. However, most Welsh were bilingual in Welsh and English by the
time of their resettlement in Carolina from northern colonies.

What of the many language varieties from Africa and from indigenous
America itself? None of them had yet been standardized in a writing system, but many were associated with governmental entities. The Europeans
referred to the indigenous groups of North America as "nations" and to
the African ones as "kingdoms." They labeled the speech varieties spoken
within these entities as "languages," following their own understanding
of the link between nation and language. In truth, many of these varieties
were certainly close enough to each other to be mutually intelligible—and
would be called dialects in our modern understanding of that term. Others were radically different from each other in both structure and historical origin, requiring the kind of bilingualism that the Welsh speakers of the
British Isles acquired for communication within the domains of trade or
government.

Today we cannot know what the early indigenous peoples of Carolina
thought of their own languages. The conquerors typically assign names
both to the conquered and to the languages they speak, as well as to the
land they inhabit. The very name *America* comes from the Italian, the name
Carolina from the Latinized version of the English king's name at the time
of settlement. The Europeans typically associated the indigenous peoples
with the rivers they lived beside, recognizing the centrality of these bodies
of water in the spiritual and physical lives of the native Carolinians. Thus,
such names as *Waccamaw*, *Santee*, *Congaree*, and *Edisto* are used for the
rivers, the peoples, and the languages they spoke. These names are all that
remain of most of these languages, however, which disappeared within the
first century of contact without any documentation of their structure or
vocabulary.

The languages and dialects of those brought in bondage from Africa are
a different matter. Many of them are still spoken in contemporary Africa,
even though the Africans in Carolina stopped speaking them within a generation. The African American linguist Lorenzo Dow Turner was able to

study some of these original languages in the 1930s when he began to suspect their influence on the creole Gullah, which is spoken today by many
descendants of the original Africans along the coast of contemporary South
Carolina and Georgia. It is this creole, a mixed language born of the contact between English and several African languages, that became one of the
most distinctive language varieties still spoken in America.

How did the many languages and dialects spoken in early South Carolina
disappear, leaving English as the common language and Gullah as a newly
formed language spoken on the coastal plantations? And how did distinctive
varieties of English that evolved among the ethnic groups and social classes
within this small state carry with them traces of earlier speech patterns—
within the relatively short time span of three centuries? Part 2 will address
these questions, looking carefully at the power relationships between the
speakers of different races and classes and the social interactions that resulted in distinctive ways of speaking: the *contact* between speakers of languages from three continents, the *language variation* that emerged from this
contact, and some rhetorical *patterns* characteristic of the three ethnic
speech communities even into the twentieth and twenty-first centuries.

4 | *Language Contact*

The term *language contact* summons up images of sentences from different languages meeting on the street somewhere, sometimes passing each other with merely a nod, other times pausing to greet and converse at length. With more prolonged conversations, these personified sentences might exchange caps, unbutton or button a vest, take off an extraneous garment, or borrow an especially attractive scarf. Over years of protracted encounters, such rearrangements become common, and the sentences come to resemble each other in significant ways.

Although misleading if pushed too far, personifications of an abstract entity such as a language can help us understand some of what happens when speakers of different languages interact frequently and intensely. In circumstances of prolonged contact with other languages, language structures can change—usually depending on the economic and social resources commanded by each partner in the conversation. The language of the more powerful speakers normally changes least, while the language of the less powerful speakers changes greatly or may even disappear. Returning to our image of the personified sentences, we observe the less powerful sentences borrowing some of the rich and stylish garments of the more powerful. The powerful sentences do not seem to borrow much from their partners, perhaps because the less powerful sentences are seen as unstylish and unfashionable, unsuited for the times.

Sometimes—infrequently to be sure—we can observe the less powerful sentences clinging stubbornly to their serviceable garments, perceiving them to be quite adequate for the needs of the moment and being unwilling to pay the high costs associated with borrowing or buying the more fashionable garments of their powerful partners. And as we look back on the various changes in fashion from a historical perspective, the adequacy of *all* the garments is evident for basic communication needs within each speech community. When conversations across different speech communities become frequent and necessary within a larger, perhaps newly formed, community, choices are made among the available languages.

   This chapter will focus on the kinds of language contact occurring between the different groups of speakers at different points in time during the
colonial era, leaving the following chapter to describe the language variation that resulted from the language contact of several generations of speakers whose ancestors spoke so many different languages and dialects.

Bilingualism

Bilingualism is the knowledge of more than one language—though speakers do not always have equal proficiency in both. *Natural* bilingualism
refers to the kind of second language one acquires in natural settings without formal instruction, somewhat the way one learns the first language:
listening, observing the appropriate conditions for speaking, engaging in
simple conversations as one's confidence builds, receiving correction in real
situations when an attempted conversational turn fails. Most bilingualism
in early Carolina was of this type. *Elite* bilingualism refers to the kind of
second language acquired through the study of written texts, often for religious or scientific purposes. This second language is most often learned
through formal instruction and is typically reserved for only a chosen few
within a society—when a society has sufficient resources to support these
elite learners for the years needed for study. In the early years of the colony,
only a limited number of young European males had access to the resources this kind of bilingualism requires. A few African men and women
had access to formal schooling in English by the mid–eighteenth century—
as did selected Indian males later in the same century.

Natural Bilingualism

Individual bilingualism. Before the coming of the Africans and Europeans,
Native Americans had used bilingual individuals as interpreters between
tribes. Typically these were adults or children captured in battle or were
young adults who married into a different tribe. Whether entering the community through war or marriage, these individuals were usually integrated
into the new group as full participants, learning the language and serving
as interpreters between the new community and the old. This widespread
practice among Native Americans provided a few bilingual interpreters for
each small group, who acted as intermediaries between it and other groups
with whom they interacted. Because only a few in each group engaged in
these bilingual conversations, the primary language of the group would
have been affected little by the presence of the bilinguals. Typically small
groups maintained different languages from their close neighbors, their
needs for interactions with others met by their bilingual members. As best

we can tell, there was no single lingua franca (or language of wider communication) spoken by all of the indigenous peoples of Carolina at the time
of African and European contact, but there is emerging evidence for an
earlier Muskogean lingua franca in use among those Indian groups who
spoke different Muskogean languages (Booker, Hudson, and Rankin 1992).

The first European contacts deliberately sought to make use of individual bilingualism for communication between themselves and indigenous
Carolinians. The Spanish sailors under the direction of Lucas Vázquez de
Ayllón, who explored the coast near the Santee River in the early 1500s,
captured native inhabitants speaking at least three different languages and
transported them to the Caribbean islands and Florida so that they could
learn Spanish. These Indians escaped on the return voyage and were of no
ultimate use to the Spanish, but this use of individual bilinguals was clearly
central in European efforts to provide needed interpreters. The first prolonged contact between Indians and Europeans in South Carolina was with
the Spanish expedition led by Soto in 1540. As we have noted in chapter
1, the Spanish relied on multilayered interpretation by an Indian guide,
Perico, who knew some of the languages along a route from Georgia to
North Carolina. With the help of a Spanish soldier who knew one of the
languages that Perico knew, the expedition made its way through South
Carolina along an interior south-to-north route. The next Spanish expeditions, led by Juan Pardo between 1566 and 1568, took an east-west route
from the southern coast to the western mountains. One of Pardo's expeditions used a young Frenchman named Guillermo Rufín as interpreter.
Rufín had been a member of a short-lived French colony on Port Royal
Bay and had stayed behind when his colleagues sailed for France in 1562.
He joined the Indians of Orista and during a year with them probably
learned a Muskogean language, which he used successfully as interpreter
from the eastern coast to the western Blue Ridge Mountains, where Cherokee, an Iroquois language, was spoken. Here other interpreters took over
from Rufín. The Spanish expedition thus made use of a French interpreter
who had become a natural bilingual during his year among the Orista Indians near Port Royal—luckily acquiring a second language that could be
understood across a wide area of South Carolina. Using Rufín's bilingual
skills, the Spanish replicated the Indians' practice of using bilinguals to
communicate between tribes who had different languages from their own.

In the most careful examination of the Spanish travel diaries to date,
Booker, Hudson, and Rankin conclude that there is some evidence that
a Creek-based lingua franca was used among speakers of Muskogean
languages throughout prehistoric Georgia and the Carolinas, long before

contact with Europeans and Africans. They cite clear evidence that multi-lingual political units existed in the Southeast prior to European contact, and they postulate that such units may have developed a lingua franca for intertribal communication. If such a contact language existed, bilingualism among speakers of Muskogean languages may have been widespread—though perhaps still confined to a limited number of individuals in each group. At this distance in time it may be impossible to know.

Within the small geographic area encompassed by South Carolina, three other linguistic families existed in addition to Muskogean: Algonquian, of which Shawnee was a member; Iroquoian, to which Cherokee belonged; and Catawban, which included Woccon, Catawba itself, and a dialect known as Iswq. Yuchi, a language isolate, also existed somewhere west of the Appalachians, with some of its speakers living in South Carolina from time to time. Booker, Hudson, and Rankin's reading of the linguistic and archeological record suggests that regional chiefdoms included more than one linguistic group in the era before European contact. The chiefdoms of the Southeast were organized around a system of tribute and deference to a paramount chief, a system that would have entailed periodic meetings between the headmen from each town. If the chiefdom was indeed multilingual, as seems probable, discussions between the headmen would customarily include the services of bilingual interpreters. Through the services of such bilinguals, meetings were conducted so that all could understand the deliberations and arrive at consensus on actions to be taken as a political entity. As we have seen, Pardo adopted this indigenous practice, at every major town he visited giving his own speech in Spanish, which was then interpreted for the assembled dignitaries into the languages they spoke.

In the period between 1521 and 1704, which Hudson and Tesser (1994) have termed "the forgotten centuries," the Spanish missions in Florida up to the South Carolina border taught the Indians some of their language (even some reading and writing in Spanish), as well as Christian doctrines and prayers. In his history of colonial South Carolina, David Duncan Wallace reports that the "first words the English heard from the Indians in 1670 were a welcome in broken Spanish" (1934, 55). By this date the Indians' way of life had been much changed by interaction with the Spanish over the intervening century, although the Spanish were no longer in Carolina itself. By 1660 an uprising of South Carolina Indians had forced the Spanish to retreat to south of the Savannah River, into Georgia (Weber 1992). During the period of interaction with the Spanish, the Indians' way of life was seriously disrupted, and the large chiefdoms of the interior South disappeared. In South Carolina only the Cofitachequi (near present-day Camden) remained an important group at the time of English contact, perhaps because of the willingness of this chiefdom to incorporate other tribal refugees from European contact. Marvin T. Smith (1994) suggests that because the Cofitachequi controlled the important fall line area (a transition zone between two different ecological systems), population remnants from the Piedmont would have been attracted to this area. Within the reconstituted chiefdom multilingualism may have been the order of the day at the time the English entered Bull's Bay, some thirty miles north of present-day Charleston.

During the hundred years between the Spanish expeditions and the first permanent English settlement at Charles Town, the Indians and the English had learned enough about each other to know that they each wanted something from the other. In the case of the Indians, the metal tools and guns of the Europeans made chores easier and subdued their traditional enemies more effectively. In the case of the English, the Indians were potential trading partners for the raw materials needed to manufacture goods in England, materials that would bring easy profits. Even before the English settlement was established at Charles Town, Indian guides had accompanied English pilots on coastal exploratory voyages along the coast. Robert Sandford recorded one such expedition in 1666, in which an Indian leader in the Port Royal area entrusted his sister's son to Sandford for a ten-month voyage; Sandford, in turn, left his ship's surgeon, Henry Woodward, with the Indians "for the mutuall learning their language" (Salley 1911, 104). In such a context, however, with Woodward as the sole English speaker, virtually all of the learning would have been on Woodward's part. Woodward stayed with the Indians of Port Royal, learning the language and customs, until the Spanish captured him and took him to St. Augustine. After some adventures with pirates and hurricanes in the Leeward Islands, he made his way back to South Carolina and joined the newly established English colony near Charles Town. According to Salley, "He immediately became a conspicuous figure in the Ashley River colony, and from his knowledge of and influence with the Indians was of great benefit to the government in dealing with them" (127). Woodward subsequently spent months at a time traveling and living with another Indian group within the colony, then reporting back to the colonists on the land, its resources, and the living conditions of the people he encountered. Woodward was the first Englishman of consequence to become naturally bilingual in Indian languages of South Carolina, but he was far from the last.

The Indian trader was one of the most important bilingual figures in the colony. Employed by the English officials in Charles Town, he typically lived with the Indians with whom he traded—often taking an Indian wife, living in her house, and fathering her children. The second generation of Indian traders were often the sons of these bicultural liaisons—men who were full members of their mothers' social groups and somewhat acquainted with their fathers' ways and language. The Indian trader, in fact, functioned much as the intertribal interpreters had functioned before the coming of the Europeans. Both the trader and the interpreter (often one and the same person in colonial times) functioned as "weak ties" between the two groups in which they held membership (see fig. 4.1).

The African and European communities also contained bilinguals who served as bridges between their two groups. Chief among them were the African house servants who worked in the big house on large plantations for the European mistress but lived in the slave quarters with their own Gullah-speaking families and sometimes with the bilingual slave drivers who managed the field hands. Most of the house servants were women who performed the domestic chores associated with a large household: sewing, cooking, cleaning. Men, women, and some children also served as personal "body servants" for the plantation owners and their children; they probably had the most significant language interaction with Europeans and the greatest opportunity to acquire their languages. Some African and European children who spent many years together in this context would have had especially intense and frequent speech interaction. Most of the plantations used English as the dominant language, but French was also an early language on some plantations in the coastal area between Charles Town and the Waccamaw Neck. A variety of Spanish, as well, was often the home language in many of the Jewish merchants' homes in Charles Town. English, however, was the major language spoken in most households large enough to have a significant number of African members. The house servants who participated in both the speech network of the big house and that of the slave quarters served as bridges between these speech networks; they would have brought English vocabulary to the slave quarters and Gullah phrases to the plantation master's house.

Gullah was a mixed language that developed as more and more Africans speaking several different languages were brought to the colony in increasing numbers after the Yemassee War of 1715. Considered a creole language by linguists, this language that originated in Carolina will be described in more detail in chapter 5 as one of the colony's most significant linguistic contributions to the mosaic of American languages. Its vocabulary was over-whelmingly English, but much of its grammar was drawn from several of the African languages spoken by these incoming peoples. In the earliest years of the colony, when Africans made up only a small percentage of the colony's population, there had been greater opportunity for Africans to become bilingual in English (or another European language) because of the frequent daily contact between Africans and Europeans. Africans eventually came to outnumber both the Europeans and the Indians, with shiploads of newcomers entering Carolina directly from the coast of West Africa and from Angola until the Stono Rebellion of 1739, and then—after a brief pause—in greater and greater numbers until long after the Revolutionary War. These incoming Africans would have learned the language spoken in the slave quarters from Africans who had previously learned English as a second or third language. We have seen in chapter 3 that in 1734 the printer of the *South Carolina Gazette* described five "Negroe Men Slaves and a Girl" as speaking "very good (Black) English," an indication that their language was in some way distinctive, as is the case for virtually all second-language learners of any language. Increasingly the language learned by newcomers would have deviated more and more from the English spoken by Europeans living on the plantations and taken on the characteristics of the language known variously as Gullah, Geechee, and Sea Island Creole, as each successive wave of newcomers imperfectly learned the language variety then being spoken in the slave quarters. (See Thomason 2001, 183–89, for an excellent discussion of how imperfect language learning led to the development of plantation creole languages.)

Among the Europeans the women of the plantations were most likely to become bilingual in English and Gullah and to serve as links between their speech community of birth and that of the enslaved people they encountered daily. Some mistresses had more significant interaction with the Africans living on the plantation than others. Eliza Lucas Pinckney was one who did, and her letter book provides accounts of her activities over the span of five years in which she was in charge of her father's plantations, prior to her marriage to another planter (Pinckney 1972). She describes her activities as a nurse for a small slave hospital during a smallpox epidemic, as a teacher of reading and writing to two of the enslaved women on her father's plantation, and as one of the first experimenters with the indigo crop and its blue dye so valued for the European trade. Most European women were not this active in the overall management of plantation life, however, and could avoid becoming bilingual if they chose—unlike the African house servants, whose position depended on knowledge of English. Unfortunately no written records exist from the Africans themselves to give details of their personal linguistic interactions.

Among the African women, one group who would have been bilingual in Gullah and some variety of English were women merchants who dominated the Charles Town marketplace. Olwell maintains that after the 1740 Negro Act, which allowed enslaved men and women to attend market and to buy and sell on behalf of their masters if they had written tickets specifying what was to be bought and sold, these market-bound slaves came to dominate the Charles Town market to the extent that Euro-Carolinians began to resent both their control of the supplies of basic necessities and also their growing independence of their masters' control (1998, 169). Afro-Carolinian women soon came to control the selling of goods, as they exchanged news and gossip along with money in much the same manner common to West African villages both then and now. African men were more involved in procuring goods, especially fish, from the sea and from the rivers, and African men sometimes were exclusively the boatmen who provided the main transportation along the many rivers of the lowcountry (Olwell 1998, 152). Enslaved men and women who possessed special skills were often "hired out" by their masters to work at such trades as glazing, bricklaying, carpentry, and tailoring. These "hired-out" laborers could keep a portion of their wages, so long as the master received what was due to him. Olwell maintains that "slaves who hired themselves out became the practical masters of their own labor" (162–63). Almost certainly these individual wage earners had wide opportunity to become bilingual in whatever variety of English was used by their temporary employers. Among the Africans with mobility and opportunities to engage in commerce on their own, the market women would have had the widest opportunities as a group to become bilingual in English and Gullah and to serve as linguistic "weak ties" between Europeans and Africans.

The men who were plantation overseers were also influential bridges between the African laborers of the rice and indigo fields and the European plantation owners. Their familiarity with Gullah, however, was also variable. Many of these overseers were English-speaking European men, but at least some must have been African or Afro-Carolinians, as indicated by the early 1712 and 1726 enactment of laws requiring that a white man be present as supervisor for every six to ten African slaves (Van Deburg 1979). Such laws are never passed unless a problem is felt to exist. Sometimes a trusted enslaved man would be put in a supervisory position; frequently

Afro-Carolinian men served as slave drivers under the overseer, probably serving as interpreters between the Europeans and the unseasoned field hands. Whether European or African, either the overseer or the slave driver had to be bilingual in the plantation ówner's language (English) and in the common language spoken by most of the field hands (Gullah). How these men acquired their second language was probably as varied as their individual life experiences. Many of the European overseers undoubtedly relied on bilingual Africans to interpret between themselves and the new arrivals from Africa who knew no English. We have accounts of such interpreters from the runaway slave ads, which sometimes note that the jailer in Charles Town used such bilinguals in attempts to learn something about newly captured runaway slaves who did not speak English.

By the 1750s the majority of the inhabitants of South Carolina had been born in the colony (Olwell 1998) and spoke a language that was considered "English." Governor Glen in 1751 made a distinction between slaves who are "country-born" (that is, born in South Carolina) and those who are not, indicating that the former "can all speak our language" (Merrens 1977, 182–83). Because the language spoken by the Afro-Carolinians who were "country-born" would have comprised mostly English vocabulary, it must have sounded like some variety of English to the Euro-Carolinians. However, unless the European speaker was bilingual in both English and Gullah, an interpreter would have been needed for many interactions.*

Individual bilingualism and social groups. The concept of weak ties serving as crucial bridges between different social networks is one that originates in sociology and has been adapted for analysis of language use (Granovetter 1973, 1983; Milroy 1987; Milroy and Milroy 1992).

In Granovetter's original proposal for what he called the "strength of weak ties," an individual can have both low- and high-density networks. In a high-density network people all know and interact closely with each other, while in a low-density one only the individual knows every member, with little or no interaction between other members in the network. Individuals in low-density networks can act as bridges or weak ties between other groups with which they have ties, thereby providing a channel for the transmission of information or influence across groups. When the language interaction within a group is both dense (that is, all speakers speak

---

*Bilingual interpreters were still needed for the youngest Gullah-speaking children in the classrooms of public schools in Georgetown County as late as the 1970s by teachers new to the locality. Older children served as their informal interpreters.

to each other intensely and frequently) and multiplex (that is, speakers interact with each other in a variety of life roles), the members speak more like each other (in other words, have the same dialect). When the opposite is the case, the language use is less similar between speakers.

The Milroys found that individual speakers who have relatively weak ties within more than one group can function as important agents of language change across the groups. In contrast those who have strong in-group ties and rarely talk with members of another group have little effect on language change. In the South Carolina context, the individual bilinguals described here within the Indian, African, and European groups may well have functioned as weak ties between the other racial groups and eventually would have served as channels for language change.

As figure 4.1 illustrates, the Indian interpreters across tribal groups would have ties stemming from childhood experiences with their original tribe but ties deriving from adulthood experiences with members of their

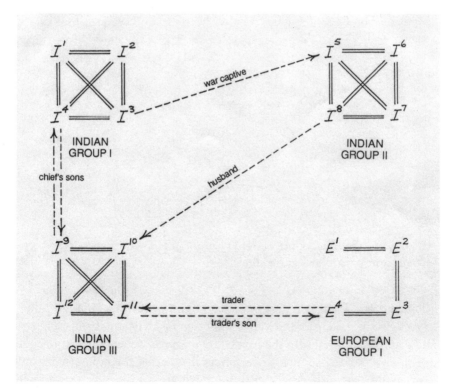

FIGURE 4.1. Typical weak ties between Indian and European groups in colonial South Carolina (dotted lines)

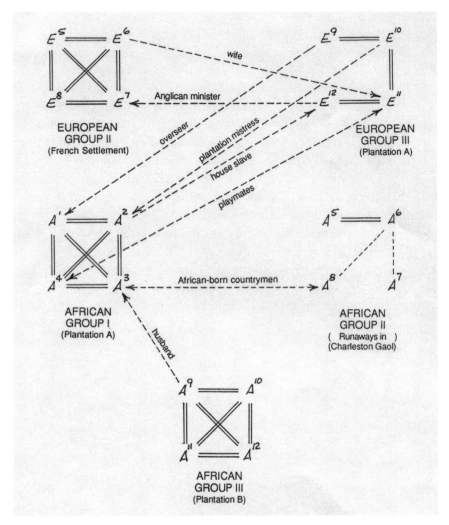

FIGURE 4.2. Typical weak ties between European and African groups in colonial South Carolina (dotted lines)

adopted tribe. They would participate in significant ways—but not fully—in each group. Likewise, the Indian traders would have ties from childhood and young adulthood with the European group, as well as occupational ties as employees of the colonial government in Charles Town, but they would acquire ties as mature adults with the Indian group they lived with, especially if they married and fathered children. Like the intertribal interpreters, they would participate in significant ways with each group, but they would

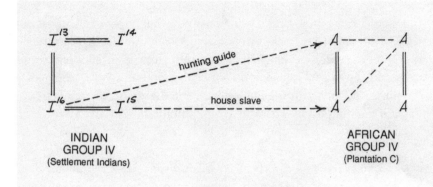

FIGURE 4.3. Early weak ties between Africans and Indians in colonial
South Carolina

lack specific experiences with language and culture within each group at
different times in their lives. Some of their sons, and occasionally a daughter, became Indian traders with weak ties to their fathers' European trading partners, as a result of accompanying them on yearly trips to Charles
Town.

Figure 4.2 illustrates the weak ties existing between European groups,
between African groups, and between Africans and Europeans. French-
speaking Anglican ministers, for example, would have language ties to the
Huguenot communities but religious ties to the English officials who gave
them their parish assignments. Likewise enslaved Africans in South Carolina would have language ties with some of the newly arrived Africans but
occupational and family ties with other Gullah speakers who had been born
in the colony; bilingual African house servants would have social and family ties to the Gullah speakers in the slave quarters but occupational and
personal ties to the English speakers in the plantation owner's house. A few
European-born plantation mistresses would have weak ties between their
households and the African slave quarters, and many European children
born in the colony would have weak ties with African women who nursed
them and with African children who were their playmates. Weak ties also
existed between the European and African plantation overseers / slave
drivers and the African field hands they supervised.

As indicated above, there was little opportunity after the early years
of the colony for Africans and Indians to interact in any systematic way
that would affect language use. Figure 4.3 illustrates the weak ties created
by Indian women who established unions with African men in the slave

quarters of the earliest plantations. African men had little or no opportunity to interact with the tribes these women came from, but the Indian women and the children born to them would interact with the Africans continually imported to the colony. The women, and ultimately their children, would have provided essential information about the foods available, the medicinal qualities of plants growing in Carolina, and the language needed to survive in the multilingual world of the early plantations. There were relatively few Indian men enslaved on the early plantations. Those captured and enslaved in the Indian wars were usually shipped out of the colony to be sold in colonies to the north or in the Caribbean. From the Settlement Indians living closest to the Europeans, Indian men were often hired as guides or hunters, but they remained free to return to their local families.

Group bilingualism. Among the Europeans themselves, there was often widespread bilingualism in two European languages for the first two or three generations in the non–English-speaking groups: French, Germans, Welsh, and Jews whose ancestral home was Spain or Portugal. Families whose home language was not that of the politically powerful in the new colony would have followed a typical immigrant pattern of using the home language for intimate interactions and the common language (English) for public ones. Because they were outnumbered and because social interaction with English speakers of an equal status was the norm for the non–English-speaking Europeans (as noted in chapter 2), there was often intermarriage between Protestant groups that required the use of English as a common home language. Several Protestant church groups recorded the need for bilingual preachers to give one Sunday sermon in the language of the home country and a later one in English, as the speech community gradually shifted to English through language choices made by its young people. Among the Protestant groups, Germans of the interior settlements appear to have retained their home language the longest, but eventually their communities also became bilingual. For the Jews there was the need to use English in business and social meetings, but their synagogue records indicate that they were using Spanish well into the nineteenth century—perhaps as a result of the strong sanctions against marriage outside the Jewish community. However, when Spanish- or Ladino-speaking Sephardic Jews intermarried with Yiddish-speaking Ashkenazim from the northern colonies, the common home language may have become English, just as was the case for bilingual Protestants.

For Indians there was not any widespread group bilingualism in English until well after the colonial period. Groups continued to use individual bilingual speakers as interpreters in public transactions between their political entities and the English government in Charles Town, but they continued to speak some version of an Indian language as their primary language until well after the Revolutionary War. Within indigenous Carolina groups themselves there was undoubtedly massive language change as groups moved further and further to the interior and joined other groups for security. In chapter 1 we saw some evidence that internal language shift may have taken place on a large scale between the Spanish marches through South Carolina in the 1500s and the first permanent settlement by the English in 1670, and it is clear that many Indian languages simply disappeared as their speakers shifted to others. Perhaps in the future, historical linguists can piece together more evidence about whether or not remnant groups became bilingual in each others' languages and shifted to new languages heavily influenced by the old ones, but at present we have no detailed knowledge of the linguistic shifts that took place during this "forgotten century." It may not be possible ever to have the required evidence. We do know that the last Catawba speaker died in the twentieth century and that the remainder of the Catawba Indians on the reservation that still exists in York County had long since shifted to English as their primary language. Compared to the Europeans who shifted to English within the second or third generation after settlement, these native Carolinians held onto some version of their native language for a long time.

There is not at present any evidence of substantial use of African languages between Africans themselves in the context of Carolina, and we are not likely to discover records of such interaction. It is certainly possible that small groups speaking the same African languages did indeed end up in the same rice fields or encounter each other on trips up and down the rivers to Charles Town, in its markets or in the jail cells where runaways were held. There simply is no record of these encounters except for the important Stono Rebellion of 1739 led by a number of African men from Angola. The colonists believed that their use of a common language, both speaking and drumming, greatly enhanced their ability to coordinate this attack, and imports of slaves from Angola were banned for some time thereafter. Recent work on this event suggests that the Angolans' common religious and military practices may have contributed to their success as well (Smith 2005), and future research may unearth other significant linguistic and cultural interaction between Africans who shared the same origins. Except for these Angolans, we lack evidence for significant group bilingualism in pairs of African languages or in one African language and English.

Elite bilingualism. Because of the economic and social resources required for the long years of study that were a prerequisite for elite bilingualism, relatively few individuals came to the early colony with these skills. Those who did typically had received educations in England or on the European continent. Even fewer had been schooled by Jewish or Islamic religious leaders in synagogues of Europe and mosques of Africa.

Once the new English colony was on a sound economic footing, young European males from wealthy families were taught Hebrew or Latin (and some Greek) as part of an elite education, and sons of prominent Anglicans were often sent to England for an extensive formal education. In England they read texts in Latin as well as English and learned to speak an elite variety of English used among the wealthy. These young men became the colony's spokesmen in negotiations with the mother country and with other colonies during the period leading up to the formation of a new nation. Daughters of wealthy families had no access to this elite bilingualism: while many were offered a smattering of French, they were denied an opportunity to learn Latin. They were not educated abroad, though they may have visited England and the Continent. Although those who took an active part in the management of plantations with large African workforces became natural bilinguals in English and Gullah, most European women of the higher classes remained largely monolingual, speaking the lowcountry dialect of English that developed in South Carolina through intensive contact between a small European planter group and the far more numerous Africans on their plantations. Unlike either the African house slaves or the European professional men, most European women found little opportunity to become elite bilinguals beyond the smattering of French learned from their personal tutors.

Literacy and bilingualism. Although literacy—the ability to understand written texts and to produce them—is not bilingualism per se, it often is a pathway to elite bilingualism for speakers of other languages. It is probable that several of the early groups in South Carolina became literate in English before they began to speak it fluently. Written English served as a bridge across the European, African, and Native American cultures. The power of the written word among the English increased dramatically after the invention of the printing press in the mid-1400s. Translations of the Bible from Latin into national languages had led to widespread literacy among Protestants throughout the British Isles (Nichols 1988), and these texts began to appear in many individual homes and in the schools associated with their churches. As the social and economic power of English speakers grew within the colony, documents in written English had significant consequences for the way all inhabitants of South Carolina led their lives. The contact across these groups was such that all speakers from all three continents came to observe the consequences of texts written in English in various domains of their lives: religious, governmental, economic, and personal. Within a century of the founding of the English settlement at Charles Town, English—both spoken and written—had become the common language. Because literacy was such an instrument of power in the early Carolina colony, it is worth considering who had access to it and who used it for what purposes.

Both Africans and Indians clearly understood early that documents written in English affected their own well-being in serious ways. We have seen that most Indian groups exchanged written letters with the colonial government in Charles Town and valued the military commissions granted to them as individuals. We have also noted that the Catawba Indians understood the value and use of official written documents to the English speakers so well that they themselves requested a written document attesting to the survey of the boundaries of their land in order to stave off encroachment by European settlers.

Although few Indian individuals learned to read and write during the colonial era, there is good evidence that many individuals within the African community did so, although they may have concealed it from their owners and even others in the African community. Because of colonial laws restricting the movement of slaves, every slave traveling was required to possess a written "ticket" while traveling, stating his or her specific mission away from home (Wood 1974, 272). The advantages that a forged ticket could bring for a person attempting to run away or to visit a family member on another plantation are obvious. There were also some advantages for the Europeans in having literate workers, such as buying and selling in the Charles Town marketplace and in keeping records on the plantation itself. Although enslaved people were legally denied literacy during turbulent times, at other times schools were established specifically to educate a select number of them. In 1742 two enslaved African men were acquired by Alexander Garden and trained to be schoolmasters for a school in Charles Town. Masters were to send one slave to study there, who would then return to the plantation and teach others. This school operated successfully for twenty-five years under the direction of one of these men (Olwell 1998, 119).

Another path toward literacy was baptism in the Anglican Church. While nearly all of the Europeans were baptized as infants, about half of the Africans may have been baptized as adults, although the records are sketchy (Olwell 1998). As adults these converts were required to have religious instruction before baptism, and as Protestants with a profound commitment to the centrality of holy texts written in the language of their members, the Anglican ministers taught prospective converts to read and recite from religious texts such as the church catechism, the Book of Common Prayer, and the Bible. Schooling in Christian doctrines was thought to increase the slaves' submissiveness and obedience (Wood 1974, 324), and ministers argued that adults who were baptized would be better workers. Converts were often given religious texts to read for themselves, which could then taken back to slave quarters and used to instruct others. The Africans who became literate in the archaic English of the King James translation of the Bible thus became a valuable resource to their wider community in more ways than the ministers foresaw. During the Revolutionary War, Euro-Carolinians attempted to censor news of the British actions in the colonial newspapers, from fear that Afro-Carolinians would learn about it—a clear indication that at least some of them were literate and had ways of spreading such news. Masters reported that news could run several hundreds of miles in a week or two among them (Olwell 1998, 229–30), and free Afro-Carolinian men were caught carrying messages across Charles Town Harbor between the British governor and the city. Olwell maintains that, because of their fear of slave uprisings, the South Carolina masters were "revolutionaries by necessity rather than choice" (243). As we have noted earlier, however, spoken communication between the British and Afro-Carolinians was difficult, probably because the British had no interpreters for the Gullah spoken by most of them.

Although at least one Indian child was among the students in the early Charles Town school founded to educate enslaved people, literacy among Indians was rare. For the indigenous peoples of South Carolina, literacy was not so clearly either to their advantage or to the Europeans'. Having their own religious practices, which were tightly connected to the topography of their native Carolina, Indians were notoriously resistant to the efforts of the Society for the Propagation of the Gospel in Foreign Parts and the missionaries it sent to the colony to instruct Indians and Africans in the abstract doctrines of Christianity. On a political level, leaders within the Indian community recognized the symbolic value of written documents for the Europeans, and they themselves made use of written letters to the colonial leaders, which they dictated to bilingual interpreters after intense community discussion. Individual literacy among the native peoples was rare, however, until well after the colonial period had ended (Nichols 1993).

For most Europeans access to written English was relatively common because of the widespread use of written texts for Protestant religious observances and for the colony's tutors and public schools. The weekly newspaper published in Charles Town was filled with local and world news and was read widely throughout the colony; only for a few brief periods (after a hurricane or financial setback) was its publication interrupted between the initial publication in 1732 and the onset of the Revolutionary War in 1776. The landowning and professional classes depended upon the newspaper's printed advertisements, shipping notices, legal documents, and news from other colonies in order to conduct informed transactions for their own personal affairs as well as those for the growing colony. The same was true for those European indentured servants aspiring to become landowners after their period of servitude. Women and girls of the landowning class were often literate because the majority of printed texts were printed in the language they also spoke: English. The switch from Latin to English as the primary language of written texts that had accompanied the Protestant Reformation in both England and Scotland, and the use of the printing press for the wide distribution of religious texts, ensured that groups previously excluded from literacy now had access to it in something close to the language they spoke daily. In fact, the fairly widespread literacy in English within the early South Carolina colony, it can be argued, preceded rather than followed the use of English as the common spoken language.

The written English used was fairly standardized, thanks to the use of the printing press. While it became the unifying common language for this multilingual colony, the spoken English used by different groups reflected social divisions associated with early settlement patterns, with racial categories, and with class divisions. It is this spoken language variation that we turn to next.

In the following chapter we will explore the effects that different kinds of bilingualism had upon the many languages of the Carolina colony, looking in turn at processes of language birth, language shift, and language death. We will also examine the structural changes in different varieties of English and the English-influenced creole language that developed, as speakers of different languages and dialects had brief or intensive contact with each other in the multilingual environment of early South Carolina.

5 | *Language Variation*

English emerged as the common language, but different segments of the population took different paths toward a common language. These paths resulted in several language varieties that "marked" speakers as members of different racial or ethnic groups, as well as of different social classes within ethnic groups.

The most famous of these language varieties is still spoken by many African Americans in coastal South Carolina: Gullah, sometimes known as Geechee in certain parts of South Carolina, as Sea Island Creole to outsiders, or simply as "country talk" among Afro-Carolinians themselves. This chapter will discuss the origins of this distinctive creole language, its grammatical features, and its probable links to African American English spoken in other parts of the country. A less well-known language variety is the dialect of English spoken by the Lumbee Indians living in the borderlands between eastern North and South Carolina. We will look at the relationships between Lumbee English and the nonstandard dialect of English spoken by many European Americans in rural South Carolina. Finally the relatively few dialect characteristics that mark a South Carolina speaker as "southern," whatever the ethnicity or social class, will be discussed in terms of how a regional dialect has become distinctive in the larger national context. Throughout, we will see that all of these distinctive varieties share more similarities than differences. Outsiders often hear only the features that mark a speaker as "southern," but native South Carolinians hear a wide range of variation that they attribute to ethnicity, class, and upcountry or lowcountry origins.

Language Birth

Early Africans in South Carolina learned English as a common language, just as did non-English newcomers from Europe. The first Africans were few in number and worked closely with European laborers in pursuit of food and shelter and then in the collection and preparation of wood products for export and trade. Those Africans who had previously lived in English colonies of the Caribbean already knew some English when they entered South Carolina. Most would have spoken it as a second or third language in addition to their African ones. Like all second-language speakers, they spoke an English reflecting interference from their first language. In other words they spoke English "with an accent," one with distinctive phonology and grammar that differed from the English of those who spoke it as a first language. Like children of other immigrants, their children and grandchildren would have begun to sound more and more like native English speakers because of their interaction with other English speakers—if their numbers remained stable relative to those of Europeans in the colony.

However, subsequent generations of Africans did not have as much interaction with native English speakers as they would have needed to become fluent in the language. Changing demographics, as well as their situation as slaves—and a society that had become more and more sharply divided between the powerful and the powerless—would inhibit a full range of language interaction with native English speakers.

Another factor that had unknown linguistic consequences was the relationship between enslaved Africans and Indians. In the earliest years of the colony both Africans and Indians had lived as slaves in the English settlement. Colonial records reveal a greater number of African men than women in the first several generations, living alongside enslaved Indian women, who outnumbered Indian males in bondage. The appearance of "mustee" runaway slaves in the newspaper advertisements of the 1730s indicate that children were born to men and women of different races, since this was the term used for someone of Indian and African parentage. The necessity for such a word indicates that a number of such children were born to couples who would have interacted across racial, as well as linguistic, boundaries. That the language they had in common would have been some variety of English spoken in the slave quarters is confirmed by the colony's weekly newspaper. If language is mentioned at all in an advertisement for runaway mustees, these individuals are invariably described as speaking English—often good English. The unknown factor in the kind of English they spoke was the extent to which it may have been influenced by the Indian languages spoken by their mothers. The coastal indigenous languages spoken in South Carolina have long since disappeared without any documentation, and it is highly doubtful that we will ever have information about their linguistic structures, much less the extent of their influence on the variety of English spoken in the early slave quarters.

The earliest linguistic interaction in the colony is clearly different from what came later. After the initial founding of the colony in 1670, the

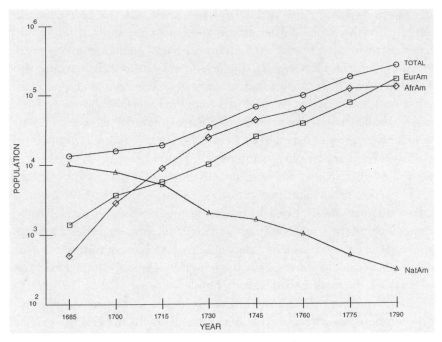

FIGURE 5.1. Estimated population by race in South Carolina (east of the mountains). Based on Wood (1989, 38); from Patricia Causey Nichols, "Creole Languages: Forging New Identities," in *Language in the USA*, edited by Edward Finegan and John R. Rickford (© 2004 Cambridge University Press). In this logarithmic graph 10^6 = 1,000,000; 10^5 = 100,000; 10^4 = 10,000; 10^3 = 1,000; 10^2 = 100; EurAm = European Americans; AfrAm = African Americans; NatAm = Native Americans.

number of Africans in South Carolina increased dramatically while that of native Indians shrank (see table 1.1). According to figures from historian Peter H. Wood (1989), there were one-third as many Africans as Europeans in the colony by 1685, but there were two-thirds as many by 1700. Only fifteen years later, in 1715, Africans outnumbered both Europeans as a group and Indians as a group. By 1721 Africans made up more than twice the total number of Europeans and Indians combined. In other words, half a century after its founding the majority population of South Carolina was of African descent (see fig. 5.1).

As we have noted earlier, the Yemassee War of 1715 was a turning point for the colonists in their understanding of the labor force that would be needed for viability of the young colony. This coordinated Indian uprising forced an understanding that Indian labor would never serve their needs, and they had also begun to understand that they could not compete with other colonies for the labor of indentured servants from Europe because of the harsh working conditions in their subtropical climate. From this time forth thousands of Africans would be imported across the Atlantic by trading companies from several European nations to be bought and sold in the slave market at Charles Town, which was the primary destination of slaving ships headed for North America. Many were subsequently shipped from Charles Town to English colonies further to the north, but the greatest number were sold within the South Carolina colony itself as laborers for the growing rice plantations. The rice crops they were bought to tend provided the grain that provisioned the ships bringing even more enslaved Africans to European colonies along the Atlantic coast. Only Africans (except for the Chinese, who grew a different variety of rice by different methods) possessed the body of knowledge needed for growing and preparing this grain in South Carolina for human consumption (Carney 2001). Thus, as participants in the emerging global economy of the Atlantic, Africans were both victims and facilitators of its enormous success. Through their efforts they provided both the labor and the knowledge that made South Carolina the richest of the original thirteen colonies in what was to become the United States of America.

The dramatic increase in the number of Africans relative to Europeans had consequences for language use. The majority of Africans entering the colony after 1715 probably would never interact to any substantial extent with native English speakers, but instead would learn the common language in the slave quarters from those who spoke English as a second (or third or fourth) language—with all the imperfections that accompany such indirect learning (Thomason 2001).

Under these social conditions a new creole language was born: Gullah. The exact place or places of this birth may be in dispute, but the conditions that gave rise to it are not. As thousands and thousands of Africans poured into the colony, uprooted from their homes and villages in what is now Angola or West Africa, they needed a common language for communication with each other. Some had been force marched from interior villages and held in seaside slave compounds for long periods, awaiting sale and transportation to European colonies in the Americas, where they would be resold as human property to colonial merchants and landowners. In these African compounds and during the long nightmare of the Middle Passage, a language used for basic communication was created and shaped by those

Africans and Europeans who were bilingual in one or more African languages and in the English of the slave traders. Because the African speakers were in the majority and because the bilinguals among them far outnumbered those among the Europeans on the sailing vessels, the language that was shaped and reshaped favored the grammatical structures found in the more prevalent African languages. The vocabulary of the new language brought to South Carolina was predominately English—the language spoken by the more powerful in the slave trade between Africa, the Caribbean, and South Carolina—but fundamental aspects of its abstract grammar were selected from the many African languages spoken by the newcomers.

Because most of the vocabulary used for this new language was English, the Gullah language developing in South Carolina was assumed to be a variety of English, though a distinctive one. As we have noted, a three-week series of advertisements placed by the printer of the *South Carolina Gazette* in 1734 characterizes four young slaves (ages fourteen through twenty), whom he wishes to sell, as speaking very good (black) English. But linguistically speaking, Gullah was a different language from English—one that probably from the beginning spanned a wide continuum. The earliest slaves imported from the crowded plantations of Barbados would have already spoken a language variety close to English. Those who came later directly from Africa and had frequent interaction with native speakers of English would have acquired more of the grammatical structures of English, while those who never spoke with a native speaker of English would retain more of the grammatical structures of their native African languages. Katherine Wyly Mille (1990) has argued convincingly that, even one hundred years after the massive immigration of Africans into Carolina, different speakers occupied different ends of the continuum and had probably done so since the beginning of the colony. Furthermore the same speaker in different social circumstances may have been able to use different portions of this continuum, as is the case for contemporary members of Gullah-speaking communities.

Take the following excerpt from a conversation between a young Gullah speaker and the white woman working in his classroom:

"He gon catch we back!"
"Huh?"
"He gon catch us again!"

This striking exchange took place in 1974, between an eleven-year-old African American boy and me as we were driving down a four-lane highway along Waccamaw Neck in coastal South Carolina.* I was passing a big eighteen-wheeler as it was gathering speed on a straight road, and my young passenger was commenting on the futility of that attempt—first in his native creole, and then in a variety closer to mine. Born some twenty miles and twenty years apart along this coast, we had learned very different language varieties in our home communities. Now, working together daily in his newly integrated local school and goofing off that day on a fishing trip, we were learning to accommodate to each other's language patterns. But as this brief exchange makes clear, the child was doing the major share of the accommodating. When my "Huh?" indicated a lack of understanding, he could make substitutions for two words used in his native Gullah, which moved his variety closer to my standard English. Having worked for two months as a classroom aide and researcher in his school, I was able to understand his use of *gon* as an auxiliary marker for future and his extension of the standard meaning of *catch*, so that I could then translate his observation to something like "He [the truck driver] is going to pass us again."

But his relatively greater understanding of my speech, and of how it differed from his, was all too typical for the school setting he was in. This young Gullah speaker exhibited in this brief exchange his ability to use a portion of the continuum between Gullah and the African American English that evolved from it, or perhaps parallel to it in different social settings.

This young boy's ability to switch between language varieties illustrates a crucial point about how both Gullah and contemporary varieties of African American English have developed: individual speakers who use more than one language often switch between the two. In the process of frequent codeswitching between their two (or more) languages, individuals may insert vocabulary and grammatical features of one language into the other—sometimes keeping separate languages for separate topics, but other times mixing the two within the same conversation if their conversational partner is also bilingual. When there is social inequality between speakers, the speaker with less social capital almost always does more of the work accommodating the other speaker—as was the case with the young boy and me. I was older, had a position of some responsibility in his school environment, and was a member of a socially privileged group in his region.

*The Waccamaw Neck is the coastal stretch of land in northeastern South Carolina that is formed by the Waccamaw River on the west and the Atlantic Ocean on the east and extends from Horry County to Georgetown County.

Even though I understood some Gullah, it never occurred to me during all my months in the community to switch to it when children did not understand me. As an educator and a white woman, I was expected to speak English and did so. However, I often observed children rephrasing their statements when their teacher or some other adult had not understood them. Some teachers, of both European and African American backgrounds, told me that during their early teaching years on the Waccamaw Neck they had used a bilingual child to "translate" the language of the Gullah-speaking children until acquiring enough proficiency to understand it. Usually a year was the length of time they needed. The linguistic obligation to switch, however, was on the Gullah-speaking children—not the English-speaking adults who taught them.*

Similar status relationships affecting language use would have existed between enslaved Africans and European landowners in early South Carolina. As we have seen, during the earliest settlement period the plantation slave quarters contained Indian women, men, and children, as well as African men, women, and children. There were also European indentured servants in many households, but their total numbers were far fewer than those of the African and Indian slaves. The first official count of the population in 1708 shows a total of 120 European servants, 2,900 adult African slaves, and 1,100 adult Indian slaves (Merrens 1977, 32). While some scholars have proposed that the Africans learned their English from the European laborers and sometimes landowners with whom they worked daily, the population distribution makes that path of language learning highly unlikely. New emigrants from Africa learned the common language from other Africans in the slave quarters and fields where they worked. A growing number of "seasoned" workers, many born in the colony, had more frequent and prolonged contact with speakers in the colony who used English in a wide range of functions, and some even became literate in this language with profound consequences for their own mobility and that of their families, as we have seen. Just because some Afro-Carolinians knew English well, however, does not mean that they did not also know how to

---

*The children were usually bilingual in English by the fourth grade and no longer needed translators, but they still used Gullah outside the classroom. Studies of the early relationship between Gullah and African American English are of course nonexistent. Weldon (2008) has recently compared how Gullah speakers in contemporary South Carolina and speakers of African American English in the Midwest use negation, finding some differences and some parallels.

speak and understand Gullah. Because so many of the daily functions of life in the colony were separated along racial lines, especially as Africans became the most numerous of the three racial groups, Afro-Carolinians of all ranks would have had significant linguistic interactions among themselves. Moreover, some Euro-Carolinians would have also learned Gullah, especially those children on the larger plantations who were cared for as infants by Afro-Carolinian women and who played with children in the "quarters" until they became old enough to go away to school. Unlike their brothers, few females were given an education or sent to "finishing" schools abroad, and we can assume that some Euro-Carolinian women had a reasonable command of Gullah for all of their adult lives. Eliza Lucas Pinckney is probably unusual in the extent of her interaction with the slaves on her father's plantation, but her letter book kept between 1739 and 1762 provides descriptions of the kinds of daily language interaction that could take place between mistress and slave (Pinckney 1972).

What were the characteristics of this new language, which can still be heard today in the homes and playgrounds of coastal South Carolina and Georgia, though rarely in public? There is no real documentation of the early creole, and neither is there extensive documentation of many of the source languages that were spoken in Africa itself (Heine and Nurse 2000). The most extensive literary representation of a late stage of Gullah is that provided by Ambrose Gonzales, a Euro-Carolinian who spent his childhood among Gullah speakers on the Sea Islands of Edisto and Hilton Head in the second half of the 1800s (Mille 1990), just after the Civil War, when African Americans were freed from slavery. His Gullah sketches were published in the *State* newspaper in 1892, followed by four collections of published tales in the 1920s. The most comprehensive linguistic study of Gullah remains that of Lorenzo Dow Turner, an African American scholar who has been called the "father of Gullah studies" by Wade-Lewis (2007, xvi and xvii). Turner was born in Elizabeth City in 1890, a coastal area in northeastern North Carolina, where he may have heard some Gullah as a child. After obtaining a B.A. from Howard University, an M.A. from Harvard University, and a Ph.D. in English from the University of Chicago, Turner studied linguistics with Hans Kurath and was invited to be one of the early field workers for the Linguistic Atlas Project of the United States. He recorded Gullah speakers along the South Carolina and Georgia coasts in the 1930s, then later studied several West African languages that he thought might be possible source languages for the Gullah speech he had recorded (Wade-Lewis 2007). His conclusions were summarized in

Africanisms in the Gullah Dialect, first published in 1949 and twice reissued because of the value to contemporary scholars of the extensive texts it provides from Gullah speakers who were born in the nineteenth century. Turner gives both conventional spelling and linguistic transcriptions for many of these texts.

We have no firsthand data on Gullah speech of the earliest years of the colony, but Mille's analysis (1990) of Gonzales's literary renditions of the creole he heard as a child in the late 1800s reveals a wide range of creole features. Both Mille's literary analysis and Mufwene's comparison (1991) of spoken Gullah from the 1930s and 1980s speculate that such variation probably existed from the early 1700s and continues into the present, given the social conditions we have documented here. Newcomers to the colony would have always used far more of their African grammar and sound systems than would "country-born" Afro-Carolinians who had been exposed longer to the language of the slave quarters. Since the number of new Africans continued to increase until the transition from colony to state (and even into the early nineteenth century), the number of African features in their language would continue to be great, especially for those whose labor was confined to the rice and indigo fields. At the same time, those "seasoned" Afro-Carolinian laborers with skills in such areas as carpentry, boating, tailoring, marketing, and labor management would be exposed to more functions of English and often would interact extensively with English speakers. In the meantime Africans talked to each other frequently, which meant that few if any of them spoke English exclusively. The probability is high that increasing numbers of Afro-Carolinians were both bilingual in Gullah and English and also used these two languages in different contexts, somewhat as I have described the young boy interacting with me on the Waccamaw Neck in the 1970s. What is *not* probable is that there were significant numbers of newly arrived Africans who were able to continue speaking their African languages with each other and to codeswitch between those languages and English. Except for the Kongo or Angolan group that precipitated the Stono Rebellion in 1739, the records contain no evidence of Africans communicating extensively in their native languages once they arrived in South Carolina. Gullah and English would have been their major languages from the early 1700s until well after the Civil War in the mid-1800s.

This distinction is important for development of the creole language. In a social setting where Africans outnumbered the more powerful English speakers but where they had little or no opportunities for full communication with these speakers, Gullah became the common language among

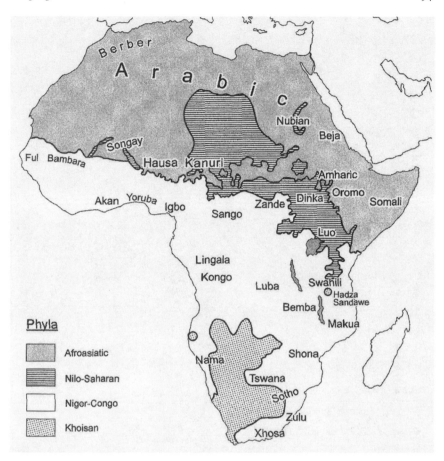

FIGURE 5.2. Language phyla of Africa; from Bernd Heine and Derek Nurse, eds., *African Languages* (© 2000 Cambridge University Press). Reprinted with the permission of Cambridge University Press

themselves. Cut off from their specific native languages, the newly arrived Africans had to select, probably by trial and error, those structures held in common among the various African languages that could serve as the grammar of the language they were forging. Because so many different languages were spoken, especially in West Africa, where the more desirable skilled laborers were found, every plantation with large groups of Africans would have several of these languages represented in the quarters where they gathered nightly to cook their evening meals and socialize. A look at the distribution of languages and language families on the African continent helps us to understand the great diversity that existed there, especially along the coast extending between Senegal and Liberia.

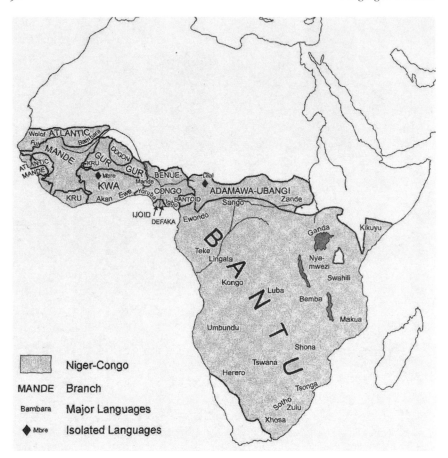

FIGURE 5.3. Language families of the Niger-Congo phylum; from Bernd
Heine and Derek Nurse, eds., *African Languages* (© 2000 Cambridge University Press). Reprinted with the permission of Cambridge University Press

Figure 5.2 reveals that the areas contributing the African population
of South Carolina did share the common language phylum of Niger-
Congo. From the distribution of the Niger-Congo phyla, a categorization by which languages deemed to have a common ancestral history are
grouped, we can see that the contributing African languages shared an
African heritage that paralleled that of the Indo-European languages ranging across Europe and into the subcontinent of India.

However, figure 5.3 shows that the West African segment contains
many different language families, while the central coast where Angola

exists has only one large language family, that of Bantu. The distribution of major branches shows that much greater diversity existed in West Africa than in the region of Angola. One large language family, Bantu, covers much of the area south of the Niger Delta, while West Africa contains almost a dozen language families. (By contrast the European languages of early South Carolina represented only three major language families— Romance [French, Spanish, Ladino], Germanic [German, English, Scots, Dutch], and Celtic [Gaelic, Welsh]—within the Indo-European phylum.)

All the languages from Africa that appeared in South Carolina in its first one hundred years as a colony probably had some basic features in common, however. None of the source languages for Gullah uses clicks (Clements 2000, 150), which are common in South African languages. Many of them seem to have had a basic word order of subject-verb-object (SVO), like English. One exception is the Mande language family of West Africa (which includes some of the languages spoken in Mali, Sierra Leone, Liberia, Senegal, Gambia, Benin, Ghana, and Nigeria); its basic word order places the object before the verb (SOV). The preferred syllable structure for most African languages is consonant-vowel (CV). Many Bantu languages have an obligatory final vowel (Clements 2000). By contrast many English words are consonant-final. Another major difference is in the prosodic system, where African languages are most unlike English. Clements observes, "The majority of African languages are tone or tonal-accent languages, in which differences in relative pitch are used to convey lexical and grammatical distinctions" (152). The commonest type in the Niger-Congo languages opposes two tone levels (high and low), with contour tones created with two or more of the tones in succession on single syllables. Because this system of conveying meaning is so unlike anything in English, it is worth noting because the initial impression one often has on hearing Gullah for the first time is the unusual prosody or "music" of the phrasing. No extensive study has yet been made of Gullah prosody, although Turner made some preliminary observations (1949, 249–53).

One of the factors crucial to the spread of the common language that developed from all the many African ones brought to South Carolina was the practice on the large plantations of gathering all of the children too young to work into "nurseries," where their daily activities were supervised by older women no longer able to do heavy agricultural work while most of their parents worked in the fields. As "seasoned" slaves, these older women would have known Gullah and would have used it as a common language with the children. The children themselves would have passed on the language to the ones just beginning to speak, as children do the world over.*

Gullah. Based on what records we have, Gullah can be linked to its African source languages in some of its vocabulary, aspects of its sound system, and a fair number of its grammatical structures. The vast majority of vocabulary items that Turner found to derive from African languages were personal names, often given to coastal African Americans as children to represent something about the day of their birth, their physical condition, or any number of attributes significant to them. Such naming practices still exist in Gullah communities of South Carolina, even though the nicknames given to children are English ones rather than African. I have heard a boy called "Nappy" because of the texture of his hair and another called "Daddy Man" because he was born on the day that his father died. Such nicknames are used only among intimates; other more traditional English names are used for public records. (Teachers of contemporary Gullah-speaking children sometimes become confused at the disparity between the two, or sometimes three, names that children have among their peers.) Turner also identified many African-derived words for objects in the natural environment, such as *benne* for sesame seed, *buckra* for white man, *fufu* for a mush made of a thin batter, *juju* for magic or evil spirit, *coota* for a tortoise or turtle, *nansi* for spider, *pinda* for peanut, *tote* meaning "to carry," and *yam* for a tuber similar to the American sweet potato. A few of these words have passed into mainstream English. Other words are heard only in prayers or stories and songs—typical places where words are found long after their meanings are lost to their speakers. (Think about *I plight thee my troth* in some Anglican or Episcopal wedding ceremonies.) Other words that appear in Gullah speech are obviously calques, or direct translations, from older African phrases. One such phrase that appears both in Brazilian Portuguese, according to John McWhorter (Heine and Nurse 2000, 9), and in the Gullah of South Carolina recorded by Turner and still heard today in South Carolina is the beautiful phrase *day clean* for the dawn of the day, a phrase originating in Yoruba of present-day Nigeria. Hazel Carter, professor emeritus of African languages and literature at the University of Wisconsin-Madison, has brought her extensive knowledge of Bantu languages to Turner's list of lexical items in Gullah having African meanings,

---

*While visiting a plantation on the Waccamaw Neck in the 1970s, I was shown the "nursery" house by an elderly African American woman whose father had been a slave on the plantation. She explained to me this child-caring practice.

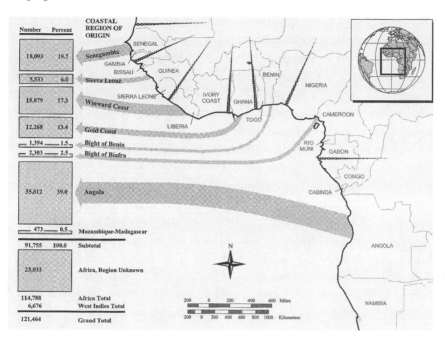

FIGURE 5.4. Sources of slaves imported to South Carolina, 1616–1806; from William S. Pollitzer, *The Gullah People and Their African Heritage* (© 1999 University of Georgia Press). Reprinted with the permission of the University of Georgia Press

and she presents evidence that much more of Gullah's vocabulary has Bantu origins than Turner realized from the resources available to him. Like Turner, Carter concludes that Bantu languages contribute more vocabulary than those of West Africa, but she suggests that there is little evidence for their contribution to the syntactic structure of Gullah. Rather, West African languages may have made more of a contribution to its grammar, she believes (Carter 1978).

A look at William S. Pollitzer's careful analysis of the percentage of slaves imported into South Carolina between 1716 and 1807 (see fig. 5.4) shows why the prevalence of Bantu vocabulary might be predictable, since more Africans arrived in South Carolina from Bantu-speaking regions than from any other single region of Africa. Typically later arrivals, these Bantu speakers would have learned the grammatical structures of the existing creole language but might have retained some of their native vocabulary.

Gullah phonology can most easily be understood by linking its more distinctive sounds to those of the West African languages, according to

Turner (1949). In particular the vowels have the most striking resemblances. Using the vowels of Yoruba as his primary basis of comparison, Turner finds the vowels (*i, e, ɛ, a, o, u*) to be similar in quality. In common with English, Gullah has several additional vowels not found in the West African languages with which he was familiar: *ɪ, ʊ,* and *ə*. Unlike English, Gullah does not have the low front vowel (*æ*) of the two English word *bag*. Among the consonants, Gullah does not use the English sounds spelled as *th*, which represents the voiceless and unvoiced sounds (*θ, ð*) of *ether* and *either*. Gullah uses *t* or *d* initially for words such as *thing* or *this* and *f* or *v* finally or medially for words such as *tooth* or *mother*. The substitution of *ting* for *thing* and *dat* for *that* is common for many dialects of English the world over, as well as for children learning English for the first time, probably because the English interdental fricatives spelled as *th* are not common consonants in languages of the world and are relatively difficult to produce. Gullah has two bilabial fricative sounds that do not occur in English but are found in several West African languages: *ϕ* and *β*. Instead of the English labiodental voiceless *f*, Gullah often uses the voiceless bilabial fricative *ϕ*. Instead of the English labiodental voiced *v* and the voiced labiovelar semivowel *w*, Gullah uses the voiced bilabial fricative *β* as one possible pronunciation. An example of how this particular difference in the use of consonants seems to persist in ways that can cause misunderstanding with non-Gullah speakers can be found in my experience with one of the children on the Waccamaw Neck in the 1970s who used the name *Ervin/Erwin* as his school name. The teacher spelled it one way and the parents spelled it another. In separate settings the teacher complained to me that those parents did not even know how to spell their children's names, and the parents complained that the teachers were always getting the spelling wrong. I suspect that the teacher was hearing neither *w* nor *v*, but instead the non-English bilabial fricative. The parents, on the other hand, were giving that Gullah sound its closest English spelling and disagreeing with the teacher on what that should be.

One of the many difficulties in determining what the sound patterns of early Gullah might have been is the variation that seems to have existed from plantation to plantation. Perhaps conditioned by the approach to phonological analysis typical of his era of linguistics, Turner did not analyze the variation that obviously exists in his texts. Taking another look at these texts, Klein and Harris (2000) have examined eight of the narratives that Turner presented in phonetic transcription and find that the dialect spoken on Edisto Island has more creole-like features than do those from Waccamaw, James Island, Johns Island, St. Helena Island, and Wadmalaw

Island. Although this variation is not noted in Turner's published analyses, he does mention it in a 1933 interview cited by Wade-Lewis (1991, 14–15). Because of the relative isolation of many speakers on the larger plantations of the Sea Islands, it is likely that dialectal variation existed from community to community. One consistency in the sound system throughout the larger Gullah-speaking area, however, seems to be that of the syllable structure, which is patterned after that of most African languages spoken on the African continent. The clearly preferred syllable is a consonant followed by a vowel (CV), with an obligatory final vowel in many cases. Turner notes that this syllable preference leads Gullah speakers either to add a vowel to English words ending in a consonant or to drop the English consonant altogether. Thus, *more* is pronounced as *mo* and *hoarse* becomes *hosi*. The same syllable structure preference influences the Gullah treatment of English consonant clusters. Turner reports (1949, 247) that *stay* and *black*, for example, which both begin with consonant clusters, are often pronounced *te* and *bakə*—in one case eliminating a consonant, in the other both eliminating a consonant for the beginning cluster as well as adding a vowel for the final syllable. This difference in syllable structure is at the heart of many of the most noticeable pronunciation differences between Gullah and English.

The morphosyntax of Gullah is probably its second most distinctive characteristic, after its prosody or intonation patterns. These grammatical differences from the regional standard were the features most noticed by children's twentieth-century teachers on the Waccamaw Neck. Even though the U.S. Supreme Court decision mandating integrated schools was handed down in 1954, actual integration of children and staff was not a reality on the Neck until 1972, and about half the teachers encountering Gullah-speaking children in their classrooms were not familiar with the creole language (Nichols 1977). Many aspects of the grammar of Gullah and South Carolina English are the same. The basic word order of both is SVO, which is also the pattern of most of Gullah's African source languages. Like English, its word order is fixed, not free. The verb structure is quite different, however, with many verb forms showing no grammatical inflections on the verb itself. Rather, tense and aspect are indicated by preverbal particles, as is the case for many of its source languages.

1. *She duh hit me.* [fourth-grade girl, 1–75]
   "She's always hitting me."
2. *Dat lady look to the bottom.* [fifth-grade boy, 10–74]
   "That lady looked at the bottom (of the river)."

3. *My older sister have wake up my next older sister.* [fourth-grade girl, 9–74]
"My older sister had woken up my next oldest sister."
Note: for this child, *have* or *had* seemed to function as a past-tense marker.

4. *Somebody been around we window, try scare us.* [fourth-grade boy, 9–74]
"Somebody was around our window, trying to scare us."

Watters (2000) notes that many African languages tend to use verbs more frequently than English and to use them where European languages would use descriptive adjectives, giving as an example *He is big* expressed as a single verbal word, rather than the verb *to be* (195). Watters notes that African languages also use verbs where English might use adverbs and conjunctions. Such constructions are common in Gullah:

5. *Ee money all down there.* [fifth-grade boy, 10–74]
"Her money was all down there (at the bottom of the river)."

The personal pronoun system of Gullah is also quite different from that of English—although it should be emphasized that the lexical items are mostly derived from English. It is the distribution that is distinctive. Often there is no gender marking on the third-person pronouns, with *ee* and *um* used to mark nominative/possessive and objective, respectively. In example 5 above, *ee* is used for feminine possessive. In the following examples *ee* is used for the nominative *it* in subject position:

6. *Ee hard, John?* [fifth-grade boy, 10–74]
"Is it (the football) hard, John?"

7. *My stomach, ee roll.* [fourth-grade girl, 11–74]
"My stomach, it rolled" (on viewing a picture of the underside of a starfish).

In the following example *um* is used for the object *him* and *ee* is used for the possessive *his:*

8. *Miz L___ put um outside and let um stay fuh tape up ee mouth.* [third-grade girl, 1–75]
"Mrs. L___ put him outside and let him stay in order to tape up his mouth."

For the plural pronouns, *we* is often used for possessive and for object:

> 9. *If anybody come to we house, we dog. . . .* [fourth-grade girl, 9–74]
>   "If anybody comes to our house, our dog. . . . "
> 10. *Ain't no house up there by we.* [fifth-grade boy, 10–74]
>   "There isn't any house up there by us."

The one personal pronoun that is not English in origin is the form used in older stages of Gullah for second person: *una* or *yuna*. Turner indicates that this form is used for both singular and plural second person, in both subject and object positions. I heard this form used only for the second-person plural, and it was rare: only the very young and the very old used it on the Waccamaw Neck in the 1970s. Green and Igwe (1963) indicate that *unù* is the form used in Igbo for plural *you*, while a different form is used for singular. The distinction between singular and plural *you* in Gullah may well be the origin of the ubiquitous use of *y'all* for plural second person in southern English generally.*

The prepositions of Gullah are fewer than those of English. In fact Turner shows no use of *at* in his texts. Irma Aloyce Ewing Cunningham (1992) provides a useful comparison between the distribution of Gullah locative prepositions and English ones in her syntactic analysis of the creole, based on fieldwork she conducted in the late 1960s.

There are no examples of the locative *at* in Turner's Gullah texts collected in the 1930s and 1940s, and there are few in mine from the 1970s

Table 5.1. English locative prepositions

	ONE DIMENSION	TWO DIMENSIONS	THREE DIMENSIONS
STATIC	at	on	in
DYNAMIC	to	onto	into
	off	(away) from	out of

(adapted from Cunningham 1992, 29)

*An elderly aunt told me that in her childhood she had heard African American workers on the farm using *yuna all* for second-person plural pronoun—giving a hint of one possible pathway between Gullah and regional standard English.

Table 5.2. Gullah locative prepositions

	ONE OR TWO DIMENSIONS	THREE DIMENSIONS
STATIC	to	in
DYNAMIC	on	in
	from	out

(adapted from Cunningham 1992, 29)

(Nichols 1976 and 1986). Although Cunningham's diagram of the locative prepositions is based on a late stage of Gullah, it probably reflects an earlier stage as well. Some of the Kwa languages of West Africa have postpositions rather than prepositions, but most of the Atlantic languages have prepositions, as do Yoruba and Igbo of Nigeria and most other languages belonging to the Niger-Congo phylum. Watters (2000, 196) states that African languages in general tend to have fewer prepositions or postpositions than European languages. An example of how Gullah speakers use the locative *to* for the one-dimensional meaning *position at* can be seen in the following question and statements:

11. *Can we stay to the table?* [fifth-grade boy, 9–74]
    "Can we remain at the table?"
12. *I over here to the beach.* [fifth-grade girl, 1–75]
    (a telephone conversation with a friend)
13. *He might be to the funeral.* [sixth-grade boy, 1–75]
    (a telephone conversation with me)

Occasionally no locative preposition is used at all:

14. *My mama got ten flowers home.* [fourth-grade girl, 10–74]
    "My mother has ten flowers at home."
15. *When I been my cousin home, then I see a lizard and I run.* [fourth-grade girl, 10–74]
    "When I was at my cousin's home, I saw a lizard and I ran."

Use of the passive voice is mixed. Watters (2000) states that many African languages do not have a passive voice at all, but that the majority of Bantu languages do. An example of the lack of passive voice in Gullah speech can be seen in this example:

    16. *Chris paper tear.* [fourth-grade boy, 10–74]
      "Chris's paper is torn."

    The form of questions is often distinctive in that for content questions an interrogative word will be used along with basic word order, rather than the verb-phrase inversions typical for English questions. Watters notes that this is a typical word order for African content questions.

    17. *Why she couldn't ride a horse to school?* [fifth-grade boy, 10–74]
      "Why couldn't she ride a horse to school?"
    18. *Who dey name?* [fifth-grade girl, 10–74]
      "What are their names?"

    A final distinctive grammatical feature is the use of complementizers, which are not discussed in most descriptions of African languages. One is the use of the English lexical item *say* as a complementizer, which is more or less the equivalent of the English *that*:

    19. *She tell me say I could finish it.* [fifth-grade boy, 10–74]
      "She told me that I could finish it (my math homework)."
    20. *I dream say that Mama got up and gone back there street.* [fifth-grade girl, 10–74]
      "I dreamed that Mama got up and went back there in the street."

Another particle *fuh*, pronounced *f* and perhaps modeled on English *for* with an omitted final consonant, functions sometimes like an English modal of obligation:

    21. *Where fuh put this, Miz Nichols?* [fifth-grade girl, 1–75]
      "Where should I put this, Mrs. Nichols?"
    22. *Which one fuh read?* [fifth-grade girl, 1–75]
      "Which one should I read?"

Other times it functions like an English complementizer in infinitive constructions:

    23. *I ain't want it fuh snow.* [fifth-grade boy, 10–74]
      "I don't want it to snow."
    24. *You been ready fuh go on the bus.* [fifth-grade girl, 1–75]
      "You were ready to go on the bus."

25. *I ain't mean um fuh come on we.* [elderly woman, 1–75]
    "I didn't mean for them to come on us."
26. *Every time John L____ kill a bird, he scared fuh go in the bush fuh get um.*
    [fourth-grade girl, 10–74]
    "Every time John L____ kills a bird, he is scared to go in the bush
    to get it."

Today there is great variation for individual speakers in their use of
Gullah because of the frequency of contact with speakers of the regional
standard language variety. Although the speakers cited above did use Gullah with friends and family, even in these more intimate settings the use of
the morphosyntactic features described here varied from turn to turn in
their conversation. In storytelling activities between two or three friends,
Gullah features were frequent, but invariably when I gave children typed
versions of their recorded stories to read that preserved the grammatical
structures noted here, they changed precisely these items when reading
their stories aloud to each other and always in the direction of standard
English. Classroom reading was associated with formal standard English,
while traditional storytelling made more use of Gullah (Nichols 1977).

Like creole languages the world over that use the vocabulary of a world
language, Gullah is often considered a "broken" or imperfect English.
Nothing could be further from the truth. It is a language of a new people
who came together on the shores of South Carolina and forged a language
from what they had available to them. Probably no one today speaks it as
the only language available to them. In my observation Gullah speakers now
use it as an "inside" language, spoken only at home or with other Gullah
speakers.* When speaking to outsiders, almost all Gullah speakers speak a
variety of English much closer to the regional standard, although it often
retains some creole features. It is easy to claim that Gullah is "dying" or is
rarely heard any more if one does not have the opportunity to participate
in Gullah gatherings, but it is very much alive and spoken as a language of
the heart and home.

Language Death

Although the languages of West Africa and Angola are no longer used in

---

*Mufwene (1991, 230n17) reports a teenager's explanation of why he would not speak
Gullah in front of Mufwene but felt obligated to speak it with his peers when at home
on one of the Sea Islands of South Carolina.

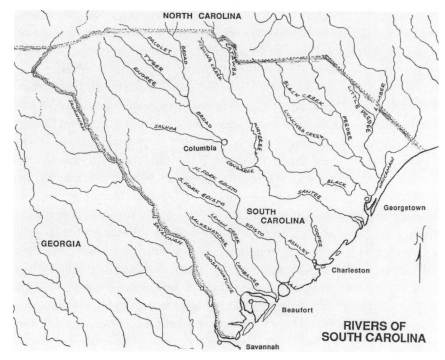

FIGURE 5.5. Rivers of South Carolina (Frank H. Nichols Jr.)

South Carolina, they still exist in Africa itself. They have not disappeared in their native lands. However, those languages native to South Carolina before the coming of the Africans and Europeans have all disappeared from this earth except for Cherokee—which is now spoken in the mountains of western North Carolina and in Oklahoma.

Cusabo. From 1562 to 1751 eighteen independent coastal tribes lived between the Santee River and the Savannah River, the area initially settled by the English colonists, and the name Cusabo was used by the colonists to refer to them all. (See fig. 5.5, Rivers of South Carolina.) Other names for them are Ashepoo, Bohicket, Combahee, Edisto, Escamaçu, Etiwan, Hoya, Kiawah, Kussah, Kussoe, Mayon, Sampa, Stalame, Stono, Touppa, Wando, Wimbee, and Witcheaugh (Waddell 2004, 254). Waddell believes that the Escamaçu, Ashepoo, Combahee, Kiawah, and Etiwan spoke the same, or a closely related, language, but few if any words of this Cusaboan language have been documented. No place names are related to Catawba except in areas where other tribes such as the Sewee and Santee were found along the river that empties into Winyah Bay; these two tribes may have been Catawban speakers (Rudes, Blumer, and May 2004). No documented words from these coastal tribes are related to the Muskogean language family except where the Yemassee lived briefly, even though previous accounts suggest that the Muskogean-speaking Creek from farther south controlled lands in and around Charles Town in 1670 when the English settled there (Eliades 1981). The Cusabo peoples do not seem to have had alliances with larger Indian nations. Prior to the successful English settlement at Charles Town, they had encountered the French at Port Royal and the Spanish who followed them. These experiences with Europeans apparently led some of them to side with the English in subsequent battles with the Spanish, and some even sided with the English during the Yemassee War. They engaged in farming, hunting, fishing, and gathering equally for subsistence along the coastal plain before European contact. Perhaps because of their prior experience with cultivation of indigenous crops, they were living mostly as farmers by the mid-1700s and coexisting with the English settlers, whom they supplied with deer and wild turkeys from their hunting. Cusabo women had only two or three children after marrying late at the age of about twenty-seven and used some sort of local root to promote abortions that kept the family size small (Waddell 2004, 261). The small size of their tribal groups and the close interaction with the English settlers along the coast meant that each generation of children would have learned more and more English, eventually speaking the colonial language exclusively as their own died with no more speakers.

Catawba. The Indian language spoken longest within South Carolina was Catawba, whose speakers recognized the power of literacy in their new world but who used it in a restricted way. Appreciating early how the Europeans used written documents much the way they used oral promises accompanied by appropriate rituals, Catawba headmen initially used documents written in English for display purposes. A few headmen carried on their person the written military commissions awarded to them with the governor's signature and colony's seal sometime after the Yemassee War of 1715 (Nichols 1993). A second use of literacy was the exchange of letters between the Catawba and the colonial government, as well as between the Catawba and a small Piedmont tribe. Also written in English, they were read and interpreted in communal meetings with the help of translators. Traders' journals document these "literacy events." Even though the Catawba creators and receivers of these documents were not literate themselves, they were active participants in these communicative acts.

By the 1760s the Catawba recognized their peril from increasing numbers of European settlers in their hunting lands, and to protect themselves in a way that the European "headmen" would recognize, they requested that English government officials give them a written deed to a fifteen-square-mile area in and around what is now the city of Rock Hill in York County (see fig. 5.6). The most interesting aspect of their approach to literacy, however, is that they subsequently chose a few select members of their group to acquire an education and to become literate in English when that kind of education became feasible for their young men. Unlike the Cherokee, they did not develop an alphabet for their own language and use it widely for personal communication. Instead, in the late 1760s they chose one of their young men, John Nettles, to attend the College of William and Mary in Virginia and to return and use his skills in encounters with the English-speaking colonists. James H. Merrell (1989, 242) suggests that having one group member perform the functions of literate communication for the larger group allowed most of the community to ignore the practice of English literacy entirely, thus continuing to preserve their own cultural and religious practices in the oral Catawba language. When Nettles became an old man, the Catawba requested of the colonial government that two or three of their young boys be taught to read and write in order to fill Nettles's now-pivotal role in the community. However, they showed no desire for all their children to be educated in a language and culture alien to them. Merrell reports that many Catawba became bilingual speakers of both Catawba and English over time, but literacy was limited to a few. He believes that this restriction kept their language and traditions alive. All of their sacred texts and traditions were kept by monolingual Catawba speakers until after the Civil War.

Although most Catawba understood English by the late 1800s, no Christian missionaries were able to convert them until the Latter-Day Saints, popularly known as Mormons, appeared among them sometime around the end of the nineteenth century. Perhaps because their theology designated American Indians as the "lost tribes of Israel" and also because these particular Christians showed a way out of the alcohol and drugs that were debilitating the Catawba (by then reduced to fewer than five hundred people), most Catawba converted to this brand of Christianity and began to enroll their children in a school run by the Mormons (Brown 1966). After some initial difficulties with funding, stronger support came from the central officials of the Latter-Day Saints in Salt Lake City in the first half of the twentieth century. The literacy in English that church membership entailed, however, probably hastened the death of their native language, and the last speakers in South Carolina died in the twentieth century. Chief Sam Blue of Rock Hill died in 1959. Red Thunder Cloud, who grew up in Rhode Island but claimed to have relatives on the Catawba Reservation in Rock Hill, died in 1996; he reportedly knew the language and worked with scholars to document it (Goddard 2000).

Why did the Catawba become dominant above all the many Native American groups in early South Carolina and continue to be, some nearly three hundred years later, the major Indian community in the state? Two factors seem to be associated with their rise, one real and one illusory. First a core group of Catawba rose to prominence on a major trade route between South Carolina and Virginia around the time of the Yemassee War in 1715. These Catawba, originating in what is now North Carolina, became allies of the English colonists after eliminating the troublesome Waxhaw. Believing they had acted out of friendship to the colonial government rather than from their own hostility to the Waxhaw, the colonists rewarded the Catawba with control of the major trade path leading to Williamsburg on the James River of Virginia. Second the Catawba, gaining strength from this special relationship with the colonial government along the coast, offered a place of refuge for smaller groups of Indians fleeing the coastal European encroachment on their traditional hunting and planting grounds. Moreover the Catawba actively recruited these smaller refugee groups, speaking many different languages, in order to strengthen their own group, whose numbers were continually diminished from the diseases imported with the Europeans. While the Indians themselves continued to be conscious of distinctions between communities northwest of Charles Town, the colonial government referred to all communities in the Catawba River valley as "Catawba," and by the mid-1700s the Native Americans had come to accept that name for themselves as well (Merrell 1989, 94–95). Thus the "Catawba Nation" as a label came to embrace many people of different origins and linguistic stock, providing yet another example of wide differences between the labels people choose for themselves and those assigned to them by keepers of the written records. Merrell provides convincing examples of the different mental maps held by Indians and Europeans that reflected their perceptions of the distribution of indigenous peoples throughout the state during the colonial period. The *South Carolina Gazette* provides what may be another example in the case of a captured Indian man about twenty years old, believed to be a slave, who "says he is Catawba (which he calls his) country, but cannot speak a word of the language" (June 4, 1753). This Indian man may have been one of the refugees speaking another language who had joined the Catawba Nation and had come to think of himself as Catawba, while continuing to speak his original language. The English colonists would have been generally unaware of the wholesale population shift that was taking place among the Native Americans themselves, although individual Indian traders and travelers may have been well aware.

Some of these individual Europeans have left intriguing records of their visits to the people known as Catawba, dating from the early expeditions into the interior soon after the founding of the Charles Town settlement in 1670. Hodge (1907, 1910) has summarized information from these early documents in his *Handbook of American Indians*, written for the Bureau of American Ethnology. John Lawson passed through their territory in 1701, reporting that they were a powerful nation, whose territory was thickly populated (Lawson 1967). In 1728 they were reported to have six villages along the Catawba River within a stretch of twenty miles. Their principal village was in what is now York County (see fig. 5.6), opposite Sugar Creek. Throughout the colonial period they were friendly to the English, except for a brief alliance with the Yemassee during the uprising of 1715. They were frequently at war with the Iroquois, Shawnee, and Delaware, but their ultimate enemy was the smallpox introduced by the Europeans; by the end of the 1700s their numbers had been greatly reduced. During this century their contact with the English colonial government became extensive, and by 1727 the Catawba were using their own bilingual interpreter rather than relying on one supplied by the English (Merrell 1989, 123). By midcentury an English-speaking traveler had no difficulty in finding someone to translate for him in any Catawba village. Meanwhile encroachment of backcountry European settlers, primarily from the "border areas" of northern England, the Lowlands of Scotland, and northern Ireland, proceeded relentlessly. The Catawba's requested survey of their lands by the English colonial government in 1764, giving them a pre-Revolutionary reservation on both sides of the Catawba River within York and Lancaster counties, reflected their understanding that only by appealing to the laws recognized by the Europeans could they retain some measure of control over their lands. After the Revolution the Catawba used their land as a source of regular income, signing ninety-nine-year leases with European settlers in exchange for yearly rents (Merrell 1989, 210). These rents were supplemented with income made by peddling pottery, baskets, and moccasins made by Catawba men and women throughout the upcountry and sometimes in the city of Charleston as well.

From a modern perspective, it is difficult to determine what constituted the Catawba language over the three centuries of its documented use. In his

1775 *History of the American Indians* James Adair maintained that Katahba (Catawba) was the "court dialect" of a nation comprising almost four hundred warriors, who were speaking more than twenty different dialects. Only in 1945 do we have a detailed sketch of the grammar of this language, classifying it as a member of the Siouan linguistic family (Siebert 1945). With the help of three informants from York County, who in 1941 were the only remaining fluent Catawba speakers on the Catawba Reservation, Frank T. Siebert Jr. established its relationship to the Siouan languages of the western prairies. He proposed that it was the last surviving member of a once extensive Eastern Siouan language group. Surely this was a very different language from that spoken in the villages Lawson visited in the early 1700s, even though it is called by the same name. It would have gone through extensive structural and vocabulary changes, resulting both from the contact with numerous other Native American languages spoken by refugees who joined their nation and from the two centuries of contact with English speakers. As the "last" speakers of the language, the informants whom Seibert interviewed would have been bilingual in Catawba and English. Furthermore, Catawba would have been used by these remaining speakers in few social contexts and would have reflected the contracted structures and vocabulary that accompany such a reduction in function. Nevertheless Siebert's contribution to our knowledge of Catawba is considerable.

From Siebert's analysis of Catawba at the last stage of its history and his comparison of its structure with that of related Siouan languages, we see that one grammatical category has been lost entirely (gender distinctions for address forms) and another has been fossilized (verbal prefixes expressing instrumentality). Such changes are characteristic of languages that have had extensive contact with related languages and that have also had extensive contact and social pressure from unrelated languages (Thomason and Kaufman 1988). Speakers of related languages who joined the Catawba would have learned their language imperfectly, thus producing the leveling effects on the grammar transmitted to successive generations. The dwindling number of people living together as Catawba would have become bilingual in the English spoken by their neighbors. As they became less and less self-sufficient within their own community, the Catawba would have had more occasions to use English in interactions with these neighbors— selling their pottery, purchasing tools, in time even sending their children to public schools where English was the language of instruction. Gradually all members of the community would speak at least some English, with younger members speaking only English, though understanding some of

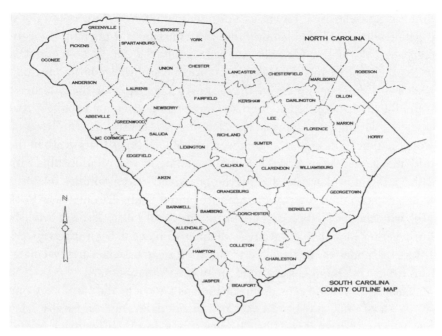

FIGURE 5.6. Robeson County, North Carolina, and modern counties of South Carolina

the Catawba spoken by their elders. At the time that Siebert studied the dying language, occasions for using the language actively would have been limited, though speakers might remember from their childhood more of the language than they actually used themselves.

Although Catawba is classified as a Siouan language in most scholarly analyses of it, Campbell and Mithun (1979, 32–33) in their survey of American Indian languages note that it has sometimes been classified as a language isolate with no known relatives because of the great differences between Catawba and other members of the Siouan family. In recent years some scholars with access to colonial Spanish documents have suggested a relationship to the Muskogean language family, based on interpreter language use during the early Pardo expeditions of the 1500s (Booker, Hudson, and Rankin 1992). Even if it is not a Muskogean language, they believe it is a mistake to consider it Siouan because of the language mixture that was evident at an early stage, pointing to the use of place names that are compatible with a Muskogean classification. In the most recent overview of languages of the Southeast Indian groups, Martin (2004) notes that some linguists now classify Catawba as a different family from Siouan but put it together with the Siouan family under the same language phylum, "Siouan-Catawba." Within the Catawba language family, the Catawba once spoken in South Carolina and the Woccon of North Carolina are both quite distinct from other members of the Catawba languages of the Southeast (Ofo, Biloxi, Tutelo). No doubt the extensive undocumented changes that occurred within the Catawba language of north-central South Carolina, from the time of its earliest presence in precolonial times to its death in the mid-1900s, prevent us from ever understanding its real relationships with other indigenous languages. Today about ninety-seven families live on a federally recognized reservation in north-central South Carolina near Rock Hill, with about two thousand people on the tribal rolls. All speak English, but whether or not that variety is distinctive has not been investigated. Efforts are underway to assemble a Catawba lexicon based on archival materials for use in school curricula (Heinemann-Priest 2007).

Lumbee. A much larger group of Indians known as the Lumbee living southeast of the Catawba does speak a distinctive variety of English that has been recently studied. The Lumbee people lost their language or languages so early that we do not know what they spoke. Linguists believe that there were originally dozens of Native American languages used in the Carolinas of which we have no record (Wolfram et al. 2002), and the Lumbee people may have spoken several of them as they were joined by native peoples of the Carolinas being pushed back from the coast onto lands the European colonists deemed less desirable. Various hypotheses exist about the origins of these peoples, but from what we have seen about the wholesale movement of other native peoples both before and after contact with the Europeans and Africans, it is likely that any original Indians living in this area were joined by other remnant groups seeking sanctuary from the growing settlements of Europeans in the more fertile farmlands elsewhere.

Although this group is not technically within the contemporary boundary of South Carolina, their swampy homeland is just north of Dillon and Marion counties and has shifted between South and North Carolina over the years, with the exact state line rarely obvious in many places (see fig. 5.6). Robeson County in North Carolina is the ancestral home of the largest self-identified Indian population east of the Mississippi, with nearly 40 percent of the population identifying as Native American in the 2000 census (Wolfram et al. 2002, 25). Having more than fifty-four thousand people on their tribal rolls and nearly forty-seven thousand of them concentrated in Robeson County, the Lumbee have only limited recognition by the federal government and no eligibility for reservation land. They have, however, been recognized by the state of North Carolina since the late 1880s, and in 1887 they established their own Indian normal school at Pembroke to train teachers for their children, with English as the medium of instruction. The institution has become part of the University of North Carolina. Like Indian groups of South Carolina, their name is associated with the river that was central to their daily lives and ceremonies, called the Lumbee River as long as a century ago (Knick 2000; cited in Wolfram et al. 2002) but now known as the Lumber River. Just below the South Carolina line the Lumber joins the Little Pee Dee River, which eventually flows into Winyah Bay at Georgetown (see fig. 5.5). Since the rivers were the major transportation routes in this area of the state until the Depression-era road-building projects, peoples were united by them in different geographic patterns from those dictated by modern highways and government boundaries. Names such as Croatan Indians, Indians of Robeson County, and Cherokee Indians of Robeson County have been used to refer to the same group of people at different time periods, which on one level indicates how long they have been a cohesive group and on another, how far from their original ancestral peoples they now are.

Losing their ancestral languages early, the Lumbee have spoken English long enough that their dialect preserves features of an earlier stage of the language. Unfortunately we lack documentation of the original languages they spoke in order to pinpoint how the original language patterns may have affected the dialect of English that developed. In an internal version of their own history, the Lumbee trace their knowledge of English to members of Raleigh's lost colony on Roanoke Island in the 1580s, which, when failing to receive necessary supplies from England, joined the Lumbee for survival (Dial and Eliades 1975; Dial 1993). It seems clear that, even though many outsiders of all three major races may have united with them over more than four centuries of contact with Europeans and Africans, the Lumbee have maintained an ethnic identity that is reflected in their distinctive spoken dialect.

This dialect is distinctive in several ways, as reported by Wolfram et al. (2002), who summarize several extensive descriptive linguistic studies done in recent years. Because the Lumbee of Robeson County interact with their African American neighbors (25 percent of the population) and with their European American neighbors (33 percent of the population), they share many features of the neighboring dialects as well. However, within their county Lumbee speakers can accurately identify other Lumbee speakers based solely on their recorded speech more than 75 percent of the time, indicating that their dialect is "recognizable as an ethnic dialect by the Lumbee; . . . [it] is neither White nor African American speech, but distinctly Lumbee" (Wolfram et al. 2002, 17). In pronunciation, unlike either their African American or European American neighbors, the Lumbee pronounce *time* and *side* as *toim* and *soid*, which reflects the older English pronunciation of the Outer Banks. Before voiceless sounds, the same vowel is pronounced without a glide: *light* sounds like *laht; right* sounds like *raht*. The *h* sound is retained in words such as *it* (*hit*) and *ain't* (*hain't*) as in older stages of English, and there is an intrusive *t* in such words as *once* and *cliff*. Like their neighbors in Robeson County and also speakers in the Appalachians and the Outer Banks, the Lumbee also pronounce *pen* and *pin* the same, a merger of vowels that occurs in all words before a nasal sound for most Southern English speakers. Like all speakers in their county, but unlike Appalachian and Outer Banks speakers, they do not pronounce *r* after a vowel: *fear* becomes *feuh; four* becomes *fowh*. In short the Lumbee have no sounds in their speech that are unique to them, but the distribution of sounds that they use *is* distinctive for their place and time. Their particular use of the sound system of English is different from either the African Americans or the European Americans in their county and probably accounts for why speakers of this dialect can recognize each other, with high reliability, from tape-recorded speech.

Lumbee grammar, or morphosyntax, is also distinctive. Just as in older stages of English, *a*- prefixing is often used with dynamic verbs, as in *That man jumped up a-running* and *The man's hand was a-bleeding*. Another older grammatical form is the suffix *-s* as a verbal ending that can be used with plural subjects, as in *The dogs barks* or *The dogs gets upset* (Wolfram et al. 2002, 69; Wolfram and Schilling-Estes 2004, 178). This usage was found in the speech of early settlers from northern England, as well as in the speech of the Scots-Irish from northern Ireland. Another relic can be found in the use of *be* rather than *have*, as in *I'm been there already* for perfect tense, a usage also found in earlier English (Wolfram et al. 2002, 70). In another usage distinctive to Lumbee speakers, the verb *to be* is regularized as *weren't* in past-tense negative, as in *I weren't, she weren't*, and *they weren't*, while other nonstandard dialects in the area regularize this irregular verb in different ways. Finally finite *be* is sometimes used with an *-s* suffix, as in *She bes here*, but the ultimate origin of this form is difficult to pinpoint (Wolfram and Schilling-Estes 2004, 185). On the one hand Scots-Irish speakers did not use this form until well after their early settlement in the region around Robeson County, and on the other hand African American residents of the county use a similar form without the *-s* suffix for a habitual meaning, as in *Sometimes she be going to the store*. Perhaps what the Lumbee speakers have done is similar to what Gullah speakers have also done: selected English forms in distinctive ways to shape the linguistic identity of their community.

A few lexical items are used by only Lumbee speakers (Wolfram et al. 2002). The term *Lum* is used to refer within the community to another Lumbee person. A *brickhouse Indian* is one who is better off financially than a *swamp Indian*. The term *on the swamp* means "in the neighborhood," and *ellick* is the Lumbee word for coffee. The phrases *fine in the world* and *sorry in the world* mean that one is doing well or not doing well. Several distinctive items are shared with other southern dialects, and one deserves special note: *toten* or *token*. In one of the earliest examinations of Lumbee English, Brewer and Reising (1982) noted that, while *toten* is a word that can be traced back to earlier stages of English, Lumbee Indians often use it as a symbol of their identity because outsiders cannot define it. For the Lumbee the term refers to a spirit or ghost, although it can also be used "to specify a noise or a sign provided by a spirit to indicate that death or evil is imminent" (110). Wolfram and Schilling-Estes (1997) note that on the Outer Banks, which also contains relic words from older stages of English, the latter meaning is prevalent.

Other Indian Groups

The time depth of the Lumbee community and the critical mass of people who live there have helped them maintain their distinctive way of speaking English, even though their ancestral languages have long since died. Distinctive dialects do not appear to exist for several other groups of self-identified Indians who still live within the boundaries of South Carolina. According to a recent statewide conference report, there are now within the state some fifteen Native American groups and organizations, which include about thirteen thousand South Carolinians (Sheinin 2001). Listed as Indian groups on the South Carolina Cherokee Web site are the following: the Catawba Indian Nation of Rock Hill, the Cherokee Indian Tribe of South Carolina (living throughout the state but primarily in the up-country counties of Oconee, Pickens, Greenville, Laurens, Spartanburg, Richland, Newberry, and Anderson), the Edisto Tribe (Dorchester, Colleton, Charleston), the Santee Tribe (Berkeley, Calhoun, and Orangeburg counties), the Pee Dee Tribe (Dillon, Marlboro, and Marion counties), the Wassamasaw Tribe of Varnertown (Berkeley and Dorchester counties), the Chaloklowas Indian People of the Chickasaw Nation, the Chicora-Waccamaw Indian People (Horry County), the Chicora Siouan Indian Tribe (Andrews), the Pee Dee Indian Nation (Beaver Creek of Neeses), the Beaver Creek Band of Pee Dee Indians (Salley), the Midlands Inter-tribal Empowerment Group of Columbia (Richland County), the Pied-mont American Indian Association (Greenville), the Santee Indian Nation, the Croatan–Pee Dee Indian Tribe (Orangeburg), and the American Indian Center of South Carolina (Richland County). This listing is drawn up by the Indian peoples themselves. The difference in population density between the Lumbee of North Carolina, who number forty-seven thousand in a single county, and that of the South Carolina Indians, who number only thirteen thousand scattered throughout the state, is one that makes a difference in language use. In a few counties some South Carolina Indian families have identified more with their African American neighbors, and in others more with their European American neighbors. Although the En-glish now used by contemporary South Carolina Indians groups has not been studied, it is likely that their speech is closest to the non-Indians with whom they have the greatest interaction. It is possible, however, that some groups may still be using a few words and sound patterns in ways that dis-tinguish them from both their African American and European American neighbors. Certainly that is the case for a small community of Cherokee in a remote region of North Carolina that is now in the process of shifting to English (Anderson 1999).

Language Shift

Unlike the indigenous languages that no longer have any living speakers, one of the original languages of South Carolina is still spoken outside the state, as are all of the European languages of the early settlers. The descen-dants of the original speakers of Cherokee who still live within the state, as well as of those of Scots, Welsh, French, German, Spanish, and Spanish-related Ladino, have shifted to English. The Snowbird Cherokee have made this shift just in the last generation, allowing us a better understand-ing of the origins of their dialect than we have for the Lumbee dialect.

Cherokee. The only member of the Southern Iroquoian language family to be spoken in the Southeast, Cherokee is still spoken on the Cherokee Qualla Reservation and in the Snowbird Community of western North Carolina (Martin 2004) and by many Cherokee whose ancestors were re-located to Oklahoma along the infamous Trail of Tears in 1838–39. The vitality of this language, once spoken in the western corner of colonial South Carolina, has benefited greatly from having its own syllabic alphabet created by a Cherokee who was not literate himself in any language but recognized the principle of converting sounds to written symbols that could be read separately from the spoken word. Sequoyah Guess created a syllabic alphabet for Cherokee and demonstrated it before Cherokee leaders at New Echota, Georgia, in 1821 (Walker 1981). Within a few years literacy became widespread among the Cherokee people, as they used it for personal letters, accounts, copies of sacred songs, and healing formulas. A newspaper was printed even before the forced removal, as well as translations of parts of the Bible, Christian religious writings, and legal documents. After their migration to Oklahoma the Cherokee were able to build on this experience with literacy and to print millions of pages in their own language in the new territory. Today several active Web sites are extending this tradition of literacy into the electronic age.

A few members of the Cherokee Nation had significant interaction with the colonists during the colonial period, but the South Carolina territory they controlled was limited to a small corner in the west. Traditional enemies of the Catawba, the Cherokee occupied lands separated from the Catawba lands by a large, uninhabited buffer zone during the early colonial period. Later, with the encroachment of Europeans into the upcountry, many of them appear to have joined the Catawba population from time to time, as indicated by the stories that Speck (1913) collected. As a group the Cherokee interacted with the South Carolina colonial government primarily in conjunction with the trade in Indian slaves and deerskins that flourished prior to the Yemassee War of 1715. After that uprising their role diminished and that of the Catawba rose. Because of their limited interaction with English speakers, it is unlikely that the Cherokee language had any significant effect on English spoken in the early colony.

From their homeland in the mountains of North Carolina, the Cherokee periodically launched raiding parties in the upper northwestern corner of South Carolina. Initially these sorties were for retaliation against those who had harmed them in some way, but later they were to secure slaves from other Indian groups as trade items with the Europeans. A regular trading route was established between their lands and Charles Town, and European traders lived with them from about 1711 (Perdue 1979). Dependence on English goods led to the growth of the Indian slave trade and later, as the African slave trade increased, to their employment as slave catchers. Some of the African runaways were adopted into their group, and the Cherokee also came into contact with enslaved Africans taken illegally into Indian territory by the European traders. Perdue observes that these Africans and Native Americans forged bonds despite European efforts to separate and set them against each other. Those Cherokee Africans who knew English often performed critical functions within their new communities (Miles and Naylor-Ojurongbe 2004). In addition to having skills in European domestic and agricultural activities, they served as diplomatic interpreters and treaty negotiators. This Cherokee use of African interpreters for interaction with English speakers can be seen as yet another example of limited bilingualism among Southeast Indians.

The Cherokee shift to English now underway in the Snowbird community of western North Carolina reflects processes that may have been found among Lumbee speakers of an earlier period. Unlike the Lumbee, however, these Cherokee speakers have never been in frequent contact with African Americans, because no African Americans have ever lived in their remote community in Graham County on the border with Tennessee. Rather, their neighbors and schoolmates have all been of European descent and are speakers of Appalachian English (AE). The AE dialect retains some features of older stages of English, in common with the English dialects of the Lumbee community and the Outer Banks community. However, the retentions that appear in Cherokee English have different patterns from those of either the Lumbee, the Outer Banks speakers, or the Appalachian English speakers of Graham County (Anderson 1999). Because the Cherokee language is not dead, it is possible to pinpoint links between Cherokee English and their ancestral language. Although the Cherokee constitute only 6 percent of the population of Graham County, Anderson shows that certain vowel patterns and a preference for a consonant-vowel syllable structure are some of the ways in which their English dialect is distinctive. She maintains that patterns from the Cherokee ancestral language account for the distinctiveness of Cherokee English after a recent and rapid language shift within the community (364).

Europeans. Like Cherokee and the colonial African languages, all the languages once spoken by colonial Europeans are now spoken elsewhere. By the end of the colonial era, most of the Europeans who were not English speakers had shifted to English for their primary language, and for most of the following two centuries only English and Gullah were spoken in the homes of South Carolinians. Recently, with the introduction of new businesses from Germany and France in the upcountry and emigration of Spanish speakers from Mexico and other Latin American countries throughout the state, Spanish, French, and German can be heard once again in homes of contemporary South Carolina. In this more recent round of immigration, Italian, Greek, and some non-European immigrant languages—Tagalog, Indic, Chinese, Korean, and Japanese—can also be heard. The total percentage of these speakers, however, is quite low, constituting only 5 percent of the overall population in the 2000 census. Greatly outnumbered by their English-speaking peers, the children of these new immigrants will speak English in their schools and workplaces, although they may speak an ancestral language at home (Nichols 2006). Most of their grandchildren will speak only English.

In colonial times French speakers shifted early to English in their coastal settlements around Charles Town and Georgetown, when Anglican churches began supplying bilingual ministers for congregations where they had settled. As the original Huguenot colonists began to intermarry with the English landowners and as their children spoke more English than French, descendants of the original French settlers all knew English by the mid-1700s. Some important place names retain a non-English pronunciation even to this day, however. Huger (*YU-gee*) Street in Columbia and Horry (*o-REE*) County on the coast are but two examples of names that often trip up outsiders unfamiliar with their French origins.

Spanish missions disappeared from the South Carolina coast with the Spanish withdrawal to the Florida peninsula after a treaty with the English in 1670 (Rogers and Taylor 1994), but the Spanish language did not disappear altogether. Instead a variety of Spanish reentered the colony from the Iberian Peninsula with Sephardic Jews, who spoke a dialect known as Ladino. Also known as Judeo-Spanish, Ladino is based on Castilian Spanish structures and contains some Hebrew vocabulary (Gordon 2005). Because early Jewish families in Charles Town were a small, though influential, portion of the total European population, Ladino would have been used only as a home language. When Jews from a large London congregation entered the colony in 1750, both Ladino and Hebrew were used in their synagogue. By the early 1800s English was used for prayers in their services rather than Ladino, an indication that the Jewish community had completed the shift to English. This variety of Spanish is still spoken today in Israel and parts of Turkey.

German was spoken longer in the colony than either French or Spanish, both because their settlements were established in the interior further from the English-controlled center of government and commerce, and also because of the long presence of German literacy among their preachers and teachers. Orangeburg was the first major long-term German settlement and continued to attract German speakers until just before the Revolutionary War. Counties further inland from the coast in the old Saxe Gothe area were even better able to resist the shift to English. In his recollections of his life in the nineteenth century, an elderly resident of Lexington County (see fig. 5.6), who had been a tax collector and thus knew most of the county residents, tells of knowing an old Lutheran preacher who had been a Hessian soldier in the Revolutionary War and had deserted from the British army in Charles Town, making his way to Lexington (Scott 1884). Having been sold by a German prince to the king of England to fight the American rebels, this soldier, Yost Meetze, neither spoke the language nor shared the cause of the British. After establishing himself as a prosperous farmer, businessman, and Lutheran minister in the Lexington area, he corresponded with his German family in his native language and was able to bring other German immigrants to join the community in 1832. The county longest to hold on to its German heritage, and probably to its language as well, was Newberry (see fig. 5.6). As we have noted, at the 1980 census it contained more Lutherans, adherents of the religious faith followed by most German Protestants, than any other county of the state. Highlighting its cultural prominence, Newberry has been home to a seminary for training Lutheran ministers.

Welsh speakers entered the colony in the 1730s and shifted to English within a generation or two. From their initial settlement along the Pee Dee River in Florence and Darlington counties (see fig. 5.6), their inclusive missionary activities resulted in the establishment of more than three dozen Baptist churches and furthered the interaction of their children with non-Welsh speakers. The inevitable marriages that occurred between these children and English speakers hastened the shift of the community to English.

The language situation of the Scots and the Ulster Scots was more complicated, since they used two major languages in addition to English: Gaelic and Scots. Gaelic is a Celtic language in the same family as Welsh and now-extinct Cornish, while Scots is a Germanic language in the same family as English. The Gaelic-speaking Highland Scots who settled the Cape Fear region in the 1730s just north of the Welsh settlement (then part of South Carolina) were unable initially to find a Gaelic-speaking minister. Although they eventually obtained one who was bilingual in English and Gaelic, church school instruction for their children was in English (Meyer 1957). Like the Ulster Scots, this group used English for literacy and another language for speaking. At least some people among the Highland Scots were speaking Gaelic as late as 1860, when the final sermon was preached in their home language for the community (Meyer 1957, 119).

Scots-speaking settlers entered the colony directly from Ulster about the same time as the Gaelic speakers entered. They attempted settlements further south in the coastal plain, a successful one in Williamsburg County and an unsuccessful one in Horry County. The Ulster Scots had already experienced one uprooting from the Lowland counties of Scotland when their families were "planted" in Ulster. For several centuries they had been speaking a variety of Scots based on the West Mid Scots of Ayrshire and Renfrewshire and the South and Mid Scots of Galloway and Kirkcudbrightshire in the Scottish Lowlands (Montgomery and Gregg 1997). In the northern counties of Ireland known as Ulster they had mingled with speakers of both English and Irish Gaelic, and a variety of English heavily influenced by Scots and Gaelic had developed as their primary language by the 1700s. In other words the shift to a variety of spoken English known as "Ulster English" had begun before their immigration to North America. Like the Highland Scots, these Ulster Scots were literate in English, which was the language of government and education in Ulster. Literacy was high among the Scots because their King James VI had authorized an English translation of the Bible when he also became King James I of England and had mandated that every household above a certain income possess this particular translation. Church schools were started in Scotland expressly to teach people to read this text—which not incidentally upheld the monarchy in ways that a previous translation had not. Montgomery and Gregg maintain that "by the second half of the seventeenth century Scottish forms had all but disappeared from writing" in formal documents written by Ulster Scots (585).

The second wave of Ulster Scots to enter South Carolina (1763–75) came in much greater numbers than those settling near the coast. They set up villages or single households primarily in the upcountry, entering the colony down the Great Wagon Road through the Appalachians from previous settlements in English colonies further north. The settlement of these Ulster Scots in South Carolina would have been the third major upheaval in memory for this group: from Lowland Scotland, to Ulster, to Pennsylvania or Virginia, and then to South Carolina. Every move had meant further contact with English speakers, which would have been solidified by their tradition of literacy in English. These latest settlers, however, continued to speak (though not read and write) a dialect distinct from those found along the coast. The backcountry contained few, if any, Gullah speakers to influence their speech patterns, nor did it contain many from the south of England. Most of their new neighbors would have been Indians and Germans.

The divide between the upcountry (sometimes labeled *backcountry*) and the lowcountry developed initially because of earlier settlement of the coastal region, but historical animosities between the Ulster Scots of the upcountry and the dominant English of the lowcountry exacerbated this divide. Shortly after the colony became a state, the legislature authorized a publicly funded state college to be built in the center of the state "in order to promote greater unity" (Rogers and Taylor 1994, 69). In 1805 the State College of South Carolina opened in Columbia, later to become the University of South Carolina. One governor at the time expressed hope that the young people meeting there together would get to know each other in ways that would "tend to the complete annihilation of all divisions within our State" (Klein 1990, 241). These young people would of course have been white men, the future leaders of the new state.

Certain differences in dialect between the two major sections of the state have continued to manifest themselves for more than two centuries. Two of the most salient differences are found in the sound system and in the pronominal system:

1. r *after vowels and in word-final position*
One of the major distinctions between upcountry and lowcountry English has been the presence or absence of *r* constriction after vowels. The Ulster Scots originally had a strong *r*, even trilled in some contexts, while English settlers from around London did not (Wells 1982). For much of South Carolina's history the nonrhotic dialect was more prestigious since it was associated with the speech of the gentry and the well-educated, and even into the twentieth century two governors illustrated the contrast in their public speeches. Richard Riley from Greenville, later U.S. secretary of education, used a constricted *r* after vowels, while Ernest Hollings from Charleston, later a U.S. senator, did not. For Riley, *board* was pronounced *bored*, while for Hollings it was pronounced *bode*—at home and abroad. Montgomery (2001) notes that the loss of *r* results in some revealing spellings in immigrant letters: *hoss* for *horse*, *bust* for *burst*, *passel* for *parcel*. The rhotic dialect seems to have prevailed, however, despite the prestige of the nonrhotic lowcountry speech. Raymond O'Cain (1972) studied pronunciation changes in Charleston after World War II and found

that the introduction of postvocalic *r* coincided with the movement of working-class Euro-Carolinians from inland areas to the coast in search of jobs, while for upper-class Afro-Carolinians a similar change occurred among longtime coastal residents with wide contacts outside the state (94). During a year of teaching at the University of South Carolina in Columbia in the early 1980s, I heard virtually no speakers without the constricted postvocalic *r* among young people who had come from all parts of the state, although I had certainly noticed this usage among young women from the lowcountry when I was a student at Winthrop College during the 1950s.

2. hit *used as third-person neuter pronoun for subject and object*
Old English had an aspirated form for the third-person neuter pronouns, in both subject and object position, which is spelled *hit*. By the time that South Carolina was settled, this pronoun had lost its aspiration in the English of southern England, and the spelling of *it* in written English reflected this loss. However, the old form persisted in both northern England and Scotland and was brought to the colony by the Ulster Scots. It can still be heard in rural parts of the upcountry and the Pee Dee area among elderly speakers of European descent today. I heard it only once among African Americans along the Waccamaw Neck, but a colleague reported its use in the York County and Lancaster County areas, where African Americans are less numerous (Shirley Brice Heath, personal communication, 1974). The more frequent nonstandard usage for neuter pronouns among Gullah speakers along the coast is *ee* for subject and possessive case, *um* for objective case, reflecting the influence of ancestral languages during formation of the creole language.

Two other features are shared by most South Carolina speakers of every ethnic group, age, and social class, as well as by many other southerners:

1. The vowel *ai* is pronounced with a upward glide in most dialects of American English, but a distinguishing feature of southern English is a pronunciation as a single vowel or one with a much slighter glide, sounded like the *a* of *father*. Pederson (2001, 277) believes that this pronunciation originated in the South Carolina Piedmont but is general enough to be classified as southern dialect. Charles Jones reports that an anonymous treatise on Scottish "vulgarities" of speech in 1826 attributed this pronunciation to Scots (1997, 315–16).
2. The use of more than one modal verb in a single verb phrase is used in speaking, though not in writing. Joan Beal (1997) describes this as one

way that Scottish English is massively different from standard English, citing forms that are frequently heard in the southern United States and northern England but that have been ungrammatical in most of England since the early modern period:

    a. "They *might could* be working in the shop."
    b. "They *maybe could* be. . . ."
    c. "You *might would* like to come with us."
    d. "You *might should* claim your expenses."

All of these so-called double modal constructions, and many more, are alive and well in South Carolina speech (Mishoe and Montgomery 1994).

One final contribution from Scottish English is worth noting, primarily because it is a source of misinterpretation of the state of mind of southern speakers: the intonation pattern used for "information" questions that begin with a *Wh*-word (Jones 1997). For such questions as *Where are you going?* standard English uses a falling tone at the end of the question, while Scots has a falling, then rising, one. To a speaker of standard English this particular intonation sounds as if the speaker is "uncertain," which was the national spin on the speech patterns of former President Jimmy Carter of Plains, Georgia.

In sum, many of the speech patterns that distinguish someone as "from South Carolina" today are shared across the state, while others may be shared only regionally or ethnically and still others throughout the entire South. Speakers everywhere use speech patterns similar to people they love and feel closest to, and those in South Carolina have been no different. The language variation within the state has long been noted as complex, and it can be used to study both the past and the present.

6 | *Speech Communities*

Rhetorical Patterns

Speech communities are groups of people who not only share such language structures as the ones described in the previous chapter, but also ways of using language. This chapter will focus on ways of using language, patterns that are distinctive for each of the three major ethnic groups that developed in early South Carolina. Sometimes the distinctions between the different ways of using language are subtle, as we saw with the language structures themselves, and often the differences are not obvious to outsiders. To insiders, however, these ways of using language—even the "same" language— are some of the basic means of identifying who "belongs" to a group and who does not.

Often, as is the case in South Carolina, these subtle and not-so-subtle differences in language use reflect ancestral patterns carefully preserved through song and story across the centuries, at both the sentence and narrative levels. This section will describe some of those old rhetorical distinctions that can still be observed today among communities that identity with either an Indian, African, or European ancestral past. Within each of the three broad ethnic groups, there are several subgroups, and people shift between them from time to time.

The first rhetorical pattern to be discussed is that of the narrative, a genre common to all speech communities throughout the world as a way of transmitting cultural knowledge and beliefs. Recent interdisciplinary work on narratives argues that stories help us to organize multiple knowledge domains and guide us in problem solving (Herman 2003). Storytelling is an activity in which speakers of all ages participate to some extent, and differences in both the patterns and the content of community stories can be seen in stories told at an early age among children. The second pattern to be examined is a broad one, that of religious discourse, which can include prayers, sermons, song, and dance. Since the majority of South Carolinians are Protestant Christians sharing the same sacred texts and many of the same rituals, differences between their ways of using language in public meetings give a window onto other genres used by the three speech communities. Finally record keeping presents another way of using language that was initially specific to European Americans because of its association with literacy. How the three groups constructed their own "literacy events" also speaks to different ways of using language.

Narratives

> When the people sat around on the porch and passed around the
> pictures of their thoughts for the others to look at and see, it was nice.
> (Zora Neale Hurston, *Their Eyes Were Watching God*, 1937)

One of the pervasive images of the American South is the front porch, where men and women sit in the shade on a hot summer's day and tell stories to each other. In *Their Eyes Were Watching God*, one of the finest of all American novels, Janie Crawford Starks listens to the men sitting on the porch of her husband's store as they tell story after story about an old yellow mule that wanders around their Florida town. On front porches of stores such as this, on piazzas of farms and plantations, under tobacco sheds, on the rough boards of shanties and under spreading oak trees or grape arbors, stories like this have been told. Before air conditioning and television was widely available, these front porches and shaded yards served both as places to catch a cool breeze and to take part in the common discourse of the community. Often stories were prompted by a passing character, like that of the town's yellow mule in Hurston's novel. Always they have been used to transmit the accumulated wisdom and traditions of diverse peoples, as well as social commentary on contemporary events. Many of these stories have found their way into the more formal discourse of the Sunday sermon in Protestant churches, serving to supplement and interpret the older stories from holy texts originating in Hebrew and Greek.

In this chapter we will take a look at some of the themes common to stories told by the three pancultural groups of modern South Carolina, and we will examine also the rhetorical structures used by the three groups. In doing so we will see some of the results of nearly three centuries of speaking together and across ethnic divisions in stories told by twentieth-century children.

Even though the three ethnic groups of South Carolina long ago adopted some variety of English as their only language and have lived among the flora and fauna of the southeastern United States as their only home, each group has continued to tell stories in ways that reflect ancient patterns of storytelling. For African Americans the themes of stories once told in other languages have been transported to English not only in South Carolina, but also in communities throughout the country where concentrations of African Americans live and interact (Nichols 1989). Perceptive educators have documented shared patterns of language use among African American children in a variety of classroom settings (Heath 1983 and 1989; Michaels and Collins 1984; Ball 1991). For European Americans the same continuity with old traditions exists, but the distinctiveness of their traditions is not often noticed because theirs are so often the "norm" for public writing, for classroom language, for committee discussions, for books on the best-seller lists, and for many other areas of public discourse. Native American storytelling traditions have been the least documented, and the texts that do exist have not yet been compiled in the kind of motif indexes available for West African and European sources (Clarke 1958; Thompson 1955–58). Such indexes are invaluable for scholars in systematically cross-referencing storytelling motifs between cultural groups and revealing which motifs are specific to one group. Until such indexes are available to compare the themes and structures of stories told by all the representative groups of South Carolina, listening to children's voices is one of the best reflections of what the narrative traditions of early South Carolina might have been. These children's stories reflect the patterns of their homes and communities, and they let us listen to the echo of voices from the past, preserved in stories from the front porch.

The initial children's stories that I collected on the Waccamaw Neck in 1973–74 from children of African and European ancestry were a by-product of a research project on the grammatical structure of Gullah. Although the adult population was the focus of my study, I worked as a volunteer teacher's aide in a local classroom in order to make a contribution that would be recognized and valued by the community. In the process I obtained invaluable information about the wide range of language used by the children across age and ethnic groups. Nearly a decade after collecting these stories, I became aware of their distinctive rhetorical features through the groundbreaking research of Shirley Brice Heath's *Ways with Words* (1983), which describes language use by communities of blacks and whites in the Carolina Piedmont. In 1993 I undertook further classroom research among Lumbee Indian children in a school just north of the South Carolina border, to discover what linguistic and rhetorical features might be distinctive for stories told by children of that background. Robeson County in southeastern North Carolina has for centuries has been the home of a group of Native Americans who have staunchly maintained their self-identity over the centuries as neither "white" nor "black" (Dial and Eliades

1975; Blu 1980; Sider 1993). They have been known by various names at various times and struggled to secure recognition from the federal government without success, but they are now officially recognized by the state of North Carolina as Indians. While they have never known life on a reservation, the Lumbee and Tuscarora Indians are the fifth largest Indian tribe in the modern United States (Tyson 1988). Here we will examine some of the features of stories told by African American and European American children of the Waccamaw Neck in northeastern South Carolina and by Native American children in southeastern North Carolina.

Thematic Continuities

Memories of Africa filter through the tales told by children on the Waccamaw Neck, particularly at Halloween—a time when both children and adults in this community delight in telling stories of the supernatural, of ghosts and spirits who roam their swamps and woods and dirt roads, reappearing from generation to generation. In 1974 I recorded such stories told in a large group of about thirty children, with two adult classroom aides present. Later I recorded smaller groups of three or four children telling some of the same stories, along with other nonsupernatural narratives. I subsequently used many of these stories as part of a reading activity in my capacity as a volunteer classroom teaching aide, typing them up verbatim and giving copies to the storytelling groups to read aloud. I worked in this elementary school, whose student population was 90 percent African American, for five months and interacted with more than one hundred fourth, fifth, and sixth graders on a daily basis. Often I visited some of these children in their homes, invited them to mine, went fishing with them, and attended churches in their community. My knowledge of their lives outside school proved essential to interpreting many of the stories I recorded.

The stories of the supernatural discussed here were told by the African American children exclusively, never by their European American classmates. They contain themes common to African American communities in North America and in the Caribbean, as well as in Africa itself. The first of these stories is about a supernatural "hag," who also appears in stories from the Bahamas (Parsons 1923), on the Upper Peninsula of Michigan (Dorson 1956 and 1958), and in a village of Guyana (Rickford 1986), as well as in Vai folklore of Liberia (Ellis 1914).

Hag

One day me and Shewana and Jimmy been walking down the road.
We been going carry the trash to the garbage disposal. And then,

Mary, she been a-going down the road. And then she say, she tell me, Jimmy, and Shewana that she want us to come to her house fuh get a package. And then we say no, and then she keep on following us everywhere we go. And then it got dark—we been walking down Parkersville Road—then we see she jump out her skin. And then Jimmy gone to _____ and get a box of salt and put the salt down on her skin. And then she come back and say, "Skin, skin, you know me." She keep on sayin, "Skin, skin, you know me." And then we tell our mama, and mama say that what the ghost-dem always say, say when somebody put salt or pepper in their skin, they come back and say, "Skin, skin, you know me." [told by African American girl, fifth grade, 1973]

Stories of hags, usually a female witch who assumes a mortal shape in the daytime but shifts her skin and goes out to "ride" humans or animals at night, are common in coastal South Carolina. The child who told this particular version told it at the large Halloween session and again in a smaller group. Characteristically the teller has actually seen a hag or the results of her work, thus adding an immediacy and vividness to the tale that goes beyond a reported version. The belief that one can control the activities of a hag by sprinkling her skin with salt and pepper is a strong one; both African American and European American inhabitants of the coastal Sea Islands sometimes sprinkle their bedrooms with salt or pepper before retiring for the night. Several children told stories about hags, or about family members pretending to be hags as a joke in order to frighten them.

While the theme of skin shifting itself is fairly common among folk stories of the world, none of the European-derived skin-shifting tales has precisely the features of the Waccamaw Neck version (Henderson 1866). The belief in this kind of hag is one of long standing in this area of coastal Carolina, as indicated by the earlier WPA collection containing a story using virtually the same words by an African American storyteller on the Waccamaw Neck: "Skin, skin, you know me? Skin, skin, dis me" (Writers' Program 1941, 89). Dorson's 1956 tale from an elderly African American man in Michigan contains the line, "Skin, don't you know me?" three different times. Rickford's 1986 Guyanese tale has the hag speaking virtually the same refrain: "Skin, da me!! Yu no noo mii?" *The Dictionary of Jamaican English* (Cassidy and Le Page 1980) devotes an entry to "Old-Hige," and Cassidy adds (personal communication, 1974) that the oral tradition held that, if one found the witch's skin and sprinkled salt and pepper into it, she could not put it on again without serious pain. According to him, the chant

"Pepper and salt to your mammy!" is a way of accusing someone's mother of being a witch.

The widespread occurrence of stories about the hag who sheds her skin at night to ride people and animals bespeaks a shared cultural and linguistic heritage among African American communities of both mainland North America and the Caribbean. The absence of such a tale in the major folklore motif indexes of the British Isles (Baughman 1954; Thompson 1955–58) and the presence of similar tales in the major motif index of the West African cultural area (Clarke 1958) point to continuities between African American speech communities and those of Africa itself.

A second tale is about a supernatural creature known as the Plat-Eye, appearing in African American stories told in Georgetown and Williamsburg counties in South Carolina—an area where thriving rice plantations were tended by African slaves in the low-lying, swampy land fed by a network of tidal rivers. Other sections of South Carolina do not feature this creature in their stories. The Plat-Eye is an evil being who can assume a variety of animal shapes. Its appearance is often associated with a new moon (Davis 1914). The Plat-Eye's encounter with a human being is the occasion for a struggle between good and evil. When the children of the Waccamaw Neck hear the Plat-Eye playing the piano in their church, they stand by a grandmother's grave so that her good spirit can protect them from the Plat-Eye's evil one:

Plat-Eye

> To our church, we had a old piano in our church, but now we got
> nothing. And some Plat-Eye—see, me and Gregg-dem and some
> more children, we used to go back there. And then one day we gone
> back there, we hear the thing playing and we went back there, and
> then—we see the keys just a-move like this here, and then—the night
> come—I say, "Gregg, look-a-there!" And then been a Plat-Eye mov-
> ing the keys—the piano keys—and all that. And then we went by the
> grave, and then I gone and stand up by my grandmamma grave and
> then they wouldn't come over there. But they stay right there, play
> that piano. [told by African American boy, fifth grade, 1974]

An earlier story collected on the Waccamaw Neck by Genevieve Wilcox Chandler (Writers' Program 1941, 88) has the Plat-Eye take the shape of a black cat, appearing "wid he eye lak balls ob fire, en he hair stan on end." Some three decades later children were using similar words to describe this folk creature to their European American teachers who were newcomers to the Neck: "Fire come out ee eye!"

The Gullah-speaking narrator of Chandler's WPA tale tells of singing a hymn to ward off the evil power of the creature. The storyteller runs away from it, praising God for delivering her from that cat. Like the hag, this supernatural being has no counterpart in oral traditions of the British Isles. Frederic G. Cassidy reports that he has often heard of the Plat-Eye as an American creature but knows of no exact counterpart in the Caribbean (personal communication, 1974). He suggests that the Rolling Calf (Roaring Calf) in his *Dictionary of Jamaican English*, which has fiery eyes and pounces on people at night, is similar to the Plat-Eye.

A third tale told by African American children on the Waccamaw Neck concerns not supernatural beings, but human beings who have powers to see supernatural beings. A child who is born with a veil or caul (part of the afterbirth) over its face has power to see ghosts until at least early adulthood. One child tells of an older brother who had such powers as a child:

Born with a Caul

This about my brother name T_____. And he was born with—
I don't know, but he was born with something on ee face and he could
see ghost when he was little but now he can't. And my mother—and
he the second oldest in the house—and my mother used to carry him
everywhere she go, because he wouldn't let um—my mother—go by
eeself. Then one night my mother and my brother went to school.
And then—big schoolhouse where Mrs. N_____ teach right in
that—and my brother see—my brother see a ghost, but my mother
couldn't see it. And then my brother tell my mother say he wasn't
scared. But my mother say it might hurt you. And then ee tell um,
"Let's turn back wait till some other people get there." But my
brother he ain't paying no attention to Mama and he went right on.
And he came back and Mama ask him if he see anything. And ee say
he see a white dog—a white ghost dog. And ee run back there and
he say he been gon run behind um but ee been too fast for um. So
he turn back and—I forgot. That's all. [told by African American boy,
fifth grade, 1974]

The folklorist Richard Dorson (1958) has collected a similar story from an African American storyteller on the Upper Peninsula of Michigan. The belief that children born with a veil are somehow special or lucky can be found in the early British oral tradition (Henderson 1866), but the ability to see ghosts appears to be shared among the African American and Native American oral traditions.

A tale appearing in a 1971 North Carolina folklore journal contains a similar characterization of a person who has been born with a caul, which appears in the folklore of the Lumbee Indians who live along the Lumber River, just north of the South Carolina border: "'As I've told you before,' Papa said softly, his clear bright, greenish-blue eyes sparkling with excitement, 'anyone born with a caul over his eyes is gifted to see and hear spirits. That's how I was born. And that kind o' person ain't a-scared of spirits, being as he's seen and heard so many of them . . .'" (Barton 1971, 173).

Barton's tale goes on to mention the *tok'ns* believed by this community to appear before or just after someone dies. Brewer and Reising (1982) discuss this belief in conjunction with an analysis of the variety of English spoken among the Lumbees. The specific capacity to foresee death through some noise or sign from the spirit world, known as tokens, is mentioned only in the Lumbee folklore, not in the African American sources.

In 1993 I was able to spend several months among Lumbee Indian children in a sixth-grade classroom in Robeson County, North Carolina, conducting writing and reading activities on a weekly basis. All but one of the children in this classroom self-identified as Indian. The staff in the school was multicultural, with African American, Native American, and European American teachers and a principal who self-identified as Indian. The teacher of the class was European American but lived with another teacher at the school who was Lumbee. In addition to writing and reading I also taught occasional lessons in math and science for this teacher, as well as observing the children in the classroom, on the playground, and in the lunchroom. Storytelling sessions were conducted after we had spent several weeks together. Each child who wanted to tell a story selected a friend to introduce him or her with a handheld microphone, standing in front of the entire class and announcing what the story would be about. Either immediately after the session or on my next visit, I played their stories back to them. I also brought printed copies of their stories to the class for them to read to each other and keep in their writing folders, along with other work they were doing with me. Near the end of my time there, groups of children selected one of the stories told before the class to illustrate on large poster paper, which we mounted on the classroom wall. With the teacher's help, each child selected a piece of writing to go into a class booklet and often illustrated it as well; we laminated and bound these, placing the finished booklet in the school library. Because I was living about one hundred miles away from this community, I was not able to participate in community and church activities with the children as I had done in the African American community. My lack of knowledge of their out-of-school activities affects the extent to which I have been able to interpret their stories, although I continued to correspond with several of the children just as I did with the African American and European American children on the Waccamaw Neck of South Carolina. During our months together I collected a wide range of their oral and written English used in a classroom setting.

The stories that I collected among these Lumbee children contain no supernatural beings like the hag or the Plat-Eye, but they do show human beings having supernatural powers. A Native American girl tells of three separate occasions on which the "smell of flowers" signals her special ability to foresee the imminent death of someone she knows. Her mother's confirmation of the meaning of her experience suggests that this is a widespread belief in her community.

Smelling Flowers

It was one morning when I woke up, and my uncle came to my house. We went, was going go to the store, and he said, "We'll wait a little while." And so I waited a little while, and he said, "Well, let's go. Get in the car." So we went into the car. He must 'a been drunk. And when we got there, he run it off the road. And he went in the store, and he said, "Get you five bags of candy, 'cause this might be the last time you'll see me." And so we went in the store, and we got five bags of candy. We came back out, and we drove home. And when we turned in the road, he went to going in the field, and we got stuck. And so I walked home and got Daddy, and Daddy came down there and pulled him out. And so he rode back to the house, and he said, "Can I live in your building? Just for tonight." Daddy said, "You picking with me?" He said, "yeah." And so he drove back home, and the next morning when I woke up, I smelled flowers, like it was a forest. And they called and said he had died.

And so I smelled flowers again, and some kid in the family had died, and I don't know . . . I forgot their name. And so we came back to the house from cleaning up, the blood and everything. He had got shot three times. And then that night I went to smelling more flowers and kept on smelling flowers until I fell asleep. Then that morning when we got up, I got sick.

Then the next two days, we went to setting up, and I went to smelling flowers again. And I told Mama what I been smelling, and she said, "Somebody's dying, and you know about it." And then that night, we found out that I knew something about a uncle that nobody knew. I forgot . . . it was about I knew he was gonna die and I didn't tell nobody. And what had happened is he had told me he had went to Raleigh and these men tried to killed him, and he said one day that they's gon come back and they will not leave him living. That's the end. [Native American girl, sixth grade, 1993]

Although the child did not use the term *token*, her description of her supernatural ability to foresee a death is consistent with similar beliefs among the Lumbee described by Barton (1971) and by Brewer and Reising (1982). Brewer and Reising cite several examples from a 1978 oral history project of Lumbee speakers describing different manifestations or tokens from the spirit world warning of death. Their examples are either visual or aural; none entails the sense of smell described by the child above.

Structural Contrasts

A second set of stories told by children from the three different ethnic groups reveals contrasting rhetorical structures. These structures are accompanied by distinctive linguistic features, some of which have been discussed earlier. For many children both the rhetorical structure and the linguistic features of their oral stories carry over into their early attempts at written texts.

The first story in this set is told cooperatively by two boys who had been hunting together with the father of one of them. Both of these boys are African American and use a storytelling style common to their community: all of the participants in the storytelling session take active roles in the telling, audience as well as primary storyteller. A listener often actively contributes endings, adds further details, or serves as a sort of chorus for the main action related by the primary teller. In this story, which I have titled "Hunting for Squirrel," the two boys negotiate the topic of the story at the beginning, selecting the primary listener as the "butt" of the story. At the end this listener does not like the resulting picture of himself and suggests a different ending, complete with dialogue. The teller complies in part, reducing the reported speech somewhat but leaving the subject of the story in a more favorable position than his original ending.

Hunting for Squirrel

RW: Lemme see what I can talk about. You.

JL: Tell um bout that buckshot, shotgun.

RW: Oh. Yeah. One day, me and John L_____ been going hunting for squirrel, him and my daddy and John L_____, we were
going hunting. And John L_____ see a squirrel. John L_____ say,
"Daddy, let me hold the rifle." Then ee daddy say, "No, the rifle
might kick you. Shoot with your pellet gun." John L_____ say, "No,
I'm going to kill the squirrel." Then John L_____ say, "I gon shoot
my pistol." And ee say, "O.K., shoot your pistol." John L_____
shoot at the squirrel and brush the squirrel. Then John L_____ say,
"I'll get him this time." Then John L_____ shoot the squirrel in ee
tail. Then John L_____ say, "The next time I bet you I can get him,
R_____." And so when John L_____ shoot, he daddy blow the squirrel out the tree. Boo-ow! John L_____ was mad. John L_____ say,
"No. I going hunting by myself." John L_____ gone up in the woods.

JL: Say, "John L_____ say, 'Poop he daddy! Daddy can't do nothin
for me. I'm 'on get that shotgun and I'm 'on haul boogie, Boy!" Say that!

RW: John L_____ say, "Poop ee daddy! Gon get that shotgun and
haul boogie!" [told by African American boys, fifth grade, 1973]

The participatory storytelling style of these two African American children can be compared with a Bahamian storytelling tradition described by
folklorist Daniel J. Crowley (1977, 20); a Bahamian storyteller literally cannot continue a story without periodically receiving the message "Bunday!"
from the audience, which indicates their appreciation of it and their desire
to hear more. A storyteller who does not receive such vocal encouragement
must discontinue the story, Crowley reports.

Three personal-experience narratives, using the roughly similar theme
of a dog that is somewhere it does not belong, demonstrate both linguistic and rhetorical differences for African American, European American,
and Native American children of approximately the same ages and socio-
economic backgrounds. Two of the storytellers were fifth-grade classmates
on the Waccamaw Neck in 1974. The third was a Native American living
in Robeson County, North Carolina, where I recorded him in his sixth-
grade classroom in 1993.

Unlike the two squirrel hunters above, the European American boy tells
his story as a solitary storyteller, neither expecting nor inviting participation from his audience. He produces the kind of autonomous text that Wolf

and Pusch (1985) associate with book-based cultures. He provides background information for his listeners, giving family relationships but no personal names for an audience that is not expected to know his main characters:

Dog and Chickens

I have this dog, and we have a bunch of chickens back at my uncle's and at my house. And this dog, he went after the chickens the other day, and he killed two roosters and four hens and went after some more. And when he did, my uncle shot him in the leg and made him go on. And he came back yesterday and almost got some more. We ran him off again. And when we did we had to go take him to town and put him to sleep 'cause he was real badly hurt. So we had him pretty well fixed up, so we could bury him. [told by European American boy, fifth grade, 1973]

This storyteller provides an account of cause and effect, leading up to the uncle's shooting of the dog. Characteristic of the oral tradition of his speech community, he provides a coda, or summary of the consequences, as well as an implied moralistic comment on the killing of a dog and its burial: you do not leave a badly wounded animal alive to suffer, and you bury a dead one with proper observances.

His African American classmate tells a story, which I have titled "Dog and Car," immediately on the heels of "Dog and Chickens." Even before his classmate finishes, the African American child exclaims, "Oh, I got one!" indicating his eagerness to participate in the topic on the "floor" (Edelsky 1981). He proceeds to contribute another story of a dog that was killed, displaying quite different assumptions from the first storyteller about what his audience needs to know. He takes pains to locate the narrative in time and space but does not identify the relationships between the characters. Instead he calls them by name, assuming his audience will know them. In contrast to the previous story, this is not an autonomous text:

Dog and Car

Oh, I got one! [overlapping previous story] One day, yesterday, me and Darryl, we were going in the yard. Me and Darryl hear a car say, "Bump, bump." And then Teria dog—and he say, Darryl said, "Teria dog done get hit." Then me and Darryl run up there and the dog bleed all over. Then Bubba bring um in the yard. Then Bubba gone get ee gun and shoot um.

[questions from his audience about the end result]
He been dead. [told by African American boy, fifth grade, 1973]

The story includes direct quotation from the characters he has called by name, further personalizing his story and giving immediacy to the action. This child does not summarize or evaluate the final outcome for the dog, but concludes with the most dramatic action for participants in the drama: the shooting of the dog. Again we see the quality of immediacy, as opposed to reported action. The audience feels free to elicit further details needed to learn about the result of the shooting, just as the listener in "Hunting for Squirrel" felt free to suggest a revision of that story's original ending. No moral comment is either given or suggested about the shooting of the dog at the conclusion of this story.

A narrative told by a Lumbee Indian boy, which also includes a dog that is somewhere he should not be, displays some rhetorical features of both stories above. Like the African American child he uses direct conversation, as well as sound effects that are not possible to reproduce in print. He also uses a personal name for his main character but specifies his kin relationship to the narrator in a fashion similar to the European American child. As in the other two stories, a dog is shot, but that action is a side event—though one that reveals the point of the story. The ending includes a coda that summarizes and explains the meaning of the action, similar to the European American child's story, but it contains no hint of a moral or lesson to be learned by his audience. It is, rather, an account of an experience where the storyteller learned something surprising.

Dog and Thief

One time, we was watching this game on TV, and we heard this knock on the door. So the man come in—it was a man that we never had seen him before—he come in, and he says, "Can I use your telephone? Can I use your telephone?" And he had his shirt tied in a knot, and he had something back there and it was sticking up. He'd bend over on the table like this, and it would stick up in his back pocket. So my brother Ronnie, he asked him what was that in his back pocket, and he said, "That's my flashlight!"

And then, he went in the woods, in the woods beside our house, and he got down in the woods, like, on his knees. And we got this BB gun, and there was this dog that come to our house, and Ronnie Allen tried to shoot him with the BB gun, but he missed the dog. But that

man jumped up a-running, and then. . . . The man's hand was
a-bleeding, so Ronnie come back in the house, and he says, "Good
night! I believe I shot that man in the hand!" And then the next day
we went outside: he had went in our truck and in our car. And the
flashlight he was talking about, it come out of our car. He stole it
out of our car. [told by Native American boy, sixth grade, 1993]

Although I have titled this story "Dog and Thief," the storyteller's
audience had no knowledge of the theft until the end of the story. Unlike
the African American boy, this Native American child goes beyond the high
point of the action to tell his listeners explicitly that the flashlight in the
pocket of the man who came to the door asking to use the telephone had
been stolen. He concludes the story by stepping outside the narrative proper and providing an evaluation for his audience, to make clear the point of
his story. Unlike the European American child, however, he does not go on
to provide a moral reflection on this act that is central to his story—either
directly or by implication.

One rhetorical feature that appears often in the stories told by Native
American children is that of repetition. In "Dog and Thief" we have two
examples:

"Can I use your telephone? Can I use your telephone?"
. . . it come out of our car. He stole it out of our car.

In the earlier story by the Lumbee Indian girl, "Smelling Flowers," the
audience is told of her experience on three different occasions, in roughly
similar words:

. . . and the next morning when I woke up, I smelled flowers, like it
was a forest. And they called and said he had died.
And so I smelled flowers again, and some kid in the family had
died. . . .
. . . and I went to smelling flowers again. And I told Mama what
I been smelling, and she said, "Somebody's dying, and you know
about it."

In another remarkable story, too long to print here in its entirety,
another Lumbee Indian classmate retells a story that is not one of personal
experience but one she has obviously heard often. It begins: "There's this
little boy, he had first day went to school, and there's this woman said, 'Little boy, what's your name?'" The refrain following this opening line—"I'm

a little boy from across the street. I'll whip your rump from tree to tree"—
is repeated exactly the same way for a total of ten times, following new challenges to the boy from the teacher, the principal, God, and the devil. The
story ends with a variation on this refrain, attributed to the devil, who tells
the little boy: "I'm a little boy from underground. I'll burn your rump like
charcoal brown."

As we will see, the prevalence of repetition is a structural device in the
oral rhetoric of Native Americans of the Southeast. This can be seen in
religious language from the past and in the present.

Religious Discourse

While religious beliefs of the three groups from Africa, Europe, and North
America differed in major ways at initial contact, most members of all
three groups are now members of Protestant Christian churches. (The few
Roman Catholic churches and Jewish synagogues in the region are located
mostly in urban areas.) Even though the themes of their religious observances are now similar, rhetorical interpretations of the same doctrines
reflect ancient patterns of celebrating the sacred that are distinctive for
each cultural group.

Native American. One rhetorical device that appears frequently in Native
American texts is the repetition noted in children's stories above. From the
late 1800s James Mooney records a monolingual Cherokee speaker using
repetition frequently in both stories and prayers. Mooney's informant was
one who had escaped the forced removal of his people to Oklahoma in 1835
and was, at the time Mooney knew him, living with other surviving Cherokees in western North Carolina. In a prayer before eating the new corn,
a ceremony with white beads was used with a single stanza repeated seven
times for each member of the family: "*Sgé!* O now you have drawn near to
listen, O Long Man, in repose. You fail not in anything. My paths lead
down to the edge of your body. The white cloth has come and is resting
upon the white seats. The white beads are resting upon it [the cloth]. The
soul restored has now ascended to the first upper world" (Mooney 1900,
8–9).

After seven identical repetitions of this stanza, the prayer changes with
the eighth stanza, signaling the end of the ritual. The value of Mooney's
texts lies in their closeness to the original performance by native peoples.
Mooney knew the language himself and collected texts from monolingual
Cherokee spiritual leaders who wanted them preserved in writing. Because
of their own recent use of writing in the syllabary developed by Sequoyah,

the Cherokees recognized the value of written records for legends and rituals that might be lost—especially given their experience with the expulsion of so many of their people to lands in the West.

While the Lumbee and Tuscarora of the Robeson County lowlands
are separated by many miles from the Cherokee of the hill country, native
peoples throughout the Southeast once shared common cultural traditions and presumably similar rhetorical styles. The testimony of a Lumbee
woman in a Holiness Church of Robeson County in 1988 reflects a more
constrained use of repetition. Ruel W. Tyson Jr., who collected this testimony, sets the repeated portions off in different type and comments that
these repetitions came at high points in her testimony:

> I thank the Lord today for being saved.
> I thank him for being sanctified.
> I thank him for the power of the Holy Ghost.
> Praise God! It's real, people. It's real, praise God.
> And if you don't have it, you need to seek for it.
> Praise God. Because you can have it. The Bible says you can have it,
>   praise the Lord!
> It's wonderful! Praise God! (Tyson 1988, 108)

Several repetitions occur before and after a section where she is "speaking
in tongues":

> I got it!
> I got it!
> I got it! [speaks in tongues]
> It's real, praise God! [speaks again in tongues]
>
> It's real!
> Oh yes, Jesus!
> Thank you, God.
>
> It's real!

In an earlier, more discursive, portion of this woman's testimony, similar patterns of repetitions are evident:

> Praise God. You know those old songs we used to sing . . . but I
> still feel just like they did back then . . . singing. I thought about an
> older person, you know, their hair is turned white, praise God. And
> you know, I seen some, and I heared about some, when they are just

'bout to cross over, praise God, and some of 'em say <u>they could see</u>
<u>angels</u>, and they could hear the angels sing, and ask one that was
standing by, "<u>Could you see the angels</u>?" And they tell 'em "No,"
<u>they couldn't see the angels</u>. But praise God, they are so near home
<u>they could see the angels</u>. Praise God in Glory. They were just about
to take them over [my underlining]. (107)

While the repetitions of this modern Lumbee woman do not parallel
the length of the repetitive texts collected by Mooney, this striking use of
repetition in Native American texts separated by age, time, place, and cir-
cumstance indicates its importance as a rhetorical device in these communities. This device can certainly be found in texts produced by many other
cultures, as Jones-Jackson (1987) demonstrates for African American tales
and sermons. Nevertheless, its status seems to be central to Native American storytelling and religious discourse.

At the time of contact with Europeans and Africans and long after, the
sacred for Native Americans was part of daily life, interwoven with the
fields and forests they inhabited. The Long Man in the Cherokee prayer
that Mooney collected in 1900 refers to the river, which was always a central focus for Native American religious observances in the Southeast.
Mooney (1900) reports that the towns of the Cherokee were always built
close to the riverbank, because purification in the running stream was part
of every tribal function. The river was metaphorically referred to as the
Long Man, a giant with his head in the foothills of the mountains and his
foot down in the lowland. Important ceremonies were performed at a bend
in the river, with the priest facing east and looking upstream as the sun rose.
Some ceremonies included dipping up the water, as in childbirth, while
others entailed whole families plunging into the water at the new moon.
Mooney provides a literal translation of one of the ritual prayers for
bathing:

Listen! O, now you have drawn near to hearken, O Long Man
at rest. O helper of men, you let nothing slip from your grasp. You
never let the soul slip from your grasp. Come now and take a firmer
grasp. I originated near the cataract, and from there I stretch out
my hand toward this place. Now I have bathed in your body. Let the
white foam cling to my head as I go about, and let the white staff be
in my hand. Let the health-giving âya await me along the road. Now
my soul stands erect in the seventh heaven Yû! (1900, 2–3)

This prayer and other texts collected by Mooney in the late 1800s demonstrate how firmly the religious observances were connected to the physical world that these early ancestors inhabited. It is probably for such reasons that the most frequently used name for the contemporary Native Americans in Robeson County is Lumbee, taken from the long river that winds through the lands they inhabit and was spelled *Lumber* by early mapmakers. (See fig. 5.5.)

In his description of a modern Lumbee church service, Tyson (1988) indicates that the religious discourse is still located and connected to the physical and social world that the worshippers inhabit. In his description of a modern woman who gives "testimony" during the service, he characterizes her discourse thus: "She describes herself, but she also describes a world, of places and of a people—relations and neighbors—and of her time and of the times in which she lives. The testimony discloses places and times in her history, and her assertions implicate a cosmos deeply associated with her time and the times in which she lives" (113).

Just prior to the "I've got it!" segment quoted above, which accompanies her speaking in tongues, this Lumbee woman has explicated her connection with the past in both place and time:

> You know, I used to go to Evergreen [Church] down there.
> That's where I was raised, praise God. And you know, them older
> women they wore dresses a-dragging the floor. You couldn't see their
> shoes, praise God. And my grandmother, she wouldn't wear nothing
> but cotton stockings, and she dyed them black. They had to be black.
> And that's what she wore. And you know, I was a little child. . . . I
> come yesterday evening to thinking about it. . . . I was a little child.
> I could see them older people a-shouting and a-praising God. And
> the place was filled with the spirit of God. I just feel it too, praise
> God. . . . (109)

For religious discourse of Native Americans in the past and the present, use of repetition and manifestation of a strong connection with a specific physical place seem to be central.

African American. The African Americans brought with them still different religious traditions from their villages of West Africa, Angola, and the Niger Delta. Separated abruptly from their familiar physical worlds, they nevertheless transported to South Carolina beliefs in spirit worlds linked to the physical. Perhaps because their familiar physical places were no longer reachable, the spirit world took on even greater importance.

Patricia Jones-Jackson (1987) provides a text from a contemporary speaker on Wadmalaw Island in South Carolina, who holds strong beliefs in a spirit world:

> Listen well now: when you die, you see, the soul of a man goes home to the Kingdom of God, but your spirit remains here on earth. And if you were an evildoer all of your life, then after you die, your spirit can continue doing the same kind of evil. Your soul is in heaven, but your spirit remains here on earth with the body, and that's the one that will harm you.
>
> You see, I speak of this now because a great many people don't believe. They say that ghosts do not exist. But they do exist. But now, since the automobile and other transportation has overrun the high-ways, these spirits have sought refuge in the woods. . . . (163)

Like their contemporaries from North America and from Europe, Africans believed in a High God or Supreme Creator. In addition, however, they prayed to other gods as well, and also to spirits of deceased ancestors. According to Raboteau (1978), they were most concerned with lesser gods and spirits, which they associated with natural forces and phenomena. Because the ancestors could be born again in descendants, burial rites were important. Jones-Jackson reports that the desire to be buried among one's ancestors is strong among Sea Islanders of South Carolina and Georgia, so that they can join the spirits of those who have gone before: "By ongoing tradition, Sea Island burial places are densely wooded and are considered to be the sacred abodes of the spirits" (1987, 26). In the African American graveyards on such remote islands as Wadmalaw and Daufuskie, one can still observe personal objects such as dishes, spoons, and other personal items belonging to the deceased, which have been placed on top of the grave in case they are needed or wanted in the afterlife. In the less remote cemeteries of the Waccamaw Neck, the dead are buried on an east-west axis, with their face to the rising sun. Those who experience unnatural deaths, such as drowning, are buried "cross-ways the world," on a north-south axis. Churches are built with their entrances facing east, symbolizing a connection with the rising and setting of the sun over us all.

As we have seen in the hag stories above, witches play a prominent part in the spirit world for contemporary African Americans, but these supernatural beings have roles separate from those of the dead ancestors. Often witches are identified with women in the community who can cause illness and death, during times in which their spirits leave their bodies and fly to meetings with other witches. When a person awakens tired in the morning, that weariness is often attributed to having been "ridden" by such a witch in the night. The custom of sprinkling salt and pepper around the bedroom is supposed to keep the witches away, since they cannot stand the sting of salt on their skinless bodies. Europeans in early modern times also held folk beliefs in witches, as indicated by the widespread witch hunts throughout Europe during the late 1500s and early 1600s. The characterization of European witches was quite different from the African ones, however. In Scotland, where the greatest percentage of women in all of Europe were strangled and burned at the stake as convicted witches, women identified as witches were outspoken members of the community, ones who often challenged the rising power of the Christian church and patriarchal leaders in some way (Larner 1983). Like the African witches, the European ones were believed to be capable of causing harm to individuals in the community.

A distinctive aspect of African religious rituals was that of music. Religious ceremonies of West Africa were filled with dancing, drumming, and singing as an essential part of worship. Raboteau reports that the centrality of these activities was such that religions of West Africa could be known as "danced religions" (1978, 15). In this respect Africans were like the Native Americans, for whom dancing and drumming were also an integral part of religious worship—though with different rhythms and tonal patterns. The music of African Americans, both in religious observances and in the secular music that derived from it, even today reflects the formal structure of certain West African songs. (See discussion in Pitts 1993, 81.)

Most important, the structure of religious ceremonies reveals continuity between those of the old continent and the new—even though the religions themselves have changed in name and substance. In a study of what he terms the African American "folk church" in America, Walter F. Pitts Jr. (1993) demonstrates that American Afro-Baptist religious services throughout the American South preserve ritual frames that can be linked to both African and Afro-Caribbean rituals. While serving as pianist for six years in a central Texas church, Pitts recorded religious services of as many as sixteen congregations who worshiped together on special occasions. His observations and recorded texts demonstrate the existence of two distinct "frames" within a typical worship service, for which the language and music are quite different. A frame, according to Pitts, is "like an event that is a bound segment of activity or behavior" (31). Along with anthropologist Franz Boas and others, Pitts believes that this bounded event becomes a metaphoric expression having affective value, in the process of becoming the basis of religious ritual. Through bounded metaphoric frames characterized by speech and song, the religious observance in the Afro-Baptist church moves away from abstraction and toward definiteness: "Since Afro-Baptist liturgy is not written but oral, speech and song—as metaphoric filters—become powerful tools in keeping frames, and consequently the ritual itself, intact" (32).

In Pitts's analysis, the initial frame (devotion) uses both standard twentieth-century English and the archaic sixteenth-century English of the King James Bible. Hymns are from eighteenth-century tunes that were shared with original European settlers, often "raised" or "lined" by a deacon and then sung by the congregation. In the second frame (service), the pastor often uses African American vernacular English for at least portions of the sermon, while the music employs rhythms of African American music in spirituals and gospel. Pitts observes that the more somber devotion of the first frame is conducted by a deacon as essential preparation for the more exuberant service conducted by the pastor. During the service of the second frame, prayers as well as the sermon are delivered in a participatory style that includes responses from the congregation, sometimes increasing in affective value to embrace shouts and trances. Much like the stories told by African American children, the sermon is a jointly constructed text. Pitts underscores the importance of this participation by reporting that, without appropriate response from the congregation, the preacher must cut his sermon short.

The practice of audience participation in both prayers and sermons is documented by Patricia Jones-Jackson (1987) on the Sea Islands of South Carolina. About the sermons and prayers presented in her book she comments, "While the text alone is intelligible on paper, most of the beauty of the prayer escapes, along with the force of the audience's reply and the increasing fervor of the speaker's call." In this portion of a deacon's prayer from an African Methodist Episcopal service on Wadmalaw Island, underlining indicates the audience's response:

Master Jesus, hear me
Another one of you[r] servant
Bow this evening, Jesus   <u>Bow, yes! My Lord!</u>

Sin anguished and bended   <u>Bended knees</u>

Master, it's no lower

Could I come this evening   <u>No! No Lower!</u>
Excepting my knees are down at the floor   <u>Floor! Cold floor!</u>
(Excerpt from "Opening Prayer for the Usher's Anniversary"
[Jones-Jackson 1987, 83])

The importance of audience participation is highlighted in a 1985 pres-
entation that Jones-Jackson gave before her death in 1986. Performing a
sermon for a conference on language and culture held at the University of
South Carolina, she commented that the academic "congregation" assembled there lacked the appropriate responses that typically accompanied this
sermon in a Wadmalaw Island Methodist church. A printed excerpt, along
with the responses of the African American congregation that she tran-
scribed (Jones-Jackson 1994), reveals the joint construction of African
American religious discourse. In her introduction to the text Jones-Jackson
comments, "The necessary linguistic energy, like the spiritual energy,
cannot be, and perhaps was never intended to be, captured on the page"
(124).

Pitts (1993) maintains that the Baptist denomination was uniquely suited
to a synthesis of rituals from Christian and African spirit religions in
autonomous African Baptist churches throughout America. In the wake of
the Great Awakening religious movement that swept through the English
colonies beginning in the mid-1700s, the Baptists, as well as the Methodists
(who were originally an evangelical splinter from the Anglicans), held revival camp meetings in the woods. In services far less formal than those of
the Presbyterian and Anglican services of the established churches of Scotland and England, their traveling preachers offered sermons of emotional
intensity, which fostered ecstatic conversions. In such outdoor religious
gatherings conversion was more important than instruction—a factor of
great importance to illiterate peoples, both African American and European American (Raboteau 1978). Baptists, unlike Methodists, had a loose
organizational structure, and individual congregations operated fairly
autonomously—choosing their own pastors, controlling their own funds,
and disciplining their own members for conduct unbecoming a Christian.
The first separate African American church in the United States was Baptist, initially established at Silver Bluff, South Carolina, sometime between
1773 and 1775 across the Savannah River from Georgia (Raboteau 1978,
139–40). Pitts believes it was no accident that the first autonomous African
American church was of this denomination (1993, 45).

In the Afro-Baptist church services that I attended on the Waccamaw
Neck during 1974–75 and intermittently for several years thereafter, the

language used ranged from a regional standard variety of English to the creole Gullah within a single service, following much the same organizational pattern that Pitts describes for the churches of central Texas. I attended a memorable service on a Sunday morning January 1977. The first frame was led by one of the deacons, who pitched the tune for a hymn sung by the congregation, then called for announcements after the choir marched in singing another long hymn. Another deacon read announcements from slips of paper from his position in the front row of the choir. In this portion of the service some songs were sung in a slow rhythm unknown to me even though I knew the words from my childhood experiences in a nearby Presbyterian church. Other songs were from the hymnal, but no church members used the books, even though they were available in every pew. The music increased in tempo with each verse, climaxing with a duet sung by two leading choir members; the congregation joined in on later choruses of this beautiful song, then the choir. Then heavy clapping and foot stomping began. Many older women stood, and one of the oldest moved in time to the music, almost dancing at the front of the church. My field notes from that day read at this point: "Ecstasy best describes the mood and movement. This was immediately before the sermon. . . . the preacher moved somewhat slowly into his sermon and mentioned the presence of the 'spirit'" (January 16 1977).

With the help of Pitts's analysis, I can now perceive this communal religious observance as one that did indeed preserve African rituals. During 1974–75 I had often alternated between visiting the Afro-Baptist church on the island and the Presbyterian church some twenty miles away that I had attended as a child. At the time I recognized several obvious differences in how language and music were used, but I had no rhetorical framework for comparing the two services. In these small churches where all members knew each other, the same holy texts from the seventeenth-century King James Bible were used, as well as many of the same hymns from the eighteenth century. But the differences in *how* they were used was dramatic. I will say more about the Presbyterian ritual in the next section, but here it is important to say that the use of written texts was a major distinction. Let me hasten to point out that every single person who attended the Afro-Baptist church, except one, was literate. In the Sunday School lesson that preceded the main church service, passages from the King James Bible and lessons supplied by a national Baptist organization were read aloud and commented on—often with profound insight—by the adult males and a few of the women. But in the church service itself the written text was not the primary focus that it was in the Presbyterian church.

Pitts argues convincingly that African religious rituals are retained and adapted in those of the Afro-Baptist church. According to him, the first frame parallels that of African initiation, in which future mediums are cleansed and trained. Language in this frame is characterized by slow lining and long prayers, given in archaic speech, in religious observances of West Africa. The second frame provides release from hierarchic social structure and psychological structure of routine—paralleling the sermon in the Afro-Baptist church that can lead to ecstatic trance. His insider's analysis echoes my own outsider's observation that the communal awareness of a member's troubles, reflected in oblique comments by the pastor and physical comfort by the people seated close by, functions much like the European American psychiatrist's couch or therapy group. But unlike the typical European American medical practice, these religious rituals also celebrate a member's recovery from bleak times—as on this Sunday when the elderly woman dancing and singing was expressing her joy in the life of her great-grandson, named after her husband. Part of the "spirit" pervading our celebration that cold, bright morning in January 1977 was located in our collective memory that, the last time we had been together (nearly two years earlier), the preacher had been conducting the funeral service for this woman's husband. The deep sorrow of that earlier funeral had given place to the celebration of today's church service, as the widow sang and moved with the music, while the sun streamed through the small glass windows ringing the sanctuary. It seemed as if new life were there with us, in the person of the little boy who carried his great-grandfather's name and who had been "given" by his mother to this old woman to raise. With the child and his great-grandmother lived her foster son, who had left a job in New York to stay with his mother on the island after his father (the patriarch of the community) died. This foster son sang one part of the celebratory duet that led the voices of the congregation, while his widowed mother sang and danced her praise that January morning. Her son now shared with his mother the upbringing of the great-grandchild. It seemed to me that we were celebrating the promise of new life in the presence of ancestral spirits.

European American. Unlike both Native and African Americans, European Americans experienced the sacred as sharply separate from the physical world they inhabited. As noted earlier, the majority of the European Americans in the colonial South Carolina upcountry were mainly Scots-Irish, a people who had already experienced one migration from Scotland to northern Ireland within the family's memory. Another influential group settled early in Charles Town, along the coast, and in a few inland locations:

the French Huguenots. Like the Scots-Irish they had relocated from their native land at least once before. Inheriting their religious doctrines from the Hebrews and Greeks and using for their religious observances a variety of English not spoken in their homes, their European ancestors practiced a Protestant Christianity in which the sacred was divorced from a specific time or place. The stories of the Hebrews in the land of Israel and of the early Christians in Greece and Rome were not connected with the flora and fauna of any of the geographic spaces they had ever inhabited. Consequently these stories had long been understood as metaphors for abstract religious doctrines that transcended time and place. Their holy-day observances of Christmas and Easter were celebrations of events occurring in far distant lands, in unfamiliar places. First in Europe and then in America, their Jewish and Christian doctrines were transportable beyond any specific physical environment. The natural world encountered in Carolina played no part in their ritual observances. Indeed, in the words of the Hebrew God, as translated into seventeenth-century English, the natural world was separate from humanity and placed here for the benefit of mankind—not the reverse:

> So God created man in his own image, in the image of God created he him; male and female created he them.
> And God blessed them, and God said unto them, Be fruitful, and multiply, and replenish the earth, and subdue it; and have dominion over the fish of the sea, and over the fowl of the air, and over every living thing that moveth upon the earth. (Genesis 1:28–29)

These words, heard under the blue skies of South Carolina, could be understood as a call to subdue the bears and bison, the alligators and sea turtles, the Carolina parakeets and the passenger pigeons—or at least to use them to the ends of the human beings who had been granted dominion over "every living thing that moveth upon the earth." The Europeans, unlike the indigenous peoples in South Carolina, did not hold religious beliefs placing them *in* and *among* the land in which they moved. A river was to be used, not thanked for life-giving water; a deer was to be killed for the goods that could be exchanged for its skin in England, not celebrated for its life-sustaining blood and meat. And most important, the land itself was to be bought, sold, and accumulated by those who would glorify the paternal name for future generations, rather than to be used for the limited and temporary needs of communities in the here and now.

Unbounded by specific lands or groups of people, the Christian doctrines had the potential to bring together in common worship many disparate peoples, whose roots lay in several different parts of the world. For the first century of the English settlements, Europeans united with each other over successive generations, marrying and worshipping together across tribal barriers. In the plantation belt both Europeans and Africans regularly worshiped together in the same sanctuaries—though in segregated seating. Christian missionaries actively sought to bring Indians into their religious fellowships, but their failure to win converts among them was notable. Living in their own land among spirits they recognized in every rock, tree, and living creature, the indigenous peoples were far less likely to embrace the abstract God of the Europeans than the dispossessed African Americans, who seemed to find solace in religious observances that linked in some ways to their own: belief in a supreme being, reverence for the spirit world that could not be seen but might be experienced, and perhaps above all, empathy for the enslaved Hebrew people who had been led by Moses into the promised land. (The power of this last image can be felt in the last speech of Martin Luther King Jr., just before his death in 1968, with the video image capturing for generations to come his vision from the mountaintop of the promised land his people were about to enter and his awareness that he might not get there with them into that land of freedom.)

In addition to its detachment from a specific geographic locality, the Protestant Christianity of the immigrant Europeans was strongly linked to use of printed texts and to literacy sufficient to read them. Separated from specific physical locations associated with their beliefs and holding strongly to the tenet that these beliefs were to be understood and acted on by individual believers, the Protestants of fifteenth- and sixteenth-century Europe had unchained their holy texts from the Roman Catholic pulpits and had translated them into the vernacular languages of their congregations. In the early seventeenth century the Scots had established church schools to teach at least one member of each household to read these texts and had passed laws requiring householders above a certain income to purchase a Bible for the home. Reading of the Bible and the catechism was a regular practice in many Protestant homes, and printed texts were a central part of their religious observances as communities. Making use of the mechanical printing press, invented some two centuries before the English immigration to South Carolina, the European Protestants brought with them religious texts printed in several languages: Welsh, Gaelic, French, German, and English. The Jewish synagogue in Charles Town brought Hebrew texts, along with reverence for the Old Testament that they shared with the Protestants. Because early Protestant settlers believed that all admitted to their faith should know how to read and interpret the holy texts for themselves, their educated ministers established schools or, at least, gave new members instruction prior to accepting them as full participants. Although this strong link between literacy and church membership was tempered with the Great Awakening, the early emphasis on the printed word had consequences for the language use in religious observances and in educational institutions.

Aided by printed texts, the religious observances of the early European Americans made use of rhetorical patterns that were more individual, less participatory and less attuned to the here and now, and more focused on an abstract theology that transcends the physical world than the religious observances of African Americans. After the great open-air revivals of the eighteenth century, many of the mainstream Protestant churches (Baptist, Methodist, and some Presbyterian) began to hold services that reflected influences from the African rituals that infiltrated these revival meetings attended by both ethnic groups under the grape arbors of the countryside (Pitts 1993). But earlier church services, particularly the Anglican and Presbyterian, were dominated by rituals transported from the British Isles. For a short period beginning in 1704 (Hudson 1987), the Anglican Church of England was the "established" one in South Carolina, with membership in it required for voting and its clergy supported by public taxes. This direct tie between church and state was short-lived, however, both because of the numerous competing denominations and because of the lack of Anglican clergy to serve the far-flung parishes throughout the colony. The de facto established church remained a homogenized Protestant Christian one, with participants within specific denominations switching membership with relative ease upon marriage, relocation, or simply personal inclination.

The Presbyterian religious services of my youth were strikingly different from those I experienced in the Afro-Baptist church, in that use of the printed word was primary and physical movement was minimal. As a child I was a regular participant in services held in one of the earliest Presbyterian churches established in the colony. Located approximately twenty miles from the Afro-Baptist church described earlier, the sanctuary of this church was approximately the same size and of similar architecture. There were no "graven images" in either sanctuary, no paintings on the walls, no carpet except for the aisles between the door and the pulpit. The platform on which the pulpit rested was raised about two feet above the congregation. The seating of the choir was different from that of the Afro-Baptist church. In the Presbyterian church the choir's seating rose behind a raised pulpit and was separated from the congregation by wooden partition, allowing only the heads of choir members to show. While singing they usually stood so that their bodies were visible from the waist up; they faced the congregation and provided a backdrop for the minister. By contrast, in the Afro-Baptist church the choir, deacons, and minister all sat at the same level on a platform slightly raised above the congregation, with the choir and deacons facing each other rather than the congregation. With no partition between themselves and the congregation, both choir members and deacons were able to move freely to the pulpit or front of the congregation when participating in portions of the devotional service that required rhythmic movement as well as singing. The Presbyterian choir could not move from behind their barrier; the elders and deacons sat in scattered places throughout the congregation except on communion Sunday, when they sat together in a front section facing the minister so that they might help to administer the sacrament. The deacons and elders had no prescribed seating except for this function, although deacons regularly passed the offering plates from row to row at a prescribed point in the service. Other than the offering collection by the deacons and the upright singing by the choir, ritual body movements were not a part of the activities designated to the choir, elders, or deacons in this church service.

Unlike the Afro-Baptist rituals, the Presbyterian services never incorporated the experiences of the congregation into either song or sermon. Rather, the ritual was designed to connect an individual worshipper with a personal, all-powerful, and all-knowing deity. The service had two main parts, somewhat parallel to the division in the Afro-Baptist churches described by Pitts, but the contact between the minister and the congregation was sharply different. In the European American church the singing was done in a highly regular and predictable fashion, and the sermon was a lecture—not a participatory discourse. The first half of the service, preceding the sermon, comprised congregational singing, responsive reading, and a scripture passage read by the minister. This portion of the service is similar to what Pitts labels "devotion" in the Afro-Baptist church. The hymns and texts used in this first half of the service would be chosen jointly by the minister and the choir director to complement the sermon of the second half, which was the centerpiece of the service. The order of this entire service would be presented on a printed sheet of paper, folded in half to form a four-page bulletin. While churches of all denominations and

ethnic affiliations now use printed bulletins, the functions of these bulletins
are distinctive for European and African Americans. In the Presbyterian
church I attended along the Waccamaw River, the bulletin that was handed
to each member upon entrance to the sanctuary guided a series of directed
readings. Some of these readings were ritualistic and known to most participants (the Lord's Prayer, the Apostles' Creed, and an opening hymn);
for these the hymnbooks in front of every pew were not consulted. But for
nearly every other speech act throughout the service, a printed text was
essential, and the printed bulletin directed or gave information about these
religious speech acts. Songs were designated by their number in the hymn-
book, and the congregation told by the minister which verses to read and
sing together. This hymn singing was led by the music director, who played
a brief introduction to "set the key," and by the choir standing behind the
minister and facing the congregation. Responsive readings were also announced in the bulletin by their number in the book; the alternating bold
and regular print indicated which lines were to be read by the congregation and which by the minister. After this jointly constructed reading by the
pastor and the congregation, a period of silent prayer followed, during
which music was played softly by the organist. After this period of individual silent prayer, the minister delivered a "pastoral prayer"—one often
written out in advance. There was never any vocal response from the congregation during or after this prayer, which concluded with a ritual verse
of music from the choir. Then something of a break in the service was signaled by the seating of latecomers who had remained at the back during the
prayer and by the reading of the congregational announcements by the
minister. Most of these announcements were also printed in the bulletin,
but he often used the occasion to highlight specific ones or to include new
information.

The second part of the service began with a reading of the morning's
scripture lesson from the Bible, with chapter and verse announced in the
bulletin. For the Presbyterian church this segment was more aptly characterized as lesson. Unlike the ecstatic service described by Pitts for the
Afro-Baptists, there was no exuberant display of either language or music.
Rather the focus was on the scriptural lesson from the Bible and on the lecture delivered by the minister. Many in the congregation turned to the designated passage in their own personal Bibles while the minister read aloud
from the Bible on the pulpit. For the offering that followed, the seated
choir sang quietly as the ushers passed "collection plates" from pew to pew.
The title of this offering hymn, as well as of the following anthem sung by
the standing choir, was printed in the bulletin. There was no participation

by the congregation in these well-rehearsed musical numbers, just as there was no vocal response to the sermon that followed. This sermon, its title announced in the bulletin, related to the earlier scripture reading. The minister typically used this occasion for teaching a social lesson relevant to some abstract problem of the day or for interpreting the scriptural passage in light of today's problems. One of the most memorable sermons I can remember from my childhood in the 1950s was a new minister's first sermon on the absurdity of a small community like ours having two separate school systems for the different races. (Little did I realize at the time, but we actually had *three* in one part of the county: "white," "Negro," and "Indian.") This particular minister, originally from New York, soon became one of the most popular and respected in the modern history of that church, probably signaling the beginning of church participation in the civil rights movement of the 1960s. While such a sermon would have been accompanied at various points by ritual rhythmic foot stomping on wooden floors in the Afro-Baptist church (an indication of approval), in the Presbyterian church of my youth this provocative lesson was always met by utter silence—as were all sermons, whatever the topic. Plenty might be said after the sermon over a midday meal, where the sermon and various members of the congregation alike were subjected to vigorous critique—but no response indicating either approval or disapproval was ever given by the congregation during the sermon itself. There was, in short, no extrinsic *participation* in the construction of the religious discourse. The order of the service, like the specific verses of the hymns, was set in advance. Spontaneous responses to persons and events of the moment were not appropriate from the assembled congregation, although they might be included in the minister's remarks. After the sermon the congregation sang a closing hymn, again using the hymnbooks in their pews to read and sing the designated verses. Ritualistic benedictions were pronounced by the minister and sung by the choir. The minister then came down from the platform and went to the church entrance to greet members as they left, to the accompaniment of a musical selection announced in the bulletin and played by the organist.

The importance of the centrality of literacy in controlling religious discourse within the European American churches can be seen in the admonition of eighteenth-century Anglican minister John Wesley to members of new Methodist congregations within the American colonies:

Learn these tunes before you learn any others; afterwards learn as many as you please.

> Sing them exactly as they are printed here, without altering or mending them at all; and if you have learned to sing them otherwise, unlearn it as soon as you can. ("Directions for Singing," from John Wesley's *Select Hymns*, 1761 [reprinted in United Methodist Church 1989])

Although the Methodist, Baptist, and later Pentecostal evangelicals made the written word less a focal point than their Anglican and Presbyterian counterparts, literate discourse among the European speech community as a whole was central to its existence in the new land. By contrast, literacy among African Americans and Native Americans had a different place in the development of their religious discourse and other aspects of community life. Although some Africans were Muslims and literate in the language of the Koran, they were not literate in the languages they spoke as native tongues. Like the languages of North America, those of West and Central Africa had no writing systems at the time of contact. The languages of Europe, however, had writing systems derived from the Roman alphabet (itself based on a Phoenician system adapted from Egyptian hieroglyphics). Newcomers from Europe brought with them these writing systems for the languages they spoke every day. Major settlement groups from France, Spain, Germany, and the British Isles included at least some members of their group who could both transcribe their spoken language on paper and also read messages and texts of other writers. In the new land writing was used from the earliest time between the incoming Europeans to keep records and make reports to superiors, to exchange information, and to exercise control over others. As the host tribes of America and the enslaved peoples from Africa interacted with the Europeans, literate discourse came to be a significant part of their lives as well, but the functions of literate discourse were different for the three groups from the beginning and remain so today in important respects.

As a young person growing up as a Presbyterian, I experienced the church as the focus of my early social life. Social gatherings, summer camp, religious instruction, and discussion groups made up of about two dozen young people near my own age gave opportunities for social and intellectual growth, as well as for the development of literacy and public speaking. These activities meshed seamlessly with those of school and home, where similar values were reinforced and where the language used was nearly identical. (See Lippy's 1993 discussion of the importance of religion in the life of South Carolina.) Decades later, as a teacher of remedial writing at a university in California, I came to realize that the rhetorical patterns of the Presbyterian sermon and devotional lessons in the youth groups had provided me with the rhetorical patterns valued in much of academic life throughout the United States. These patterns were in some sense "privileged" in academic circles. Having absorbed them as a child, I too was "privileged" as I entered various stages of academic life by not having to learn them as new forms of discourse. By contrast students in my California composition classes over the last two decades of the twentieth century entered academic life having learned quite different rhetorical patterns in their home communities from all points of the globe; much of their "remediation" entailed learning the European American patterns expected in the American academy. (See Heath 1983 and 1989; Nichols 1989; and Olson 1995 for further development of this point.)

Such religious observances as the Europeans conducted, I would argue, can prepare participants for inclusion in widely flung intellectual life that is separated from specific time and place and relies on printed texts. Through such texts, members of this "imagined community" can interact with each other, divorced from any specific physical setting (Anderson 1983). In addition to freeing such a community from physical boundaries, the medium of print helped early South Carolinians transcend old political boundaries of Europe. United by their overwhelmingly Protestant religious beliefs and rituals, the Europeans who settled in South Carolina interacted with each other in new physical settings in ways that mitigated differences that loomed large in the old countries. Original settlers tended to belong to specific denominations (English were Anglican; Scots and Scots-Irish were Presbyterian; Welsh were Baptist; French were Huguenot; and Germans were Lutheran), but with intermarriage and the melding of traditions among the European Americans in the new land, these denominations ceased to be closely identified with European ethnic or national groups. All of them retained a close identification with the use of printed texts, and most had a literate clergy and congregation. All adopted the use of church schools initiated in Scotland by the Presbyterians, and formal schooling included instruction in biblical texts and church catechisms. The small but significant Jewish population had an even older tradition of literacy and religious instruction, at least for males, and in the new physical setting they formed important economic and political ties with the European Protestants, as noted earlier, with one of their number elected to the first Provincial Congress in 1774 to represent one of the upcountry districts in South Carolina (Jones 1993).

Records

For the Europeans record keeping in writing was a central function of their literate discourse with each other and with Europe. They had been disbursed with licenses from their governments and expected to produce some return from their explorations and subsequent settlements in the new land. Several companions of the Spanish adventurer Hernando de Soto chronicled his early explorations of the Southeast beginning in the 1540s. They knew about the lawyer Lucas Vázquez de Ayllón, who had led a 1521 slaving expedition and in 1526 attempted to found a colony in the area of modern Georgetown County, South Carolina (Clayton, Knight, and Moore 1993, 229). As we have seen, Ayllón had taken a captured native known as Francisco of Chicora to Spain, where he learned Spanish well enough to give testimony about his native South Carolina—testimony that was written down as a guide for future explorations (Hudson 1990). The expeditions of Juan Pardo forty years later into the interior of South Carolina had access to these written records and made more records of their own. Pardo's chronicler endeavored to preserve his exact words to each group of Native Americans he encountered. Because of these written records, we can read of these contact events over four centuries later, showing a European demanding a tribute of grain from the host tribes and inviting them to become Christians and to give obedience to the king of Spain and to the pope as leader of the faith (Hudson 1990). The documents from Pardo's expeditions record that the Indian headmen repeatedly responded with "Yaa" where the Spanish orator paused in this set speech—a response that the Europeans interpreted as "Yes" but that may have meant something more like "We hear you" or "Continue." One historian of the Spanish in North America maintains that early Europeans believed that the native rulers did not have legitimate dominion of their own lands because they were not Christian and did not live according to what was understood as "natural law" (Weber 1992, 33). Whatever the interpretation by either party in these speech events, we have written records that they occurred because the Europeans used writing as a way of keeping account of what they did during such officially sanctioned expeditions.

When the English entered South Carolina in the following century, they also kept such records to send back to their English business sponsors. The British Public Record Office (BPRO) is a repository of such records, and major public libraries in the United States have transferred these records to microfilm so that they may be consulted today. The written records of early Europeans, in other words, have been accorded respect and awarded public resources that extend well into the future. The English records include accounts of explorations, encounters with indigenous peoples and with other Europeans, legal decisions of the British government and of the elected colonial assembly, business dealings with each other and with those outside the colony, and letters home detailing experiences in the new land.

Writing had the potential to unite diverse peoples in the new land, as well as to help exert control over selected groups. On the one hand, the use of written records, which may be consulted as a record for the past and a guide for the future, allowed diverse groups who were not direct descendants of the original record makers to find unity in an adopted past. Histories of the colonial past, which usually began with the appearance of the English on the shores of Carolina, detailed the struggles of the early settlers, the successful trade they established with the indigenous peoples and the mother country, the constitution they adopted to govern themselves, and their eventual break from the mother country. The written records generally excluded major categories of people—women, Indians, African slaves, and European servants—except as they entered into business dealings with those who kept the records. An occasional woman, such as Eliza Lucas Pinckney, kept a diary or record of her days, and such a diary allows us some limited access to the concerns of those rarely included in the official written records.

As well as unifying diverse peoples in the new land and providing a record of their legal and business transactions, written records served to exclude and to control. Ship captains kept records of their human cargos when bringing slaves from the Caribbean and Africa, as well as of their paying passengers from the ports of Europe. Auctioneers kept records of estate sales of slaves and other disposable property after a landowner died, as well as of the sales of captives newly brought into the Charles Town port and sold to landowners throughout the colonies in North America. Colonial officials kept records of their business dealings with native peoples of the continent—of the exchanges of deerskins and other raw materials from America for manufactured tools and other goods from Europe. Only a decade after their permanent settlement at Charles Town, the English established the Commission on Indian Affairs to regularize and control this trade. Men commissioned as "Indian traders" were required to make regular written reports to the commission, which were entered into their permanent records:

You are to cause to be entered in the book herewith sent you
all orders directions and Instructions that you shall give to Indians,
or others relating to Indians, as alsoe the Petitions and request of ye
substance of them to you made by Indians, whether it be Greivances,
Informations or otherwise, all which we desire, you or as many of you
as are or shall be present at the makeing them to attest by signing the
book att every Adjournment that our just actings by your loving
friends may hereafter appeare by the aforesaid Journall, which must
be kept by the Secretary of the Province who is requyred to transmit
the copys of it once in every yeare to us the Lords Proprieters or
oftener if occasion shall require. (Instructions for the Commissioners
appoynted to heare and determine differences between the Christians
and the Indians, BPRO, 99)

As these instructions indicate, the English financers of the Carolina
colony required that written records of activities important to the success
of their enterprise be kept and submitted at regular intervals. These records
go on to indicate that the Lords Proprietors in England reserved the right
to enter into official "treatyes" with Indians, based on written records kept
by the Carolina Commission. Given the vagaries of international mail de-
livery across the Atlantic in the late seventeenth century, this reliance on
literate discourse for decisions of peace and war seems extraordinary.

We have noted that non-Europeans recognized the importance of these
written records to the Europeans at all stages of contact. Native peoples
learned to read the brands used on deerskins, and the Catawba valued their
written "commissions" from the English colonial government to the point
of requesting replacements when the paper wore out. Even though they
themselves were not literate, the Catawba requested a written "deed" to
their territory well before the Revolutionary War because they recognized
the function of such a written document among the Europeans as a means
of protecting their lands from settlement. In a later century the Cherokee
found important uses for literacy within their own communities. When
they developed a system of writing for their language, they used it to preserve the sacred words of Cherokee religious observances and to communicate among themselves after the dislocation to Oklahoma. We have also
seen that individuals in the African American speech community made great
efforts throughout the colonial period to become literate in English, both
as a means of securing their own mobility through forged passes and as a
way of securing work opportunities that brought a better life for themselves

and their enslaved families. However, in domains where their ancestral oral traditions were strong, both the Indian and the African American speech communities used literacy only selectively and at much later dates for their narratives and for their religious activities. Records of knowledge and events within their own communities were traditionally kept as oral narratives and, as such, have not typically been easily accessible to European American communities.

Conclusion

Voices of our ancestors are echoed in the voices of speakers who have grown up in South Carolina since the colonial period, despite the normal processes of language change. South Carolinians perceive differences in the members of speech communities different from their own, just as Walt Wolfram and his colleagues have so convincingly demonstrated for the Lumbee Indians of nearby southeastern North Carolina. However, those who have grown up outside a South Carolina speech community typically hear more similarities across the three speech communities than differences. As the late Raymond O'Cain (personal communication, 1976) experienced, a South Carolinian from the lowcountry is often perceived as a member of the African American speech community, even when he or she is European American. As a graduate student at the University of Chicago while he was preparing to do fieldwork on the dialects of Charleston, Ray had to enlist his wife, who had not grown up in South Carolina, to make the telephone calls of inquiry when they were trying to rent an apartment. Chicago residents, like those of many northern cities, displayed rampant prejudices in that era and could do so legally before federal civil rights legislation was passed. I myself discovered that my California students almost universally perceived the speech of my great-uncle, who had grown up in rural Horry County, to be that of an African American when I played a tape recording of him, and they found the speech of an elderly African American woman from Georgetown County to be unintelligible without a printed transcript.

Even South Carolinians themselves, however, do not always appreciate how much their ways of speaking have been changed by the long association of the three speech communities with each other. Sometimes only when they travel or move to another part of the country do they recognize the distinctive ways in which they differ from members of their own ancestral backgrounds who did not grow up in South Carolina. A vivid example of this cultural assimilation was brought home to me on a 1987 trip to the Lowlands of Scotland with my mother, where so many of our ancestors

originated before their immigration to northern Ireland. At our first break-
fast in our hotel dining room, there was utter silence except for the clink of
cutlery. For both of us this was a highly unnatural silence because any eating place we had ever been to in South Carolina was filled with laughter,
conversation, and storytelling, not unlike what is found in the markets of
West Africa. Most South Carolinians talk more and to more people than
these speakers of the European speech community in Scotland apparently
did. The South Carolina pattern of interacting in public seemed more
like that of Yoruba speakers of Nigeria, who have greetings for a multitude of activities. Like them, most South Carolinians of European ancestry exchange greetings whenever they encounter people, even an unknown
farmer on a dusty country road. This particular way of speaking, like many
others, has been learned from centuries of interaction with the African
American speech community of the state.

Finally we should remember that no speaker talks one way all the time.
All of us adapt our pronunciation, sentence structure, vocabulary, and rhetorical patterns to the situation and to those with whom we are speaking.
In some ways our language habits are similar to the clothes we wear. We
dress up for a court appearance or for our grandmother's funeral, but the
same clothes would be totally inappropriate for a barbecue or a pickup base-
ball game with friends. Language is not all that different. I can remember
being surprised when my father spoke an uneducated, rural dialect of English in his law office in the summers when I was a teenager and filled in
for his secretary when she was on vacation. He spoke that way only with the
old farmers who came to see him as friends, never in our home or teaching
a Sunday school lesson. Having been the first of his family to graduate
from high school, he went to the University of South Carolina, where he
was on the debate team, and was elected to the state legislature from his
home county while still in law school. Only when I studied sociolinguistics
many years later did I realize that he had been required to learn a significantly different dialect of English in the process. After his death his sister
gave me one of his old high school report cards showing grades of A in
every subject except English, for which he earned only a C. His mother
and her rural speech community of Horry County used pronouns and verb
forms that dated back to a much earlier stage of English, probably close to
that used in many rural parts of colonial South Carolina. Teaching a class
on the English language in America in the 1980s at the University of South
Carolina, I had one European American student from the far western
county of Oconee come up to me after class with tears in his eyes to tell me

of how he had been teased by fellow students for using speech like that of my grandmother. Likewise, two young African American women told me at the close of a lecture on Gullah at the College of Charleston that they had both been sent to speech classes when they went to school "up North," but could never "hear" those sounds the teachers were telling them to make. Experiences such as these remind us that many people must acquire new language structures and ways of speaking if they move away from their native speech communities and especially if they find themselves in jobs that entail interaction with the general public. However, the acquisition of new structures and ways of speaking does not mean that the old ones are forgotten. Most speakers retain the older ways of speaking, using them appropriately and even joyfully when the situation warrants.

Being able to use several forms of language and dialect is a form of wealth, not poverty. Echoes of those voices from long ago are to be cherished in speech of the present.

Epilogue

Like politics, all language is local. This book has attempted to give an overview of one small geographic and political entity as part of a larger picture of how language changes, disappears, and is created anew from pieces of old ones.

Some life experiences and people have been essential in helping me to understand the language history of my home state. The earliest relevant experience is one of which I am barely conscious when I was between one and three years old, being cared for daily by a young African American woman while my mother made a long commute to teach at a country school in Horry County. During those two years I actively learned both my parents' dialect and the dialect spoken by this young woman, who was the great-granddaughter of a woman born in some part of Africa. This ancestor's picture had a place of honor on a table in her living room when I visited her many years later.

Near the end of my elementary school education, my father ran for state attorney general and took me along to almost every county in the state as he and my mother traveled to the courthouses for candidates' speeches. I became dimly aware of speech differences in the upcountry and the lowcountry as we visited my mother's relatives in Greenville County and ended the campaign in Charleston on the coast. I became even more conscious of these local speech patterns when I entered Winthrop College and came to know young white women from every county in the state. At Winthrop, then segregated along both race and gender lines, drama teachers recruited me more than once to play African American parts in college plays because of the authentic dialect I had learned from my early caregiver. Before going to Winthrop my language experiences on Saturdays and in the summers as a retail clerk in my county's leading department store brought me into contact with a range of dialects spoken in Horry County by townspeople and country farmers of both European and African descent. Even though I understood African American English, I had some difficulty understanding the occasional Gullah speaker who asked for help.

Sometimes I helped out with typing in my father's law office, and I was amazed to hear him use the rural dialect of his mother's people with some of the country farmers who sought his help. In our home, where my parents sometimes entertained other lawyers, teachers, and college professors, I had never heard him speak anything other than the standard regional English used by other professionals in our area. He had one good African American friend, in particular, with whom he spent long hours talking on the porch, but I have no idea what kind of speech either of them used when they spoke together.

This rich linguistic environment would have gone unnoticed had I not gone "north" for graduate study after teaching for a couple of years in Virginia. In an Old English class at the University of Minnesota, I learned two important facts about my own linguistic background: some of the Old English verb forms and a pronoun from 500 or 600 A.D., no longer used in standard English, had been used by my Horry County grandmother; and to my surprise the standard regional English that I spoke was a subject of ridicule in the academic setting of Minnesota. Like most young speakers of low-prestige dialects, I stopped speaking in public for several years until I learned to put the glides on my *i*'s and could constrict my *r*'s at the ends of some words. Sometimes I hypercorrected, once putting an *r* at the end of *pillow* in a book club meeting and provoking another burst of laughter in a California setting. While dialect ridicule can be painful, with a little linguistic and political knowledge it can also lead to valuable insights.

In the early days of the Vietnam War, when young males could still avoid the draft if their grades were kept up, I began teaching in California colleges and noticed that most students who failed remedial English were also speakers of low-prestige dialects, the features of which showed up in their writing. Remembering my own experience, I knew that the dialect they spoke was no reflection of their academic capabilities. Indirectly, however, the nonstandard dialects of my California-born Latino students were sending many of them to the front lines. After the fall of Saigon a few years later, when Vietnamese families began settling in California in great numbers, all our schools and colleges were presented with linguistic challenges from bright students who needed to learn the language of the academy quickly and well, and few of us were prepared to deal with them. In the process more attention was focused on the much larger number of Latino dialect and second-language speakers who had been in the state all along and whose linguistic needs had been largely ignored except in a few school districts. Searching for help, I turned to the study of linguistics at my local state university and prepared for a second graduate degree in that field.

The academic study of linguistics helped me reconnect with the speech of South Carolina. In an introductory course Edith Trager Johnson lent me her copy of Turner's 1949 book on Gullah when she learned of my background and personal interests, and she also helped me enter a network of scholars who had conducted fieldwork on the general speech of the South. A younger professor, Rebecca Agheyisi, was completing her doctoral program at Stanford and writing a dissertation on West African Pidgin English (WAPE), which she and her playmates had spoken in the schoolyard as children. With her I studied Yoruba, one of the major languages of Nigeria, as well as sociolinguistics and grammatical theory. Gradually I came to understand some of the motivations behind my father's codeswitching and also saw some connections between WAPE and Gullah. Realizing that the discipline of linguistics offered tools for learning more about this intriguing language variety still spoken along the coast of South Carolina, I entered Stanford University to study with Charles Ferguson, who was then offering one of the nation's first seminars on creole languages. After completing my dissertation on Gullah, I happened to record the speech of an elderly relative living in Socastee, one of the oldest communities on the Waccamaw Neck, all of whose permanent residents at that time were descendants of Europeans. This elderly man in his nineties had attended school only one day in his life, so his speech was relatively untouched by the more standard speech of his college-educated children. In his earlier years he had worked in the same lumbering jobs as had some elderly Gullah-speaking men I had recorded in Georgetown County, but his speech was strikingly different on the grammatical level.

Intrigued by the differences in their speech, I embarked on a small-scale study, recording residents of his all-white community who matched those of my earlier Gullah study in age and gender (Nichols 1983; 1986; 1991). At the end of a long interview of another elderly Socastee man, I happened to ask him if there had been any Indians living around the community, and he told me that a "Croatan" had run a liquor still in the nearby woods. After talking with local librarians and teachers, I learned about the Indian elementary school that had existed in my home county until the 1950s and realized that a quiet integration of self-identified Indians into white schools had occurred about that time. Older teachers knew the family names of these children, but no mention was ever made of racial differences that I was aware of as a child. Intrigued by the possible existence of yet a third speech community in the same area, I did some fieldwork in an elementary school in a Lumbee Indian community just across the South Carolina border in Robeson County, North Carolina, during a year in residence at the University of North Carolina. While there I became aware of the groundbreaking work being done at Duke University by Peter Wood and his students on Indians of the early Southeast. About that time Walt Wolfram came to North Carolina State University and founded the North Carolina Language and Life Project, directing sociolinguistic projects on North Carolina Indian, European American, and African American speech communities around the state. Without the research projects directed by Wood and Wolfram, my ability to make the connections between the South Carolina speech communities described here would not have been possible.

Much more academic research remains to be done by those who are as intrigued as I have been by the language that exists in their own families and communities. One final note, however, must be made about how awareness of one's own language background can be fostered. I became much more conscious of the connection between my own academic interests and my personal experiences when I began training experienced and prospective teachers in the multilingual frontier of California. Trying to give these teachers tools to understand what their students were experiencing, I developed a set of exercises that guided them through an exploration of their ancestors' linguistic history and their own personal experiences with language (Nichols 1993). As my colleagues who were experts on writing theory had taught me, I did these exercises with my own students—and in the process brought to my consciousness some of the critical experiences in my own background that led eventually to this book. Working with my students in California, who came from multicultural backgrounds and who went out to teach even more diverse students from all over the world, I learned about experiences of language and racial ridicule that still bring tears to my eyes. I also learned about the conditions and motivations that foster successful language learning and, often even more difficult, the acquisition of second dialects.

As more of us work our way out of what I have come to think of as our national "linguistic amnesia," my hope is that we will develop both more linguistic tolerance and more understanding of how languages and dialects are successfully learned and used.

References

Adair, James. 1775. *The History of the American Indians.* London: Dilly. Reprinted as *Adair's History of the American Indians.* Johnson City, Tenn.: Watauga, 1930.

Anderson, Benedict. 1983. *Imagined Communities: Reflections on the Origin and Spread of Nationalism.* London: Verso Editions & NLB.

Anderson, Bridget L. 1999. "Source-Language Transfer and Vowel Accommodation in the Patterning of Cherokee English *ai* and *oi*." *American Speech* 74:339–68.

Baker, Steven G. 1974. "Cofitachique: Fair Province of Carolina." M.A. thesis, University of South Carolina.

Baldwin, Agnes Leland. 1969. *First Settlers of South Carolina, 1670–1680.* Tricentennial Booklet 1. Columbia: University of South Carolina Press.

Ball, Arnetha Fay. 1991. "Organizational Patterns in the Oral and Written Expository Language of African American Adolescents." Ph.D. diss., Stanford University.

Barton, Lew. 1971. "Me-Told Tales along the Lumbee." *North Carolina Folklore* 19: 173–76.

Baughman, Ernest Warren. 1954. "A Comparative Study of the Folktales of England and North America." Ph.D. diss., Indiana University.

Beal, Joan. 1997. "Syntax and Morphology." In *The Edinburgh History of the Scots Language,* ed. Charles Jones, 355–77. Edinburgh: Edinburgh University Press.

Bernheim, Gotthardt Dellmann. 1872. *History of the German Settlements and of the Lutheran Church in North and South Carolina.* Repr., Spartanburg, S.C.: Reprint Company, 1972.

Birmingham, David. 1966. *Trade and Conflict in Angola: The Mbundu and Their Neighbors under the Influence of the Portuguese, 1483–1790.* Oxford: Clarendon.

Blu, Karen. 1980. *The Lumbee Problem: The Making of an American Indian People.* New York: Cambridge University Press.

Booker, Karen M., Charles M. Hudson, and Robert L. Rankin. 1992. "Place Name Identification and Multilingualism in the Sixteenth-Century Southeast." *Ethnohistory* 39:399–451.

Brewer, Jeutonne, and R. Reising. 1982. "Tokens in the Pocosin." *American Speech* 57: 108–20.

Bridenbaugh, Carl, and Roberta Bridenbaugh. 1972. *No Peace beyond the Line: The English in the Caribbean 1624–1690.* New York: Oxford University Press.

British Public Record Office (BPRO). *Records in the British Public Record Office Relating to South Carolina, 1663–1782.* South Carolina Archives Microcopy 1, vol. 30.

Brown, Douglas Summers. 1966. *The Catawba Indians: The People of the River.* Columbia: University of South Carolina Press.

Campbell, Lyle, and Marianne Mithun. 1979. *The Languages of Native America: Historical and Comparative Assessment.* Austin: University of Texas Press.

Carney, Judith A. 2001. *Black Rice: The African Origins of Rice Cultivation in the Americas.* Cambridge, Mass.: Harvard University Press.

Carter, Hazel. 1978. "Kongo Survivals in United States Gullah: An Examination of Turner's Material." Paper presented at "Conference on Semantics, Lexicography and Creole Studies," Society for Caribbean Linguistics, at the University of the West Indies, July 17–21, 1978.

Cassidy, Frederic G., and R. B. Le Page. 1980. *Dictionary of Jamaican English.* 2nd ed. New York: Cambridge University Press.

Clarke, Kenneth W. 1958. "Motif-Index of Folk-Tales from Culture-Area V, West Africa." Ph.D. diss., Indiana University.

Clayton, Lawrence A., Vernon James Knight, and Edward C. Moore. 1993. *The De Soto Chronicles: The Expedition of Hernando de Soto to North America in 1539–1543.* Tuscaloosa: University of Alabama Press.

Clements, G. N. 2000. "Phonology." In *African Languages: An Introduction,* ed. Bernd Heine and Derek Nurse, 123–60. New York: Cambridge University Press.

Cohen, Hennig. 1953. *The South Carolina Gazette, 1732–1775.* Columbia: University of South Carolina Press.

Coker, Caleb. 1976. "History of Society Hill." In *Darlingtoniana,* ed. E. C. Ervin and H. F. Rudisell, 24–34. Spartanburg, S.C.: Reprint Company.

Crawford, James M. 1975. "Southeastern Indian Languages." In *Studies in Southeastern Indian Languages,* ed. James M. Crawford, 1–120. Athens: University of Georgia Press.

Creel, Margaret Washington. 1988. *"A Peculiar People": Slave Religion and Community-Culture among the Gullahs.* New York: New York University Press.

Crowley, Daniel J., ed. 1977. *African Folklore in the New World.* Austin: University of Texas Press.

Cunningham, Irma Aloyce Ewing. 1992. *A Syntactic Analysis of Sea Island Creole.* Tuscaloosa: University of Alabama Press.

Curtin, Philip D. 1969. *The Atlantic Slave Trade: A Census.* Madison: University of Wisconsin.

———. 1990. *The Rise and Fall of the Plantation Complex: Essays in Atlantic History.* New York: Cambridge University Press.

Crystal, David. 1987. *The Cambridge Encyclopedia of Language.* New York: Cambridge University Press.

Dabbs, Edith M. 1983. *Sea Island Diary: A History of St. Helena Island.* Spartanburg, S.C.: Reprint Company.

Davis, Henry C. 1914. "Negro Folk-Lore in South Carolina." *Journal of American Folk-Lore* 18:241–54.

Deaton, Stan. 1999. "Self-Preservation Is the First Law of Nature: Slavery and White Anxiety in Post-Revolutionary South Carolina." Paper presented at "Conference on Slavery in Early South Carolina," Institute for Southern Studies, University of South Carolina, February 12–13, 1999.

De Jong, Gerald Francis. 1975. *The Dutch in America, 1609–1974*. Boston: Twayne.

Dial, Adolph. 1993. *The Lumbee*. New York: Chelsea Ridge.

Dial, Adolph, and David K. Eliades. 1975. *The Only Land I Know: A History of the Lumbee Indians*. San Francisco: Indian Historical Press.

Diamond, Jared. 1997. *Guns, Germs, and Steel: The Fates of Human Societies*. New York: Norton.

Dickson, R. J. 1966. *Ulster Emigration to Colonial America, 1718–1775*. London: Routledge & Kegan Paul.

Dorson, Richard M. 1956. *Negro Folktales in Michigan*. Cambridge, Mass.: Harvard University Press.

———. 1958. *Negro Tales from Pine Bluff, Arkansas, and Calvin, Michigan*. Folklore Series 12. Bloomington: Indiana University Press.

Dunn, Richard S. 1971. "The English Sugar Islands and the Founding of South Carolina." *South Carolina Historical Magazine* 72:81–93.

———. 1972. *Sugar and Slaves: The Rise of the Planter Class in the English West Indies, 1624–1713*. Chapel Hill: University of North Carolina Press.

Edelsky, Carole. 1981. "Who's Got the Floor?" *Language in Society*, 10:383–421.

Edgar, Walter. 1998. *South Carolina: A History*. Columbia: University of South Carolina Press.

Ekirch, A. Roger. 1987. *Bound for America: The Transportation of British Convicts to the Colonies, 1718–1775*. New York: Oxford University Press.

Eliades, David Klearchos. 1981. "The Indian Policy of Colonial South Carolina, 1670–1763." Ph.D. diss., University of South Carolina.

Ellis, George W. 1914. *Negro Culture in West Africa*. New York: Neale.

Elzas, Barnett A. 1905. *The Jews of South Carolina: From the Earliest Times to the Present Day*. Philadelphia: Lippincott. Repr., Spartanburg, S.C.: Reprint Company, 1972.

Equiano, Olaudah. 1789. *The Interesting Narrative of Olaudah Equiano, or Gustavus Vasa, the African*. 2 vols. London. Chaps. 1 and 2 repr. in *Africa Remembered: Narratives by West Africans from the Era of the Slave Trade*, ed. Philip D. Curtin, 69–98. Madison: University of Wisconsin Press, 1967.

Galenson, David W. 1981. *White Servitude in Colonial America: An Economic Analysis*. New York: Cambridge University Press.

Gallay, Alan. 2002. *The Indian Slave Trade: The Rise of the English Empire in the American South, 1670–1717*. New Haven, Conn.: Yale University Press.

Gleason, Henry A. 1961. *An Introduction to Descriptive Linguistics*. New York: Holt, Rinehart & Winston.

Glenmary Research Center. *Major Denominational Families, by Counties of the United States, 1980*. Atlanta: Glenmary Research Center.

Goddard, Ives. 2000. "The Identity of Red Thunder Cloud." *Society for the Study of Indigenous Languages of the Americas Newsletter* (April).

Goodman, Abram Vossem. 1973. "South Carolina from Shaftesbury to Salvador." In *Jews in the South*, ed. Leonard Dinnerstein and Mary Dale Palsson, 29–42. Baton Rouge: Louisiana State University Press.

Goodyear, Albert C., III, James L. Michie, and Tommy Charles. 1990. *The Earliest South Carolinians: The Paleoindian Occupation of South Carolina*. Columbia, S.C.: Archeological Society of South Carolina.

Gordon, Raymond G., Jr., ed. 2005. *Ethnologue: Languages of the World*, 15th ed. Dallas: Summer Institute of Linguistics International. http://www.ethnologue.com.

Graham, Ian Charles Cargill. 1956. *Colonists from Scotland: Emigration to North America, 1707–1783*. Ithaca, N.Y.: Cornell University Press.

Granovetter, Mark. 1973. "The Strength of Weak Ties." *American Journal of Sociology* 78:1360–80.

———. 1983. "The Strength of Weak Ties: A Network Theory Revisited." *Sociological Theory* 1:201–33.

Green, M. M., and G. E. Igwe. 1963. *A Descriptive Grammar of Igbo*. London: Oxford University Press.

Hagy, James William. 1993. *This Happy Land: The Jews of Colonial and Antebellum Charleston*. Tuscaloosa: University of Alabama Press.

Hahn, Steven C. 2002. "The Mother of Necessity: Carolina, the Creek Indians, and the Making of a New Order in the American Southeast, 1670–1763." In *The Transformation of Southeastern Indians, 1540–1760*, ed. Robbie Ethridge and Charles Hudson, 79–114. Jackson: University Press of Mississippi.

Hair, P. E. H. 1965. "Sierra Leone Items in the Gullah Dialect of American English." *Sierra Leone Language Review* 4:79–85.

Harris, William H., and Judith S. Levey, eds. 1975. *The New Columbia Encyclopedia*. New York: Columbia University Press.

Hartmann, Edward George. 1967. *Americans from Wales*. Boston: Christopher.

Heath, Shirley Brice. 1983. *Ways with Words: Language, Life, and Work in Communities and Classrooms*. New York: Cambridge University Press.

———. 1989. "Taking a Look at Cross-Cultural Narratives." *Topics in Language Disorders* 7:84–94.

Heine, Bernd, and Derek Nurse, eds. 2000. *African Languages: An Introduction*. New York: Cambridge University Press.

Heinemann-Priest, Claudia Y. 2007. "Catawba." In *The New Encyclopedia of Southern Culture*, gen. ed. Charles Reagan Wilson. Vol. 5, ed. Michael Montomery and Ellen Johnson, 50–52. Chapel Hill: University of North Carolina Press.

Henderson, William. 1866. *Notes on the Folklore of the Northern Counties of England and the Borders*. London: Longmans, Green. Repr., Yorkshire: E. P. Publishing, 1973.

Herman, David. 2003. "Stories as a Tool for Thinking." In *Narrative Theory and the Cognitive Sciences*, ed. David Herman, 163–92. Stanford, Calif.: Center for the Study of Language and Information, Leland Stanford Junior University.

Hickey, Raymond, ed. 2004. *Legacies of Colonial English: Studies in Transported Dialects*. New York: Cambridge University Press.

Hirsch, Arthur Henry. 1928. *The Huguenots of Colonial South Carolina*. Durham, N.C.: Duke University Press.

Hodge, Frederick Webb, ed. 1907, 1910. *Handbook of American Indians North of Mexico.* 2 vols. Bureau of American Ethnology Bulletin 30. Washington, D.C., U.S.: Government Printing Office.

Hoffman, Paul E. 1990. *A New Andalucia an a Way to the Orient: The American Southeast during the Sixteenth Century.* Baton Rouge: Louisiana State University Press.

Hudson, Charles M. 1970. *The Catawba Nation.* Athens: University of Georgia Press.

———. 1976. *The Southeastern Indians.* Knoxville: University of Tennessee Press.

———. 1990. *The Juan Pardo Expeditions: Explorations of the Carolinas and Tennessee, 1566–1568.* Washington, D.C.: Smithsonian Institution Press.

———. 1997. *Knights of Spain, Warriors of the Sun: Hernando de Soto and the South's Ancient Chiefdoms.* Athens: University of Georgia Press.

Hudson, Charles M., and Carmen Chaves Tesser, eds. 1994. *The Forgotten Centuries: Indians and Europeans in the American South, 1521–1704.* Athens: University of Georgia Press.

Hudson, Charles M., Chester B. De Pratter, and Marvin T. Smith. 1984. "The Hernando de Soto Expedition: From Apalachee to Chiaha." *Southeastern Archaeology* 3: 65–77.

Hudson, Winthrop S. 1987. *Religion in America: An Historical Account of the Development of American Religious Life.* 4th ed. New York: Macmillan.

Hurston, Zora Neale. 1937. *Their Eyes Were Watching God.* Philadelphia: Lippincott.

Jones, Charles. 1997. "Phonology." In *The Edinburgh History of the Scots Language,* ed. Charles Jones, 267–334. Edinburgh: Edinburgh University Press.

Jones, G. I. 1968. "Olaudah Equiano of the Niger Ibo." In *Africa Remembered: Narratives by West Africans from the Era of the Slave Trade,* ed. Philip D. Curtin, 60–69. Madison: University of Wisconsin Press.

Jones, Lewis. 1985. *South Carolina: One of the Fifty States.* Orangeburg, S.C.: Sandlapper.

———. 1993. "Religion in South Carolina: An Overview." In *Religion in South Carolina,* ed. C. H. Lippy, 1–23. Columbia: University of South Carolina Press.

Jones-Jackson, Patricia. 1987. *When Roots Die: Endangered Traditions on the Sea Islands.* Athens: University of Georgia Press.

———. 1994. "Let the Church Say 'Amen': The Language of Religious Rituals in Coastal South Carolina." In *The Crucible of Carolina: Essays in the Development of Gullah Language and Culture,* ed. Michael Montgomery, 115–32. Athens: University of Georgia Press.

Joyner, Charles. 1999. "A Community of Memory: Assimilation and Identity among the Jews of Georgetown." In *Shared Traditions: Southern History and Folk Culture,* 177–92. Urbana: University of Illinois Press.

Joyner, Judith R. 1985. *Beginnings: Education in Colonial South Carolina.* Columbia: Museum of Education and McKissick Museum, University of South Carolina.

Kelton, Paul. 2002. "The Great Southeastern Smallpox Epidemic, 1696–1700: The Region's First Major Epidemic?" In *The Transformation of the Southeastern Indians,*

1540–1760, ed. Robbie Ethridge and Charles Hudson, 21–38. Jackson: University Press of Mississippi.

Klein, Rachel N. 1990. *Unification of a Slave State: The Rise of the Planter Class in the South Carolina Backcountry, 1760–1808*. Chapel Hill: University of North Carolina Press.

Klein, Thomas B., and Meta Y. Harris. 2000. "Sound Structure in English: Evidence from the Narratives in Turner's *Africanisms*." Paper presented at "Gullah: A Linguistic Legacy of Africans in America—A Conference on the Fiftieth Anniversary of *Africanisms in the Gullah Dialect*," November 3, 2000, Howard University, Washington, D.C.

Knick, Stanley. 2000. *The Lumbee in Context: Toward an Understanding*. Pembroke: University of North Carolina at Pembroke Printing Office.

Kovacik, Charles F., and John J. Winberry. 1987. *South Carolina: A Geography*. Boulder, Colo.: Westview.

Larner, Christina. 1983. *Enemies of God: The Witch-hunt in Scotland*. Oxford: Blackwell.

Lawson, John. 1967. *A New Voyage to Carolina*, ed. Hugh Talmage Lefler. Chapel Hill: University of North Carolina Press. (Orig. pub. 1709).

Leyburn, James G. 1962. *The Scotch-Irish: A Social History*. Chapel Hill: University of North Carolina Press.

Lippy, Charles H., ed. 1993. *Religion in South Carolina*. Columbia: University of South Carolina Press.

Littlefield, Daniel. 1981. *Rice and Slaves: Ethnicity and the Slave Trade in Colonial South Carolina*. Baton Rouge: Louisiana State University Press.

Lovett, A. W. 1986. *Early Habsburg Spain, 1517–1598*. Oxford: Oxford University Press.

Martin, Jack B. 2004. "Languages." In *Handbook of North American Indians*. Vol. 14, *Southeast*, ed. William C. Sturtevant, 68–86. Washington, D.C.: U.S. Government Printing Office.

McDavid, Raven I. 1948. "Postvocalic *r* in South Carolina: A Social Analysis." *American Speech* 23:94–203.

McMillin, James A. 1999. "Post-Revolutionary Charleston: African Americans' Ellis Island." Paper presented at "Slavery in Early South Carolina," conference held by the Institute for Southern Studies, University of South Carolina, February 12–13, 1999.

Merrell, James H. 1989. *The Indians' New World: Catawbas and Their Neighbors from European Contact through the Era of Removal*. Chapel Hill: University of North Carolina Press.

Merrens, H. Roy, ed. 1977. *The Colonial South Carolina Scene: Contemporary Views, 1697–1774*. Columbia: University of South Carolina Press.

Meyer, Duane. 1957. *The Highland Scots of North Carolina, 1732–1776*. Chapel Hill: University of North Carolina Press.

Michaels, Sarah, and J. Collins. 1984. "Oral Discourse Styles: Classroom Interaction and the Acquisition of Literacy." In *Coherence in Spoken and Written Discourse*, ed. Deborah Tannen, 219–44. Norwood, N.J.: Ablex.

Miles, Tiya, and Celia E. Naylor-Ojurongbe. 2004. "African-Americans in Indian Societies." In *Handbook of North American Indians,* vol. 14, *Southeast,* ed. William C. Sturtevant, 753–59. Washington, D.C.: U.S. Government Printing Office.

Mille, Katherine Wyly. 1990. "A Historical Analysis of Tense-Mood-Aspect in Gullah Creole: A Case of Stable Variation." Ph.D. diss., University of South Carolina.

Milroy, Leslie. 1987. *Language and Social Networks.* 2nd ed. Oxford: Blackwell.

Milroy, Leslie, and James Milroy. 1992. "Social Network and Social Class: Towards an Integrated Sociolinguistic Model." *Language in Society* 21:1–26.

Mishoe, Margaret, and Michael Montgomery. 1994. "The Pragmatics of Multiple Modals in North and South Carolina." *American Speech* 69:3–29.

Montgomery, Michael. 2001. "British and Irish Antecedents." In *The Cambridge History of the English Language.* Vol. 6, *English in North America,* ed. John Algeo, 86–153. New York: Cambridge University Press.

———, ed. 1994. *The Crucible of Carolina: Essays in the Development of Gullah Language and Culture.* Athens: University of Georgia Press.

Montgomery, Michael, and Robert Gregg. 1997. "The Scots Language in Ulster." In *The Edinburgh History of the Scots Language,* ed. Charles Jones, 569–622. Edinburgh: Edinburgh University Press.

Mooney, James. 1894. *The Siouan Tribes of the East.* Bureau of American Ethnology Bulletin 22. Washington, D.C.: U.S. Government Printing Office.

———. 1900. "The Cherokee River Cult." *Journal of American Folk-Lore* 33 (January–March): 1–10.

Mufwene, Salikoko S. 1991. "Is Gullah Decreolizing? A Comparison of a Speech Sample of the 1930s with a Sample of the 1980s." In *The Emergence of Black English: Text and Commentary,* ed. Guy Bailey, Natalie Maynor, and Patricia Cukor-Avila, 213–30. Amsterdam: Benjamins.

Nichols, Patricia Causey. 1976. "Linguistic Change in Gullah: Sex, Age, and Mobility." Ph.D. diss., Stanford University.

———. 1977. "A Sociolinguistic Perspective on Reading and Black Children." *Language Arts* 54:150–57.

———. 1983. "Black and White Speaking in the Rural South: Difference in the Pronominal System." *American Speech* 58:201–15.

———. 1986. "Prepositions in Black and White English of South Carolina." In *Language Variety in the South: Perspectives In Black and White,* ed. Michael B. Montgomery and Guy Bailey, 73–84. University: University of Alabama Press.

———. 1988. "English as a Bridge between Cultures: Scotland, Carolina, and California." *CATESOL Journal* 1:5–16.

———. 1989. "Storytelling in Carolina: Continuities and Contrasts." *Anthropology and Education Quarterly* 20:232–45.

———. 1991. "Verbal Patterns of Black and White Speakers of Coastal South Carolina." In *Verb Phrase Patterns in Black English and Creole,* ed. Walter F. Edwards and Donald Winford, 114–28. Detroit: Wayne State University Press.

———. 1992. "Language in the Attic: Claiming Our Linguistic Heritage." In *Diversity as Resource,* ed. D. E. Murray, 275–93. Alexandria, Va.: TESOL.

———. 1993. "Literacy and Language Maintenance in Early Native Carolina." *SECOL Review* 17:97–112.

———. 2004. "Creole Languages: Forging New Identities." In *Language in the USA: Themes for the Twenty-first Century*, ed. Edward Finegan and John R. Rickford, 133–52. New York: Cambridge University Press.

———. 2006. "Language." In *South Carolina Encyclopedia*, ed. Walter B. Edgar, 534–36. Columbia: University of South Carolina Press.

O'Cain, Raymond K. 1972. "A Social Dialect Survey of Charleston, South Carolina." Ph.D. diss., University of Chicago.

Olson, David. 1995. *The World on Paper: The Conceptual and Cognitive Implications of Writing and Reading*. New York: Cambridge University Press.

Olwell, Robert. 1998. *Masters, Slaves, and Subjects: The Culture of Power in the South Carolina Low Country, 1740–1790*. Ithaca, N.Y.: Cornell University Press.

Parsons, Elsie Clews. 1923. "Folk-Lore of the Sea Islands, South Carolina." *Memoirs of the American Folk-Lore Society* 16:63–64.

Pederson, Lee. 2001. "Dialects." In *The Cambridge History of the English Language*. Vol. 6, *English in North America*, ed. John Algeo, 253–90. New York: Cambridge University Press.

Perdue, Theda. 1979. *Slavery and the Evolution of Cherokee Society, 1540–1866*. Knoxville: University of Tennessee Press.

Pinckney, Elise, ed. 1972. *The Letterbook of Eliza Lucas Pinckney, 1739–1762*. Chapel Hill: University of North Carolina Press.

Pitts, Walter F., Jr. 1993. *Old Ship of Zion: The Afro-Baptist Ritual in the African Diaspora*. New York: Oxford University Press.

Pollitzer, William S. 1999. *The Gullah People and Their African Heritage*. Athens: University of Georgia Press.

Pratt, Mary Louise. 1992. *Imperial Eyes: Travel Writing and Transculturation*. New York: Routledge.

Quattlebaum, Paul. 1956. *The Land Called Chicora: The Carolinas under Spanish Rule, with French Intrusions, 1520–1670*. Gainesville: University Press of Florida.

Raboteau, Albert J. 1978. *Slave Religion: The "Invisible Institution" in the Antebellum South*. Oxford: Oxford University Press.

Raphael, Chaim. 1985. *The Road from Babylon: The Story of Sephardic and Oriental Jews*. New York: Harper & Row.

Rickford, John R. 1986. "Social Contact and Linguistic Diffusion." *Language* 62: 245–89.

Roeber, A. G. 1993. *Palatines, Liberty, and Property: German Lutherans in Colonial British America*. Baltimore: Johns Hopkins University Press.

Rogers, George C., Jr. 1973. *A South Carolina Chronology, 1497–1970*. Tricentennial Booklet 11. Columbia: University of South Carolina Press.

Rogers, George C., Jr., and C. James Taylor. 1994. *A South Carolina Chronology, 1497–1992*. 2nd ed. Columbia: University of South Carolina Press.

Rosengarten, Dale. 1987. *Row upon Row: Sea Grass Baskets of the South Carolina Lowcountry*. Rev. ed. Columbia: McKissick Museum, University of South Carolina.

Romaine, Suzanne. 2001. "Contact with Other Languages." In *The Cambridge History of the English Language*. Vol. 6, *English in North America*, ed. John Algeo, 154–83. New York: Cambridge University Press.

Rudes, B. A., T. J. Blumer, and J. A. May. 2004. "Catawba and Its Neighbors." In *Handbook of North American Indians*. Vol. 14, *Southeast*, ed. William C. Sturtevant, 301–18. Washington, D.C.: U.S. Government Printing Office.

Salley, Alexander S., ed. 1911. *Narratives of Early Carolina, 1650–1708*. New York: Scribner.

Scott, Edwin J. 1884. *Random Recollections of a Long Life, 1806–1876*. Columbia, S.C.: Calvo. Repr., Lexington, S.C.: Lexington County Historical Society, 1980.

Shatzman, Aaron M. 1989. *Servants into Planters: The Origin of an American Image; Land Acquisition and Status Mobility in Seventeenth Century South Carolina*. New York: Garland.

Sheinin, Aaron. 2001. "American Indians in S.C. Urged to Cooperate; Seminar Focuses on How Tribes Can Preserve Their History." (Columbia, S.C.) *State*, December 9.

Sider, Gerald M. 1993. *Lumbee Indian Histories: Race, Ethnicity, and Indian Identity in the Southern United States*. New York: Cambridge University Press.

Siebert, Frank T., Jr. 1945. "Linguistic Classification of Catawba," pts. 1 and 2. *International Journal of American Linguistics* 11: 100–104; 211–18.

Smit, Pamela, and J. W. Smit, eds. 1972. *The Dutch in America, 1609–1970: A Chronology and Fact Book*. Dobbs Ferry, N.Y.: Oceana.

Smith, Buckingham, trans. 1968. *Narratives of De Soto in the Conquest of Florida*. Gainesville, Fla.: Palmetto. (Orig. pub. 1922.)

Smith, Mark M. 2005. "Time, Religion, Rebellion." In *Stono: Documenting and Interpreting a Southern Slave Revolt*, ed. Mark M. Smith, 108–23. Columbia: University of South Carolina Press.

Smith, Marvin T. 1994. "Aboriginal Depopulation in the Postcontact Southeast." In *The Forgotten Centuries: Indians and Europeans in the American South 1521–1704*, ed. Charles M. Hudson and Carmen Chaves Tesser, 257–75. Athens: University of Georgia Press.

Snell, William Robert. 1972. "Indian Slavery in Colonial South Carolina." Ph.D. diss., University of Alabama.

Sollors, Werner, ed. 1989. *Invention of Ethnicity*. New York: Oxford University Press.

South Carolina Gazette. 1732–1765. Columbia: Archives of South Caroliniana Library, University of South Carolina.

South Carolina Historical Society. 1858. "French Protestants of Abbeville District, S.C., 1761–1858." In *Collections of the South Carolina Historical Society*, 2:75–103. Charleston: South Carolina Historical Society.

Speck, F. G. 1913. "Some Catawba Texts and Folk-Lore." *Journal of American Folk-Lore* 26:319–30.

Sturtevant, William C. 2005. "History of Research on Native Languages of the Southeast." In *Native Languages of the Southeastern United States*, ed. Heather K. Hardy and Janine Scancarelli, 8–65. Lincoln: University of Nebraska Press.

————, ed. 2004. *Handbook of North American Indians*. Vol. 14, *Southeast*. Washington, D.C.: U.S. Government Printing Office.

Swanton, John R. 1946. *The Indians of the Southeastern United States*. Classics of Smithsonian Anthropology. Washington, D.C.: Smithsonian Institution Press, 1979.

Texas. 1984. *Caddoan Mounds: Temples and Tombs of an Ancient People*. [Austin, Tex.]: Texas Parks and Wildlife Department.

Thomas, Erik R. 2001. *An Acoustic Analysis of Vowel Variation in New World English*. Publications of the American Dialect Society 85. Durham, N.C.: Duke University Press.

Thomason, Sarah Grey. 2001. *Language Contact: An Introduction*. Washington, D.C.: Georgetown University Press.

Thomason, Sarah Grey, and Terrence Kaufman. 1988. *Language Contact, Creolization, and Genetic Linguistics*. Berkeley: University of California Press.

Thompson, Stith. 1955–58. *Motif-Index of Folk-Literature*. 6 vols. Rev. ed. Bloomington: Indiana University Press.

Townsend, Leah. 1935. *South Carolina Baptists, 1670–1805*. Florence, S.C.: Florence Printing Company.

Turner, Lorenzo Dow. 1949. *Africanisms in the Gullah Dialect*. Chicago: University of Chicago Press. Repr., with new introduction by Katherine Wyly Mille and Michael B. Montgomery. Columbia: University of South Carolina Press, 2002.

Tyson, Ruel W., Jr. 1988. "The Testimony of Sister Annie Mae." In *Diversities of Gifts: Field Studies in Southern Religion*, ed. Ruel W. Tyson Jr., J. L. Peacock, and D. W. Patterson, 105–25. Urbana: University of Illinois Press.

United Methodist Church. 1989. *The United Methodist Hymnal: Book of United Methodist Worship*. Nashville: United Methodist Publishing House.

Van Deburg, William. 1979. *The Slave Drivers: Black Agricultural Labor Supervisors in the Antebellum South*. Westport, Conn.: Greenwood Press.

Voight, Gilbert. 1922. *The German and German-Swiss Element in South Carolina 1732–1752*. Bulletin of the University of South Carolina 113. Columbia: University of South Carolina.

Von Gernet, Alexander. 2000. "North American Indigenous *Nicotania* Use and Tobacco Shamanism." In *Tobacco Use by Native Americans*, ed. Joseph C. Winter, 59–80. Norman: University of Oklahoma Press.

Wade-Lewis, Margaret. 1991. "Lorenzo Dow Turner: Pioneer African-American Linguist." *Black Scholar* 21, no. 4: 10–24.

————. 2007. *Lorenzo Dow Turner: Father of Gullah Studies*. Columbia: University of South Carolina Press.

Waddell, Gene. 1980. *Indians of the South Carolina Lowcountry, 1562–1751*. Spartanburg, S.C.: Reprint Company.

————. 2004. "Cusabo." In *Handbook of North American Indians*. Vol. 14, *Southeast*, ed. William C. Sturtevant, 254–64. Washington, D.C.: U.S. Government Printing Office.

Walker, Willard. 1981. "Native American Writing Systems." In *Language in the USA*, ed. Charles A. Ferguson and Shirley Brice Heath, 145–74. New York: Cambridge University Press.

Wallace, David Duncan. 1934. *The History of South Carolina*. New York: American Historical Society.

Wallace, James A. 1856. *History of Williamsburg Church*. Salisbury, N.C.: Bell & James.

Waterhouse, Richard. 1975. "England, the Caribbean, and the Settlement of Carolina." *Journal of American Studies* 9:259–281.

Watters, John R. 2000. "Syntax." In *African Languages: An Introduction*, ed. Bernd Heine and Derek Nurse, 194–230. New York: Cambridge University Press.

Weber, David J. 1992. *The Spanish Frontier in North America*. New Haven, Conn.: Yale University Press.

Weir, Robert. 1983. *Colonial South Carolina: A History*. Millwood, N.Y.: KTO.

Weldon, Tracey. 2008. "Gullah Negation: A Variable Analysis." *American Speech* 82: 341–66.

Wells, J. C. 1982. *Accents of English*. New York: Cambridge University Press.

Widmer, Randolph J. 1994. "The Structure of Southeastern Chiefdoms." In *The Forgotten Centuries: Indians and Europeans in the American South, 1521–1704*, ed. Charles M. Hudson and Carmen Chaves Tesser, 125–55. Athens: University of Georgia Press.

Williamson, Kay, and Roger Blench. 2000. "Niger-Congo." In *African Languages: An Introduction*, ed. Bernd Heine and Derek Nurse, 11–42. New York: Cambridge University Press.

Wolf, D. P., and J. Pusch. 1985. "The Origins of Autonomous Play Boundaries." In *Play, Language, and Stories*, ed. L. Galda and A. D. Pellegrini, 63–77. Norwood, N. J.: Ablex.

Wolfram, Walt, Clare Dannenberg, Stanley Knick, and Linda Oxendine. 2002. *Fine in the World: Lumbee Language in Time and Place*. Raleigh: North Carolina State University.

Wolfram, Walt, and Natalie Schilling-Estes. 1997. *Hoi Toide on the Outer Banks: The Story of the Ocracoke Brogue*. Chapel Hill: University of North Carolina Press.

———. 2004. "Remnant Dialects in the Coastal United States." In *Legacies of Colonial English: Studies in Transported Dialects*, ed. Raymond Hickey, 172–202. New York: Cambridge University Press.

Wood, Peter H. 1974. *Black Majority: Negroes in Colonial South Carolina from 1670 through the Stono Rebellion*. New York: Knopf.

———. 1989. "The Changing Population of the Colonial South: An Overview by Race and Region, 1685–1790." In *Powhatan's Mantle: Indians in the Colonial Southeast*, ed. Peter H. Wood, Gregory A. Waselkov, and M. Thomas Hatley, 35–103. Lincoln: University of Nebraska Press.

Wright, Esmond. 1969. "Education in the American Colonies: The Impact of Scotland." In *Essays in Scotch-Irish History*, ed. E. R. R. Green, 18–45. London: Routledge & Kegan Paul.

Wright, James Leitch, Jr. 1981. *The Only Land They Knew: The Tragic Story of the American Indians in the Old South*. New York: Free Press.

Writers' Program (U.S.). 1941. *South Carolina Folk Tales: Stories of Animals and Supernatural Beings*. Columbia, S.C. Repr., Norwood, Penn.: Norwood Editions, 1973. [Includes tales collected by Genevieve W. Chandler from former slaves in Murrells Inlet and Sandy Island areas of South Carolina.]

Index